Rex Ingram

REX INGRAM

VISIONARY DIRECTOR
of the
SILENT SCREEN

RUTH BARTON

UNIVERSITY PRESS OF KENTUCKY

Scholarly publisher for the Commonwealth,
serving Bellarmine University, Berea College, Centre College of Kentucky,
Eastern Kentucky University, The Filson Historical Society, Georgetown College,
Kentucky Historical Society, Kentucky State University, Morehead State
University, Murray State University, Northern Kentucky University, Transylvania
University, University of Kentucky, University of Louisville, and Western
Kentucky University.

Editorial and Sales Offices: The University Press of Kentucky
663 South Limestone Street, Lexington, Kentucky 40508-4008
www.kentuckypress.com

Library of Congress Cataloging-in-Publication Data

Barton, Ruth.
  Rex Ingram : visionary director of the silent screen / Ruth Barton.
      pages cm. — (Screen classics)
  Includes bibliographical references and index.
  ISBN 978-0-8131-4709-3 (hardcover : alk. paper) —
  ISBN 978-0-8131-4711-6 (pdf) — ISBN 978-0-8131-4710-9 (epub)
  1. Ingram, Rex, 1892-1950. 2. Motion picture producers and directors—
United States—Biography. I. Title.
  PN1998.3.I557B38 2014
  791.4302'33092—dc23
  [B]   2014022370

For Willie, Conal, Eoin, and Paddy

And in memory of
Major Reginald (Rex) Hitchcock, MC

Contents

Photographs follow pages 54 and 142

Author's Note on Sources

The only existing monograph on Rex Ingram is Liam O'Leary's *Rex Ingram: Master of the Silent Cinema,* first published in 1980. O'Leary deposited his personal archive in the National Library of Ireland (NLI) shortly afterward. The archive contains much of the source material for the book and more besides, including numerous photographs given to O'Leary by Alice Terry. It remains uncataloged. However, the NLI kindly allowed me to go through the collection. In 1970 René Predal published a French-language pamphlet titled *Rex Ingram, 1893–1950.* In 1975 DeWitt Bodeen published a two-part account and analysis of Ingram's life and work, "Rex Ingram and Alice Terry," in *Films in Review,* another invaluable source. In 1978 Paul Kozak completed a master's thesis on Ingram at the University of Southern California. He interviewed many former Ingram collaborators, and his thesis is a significant source of information both on Ingram and on filmmaking practices of the silent era. Kozak kindly donated a copy of his thesis to the Rex Ingram collection in the Trinity College Dublin (TCD) archives. Thanks to the guardianship of Geoff Balkan, TCD also acquired Ingram's unpublished memoirs, "A Long Way from Tipperary," and I have drawn on those for factual material and for a sense of Ingram's own perspective on his life. Unless otherwise indicated, quotations by Ingram in my book have been drawn from his memoirs. However, as with all memoirs, his must always be taken as only a partially reliable source. My bibliography has been restricted to book-length sources.

Seeing the films is challenging. Given that original negatives became unusable after a while, existing viewing copies may be second- or third-generation prints shot by a second camera or cobbled together from surviving material. The overwhelming impression conveyed by reading contemporary reviews is one of extraordinary visual mastery. Unfortunately, few of the prints available for viewing come anywhere close to providing that experience, the version of *The Four Horsemen of the Apocalypse* that Kevin Brownlow and David Gill restored being an exception. By all accounts, *Where the Pavement Ends* was a masterpiece but is currently a lost film. I was also unable to view *The Garden of Allah,* although a copy is held in the MGM archives. As a result of the poor condition of many of the prints I viewed, I have drawn heavily on critical reviews for a sense of what audiences would have seen when these films were released. A full filmography is to be found on the Rex Ingram website, www.rexingram.ie, hosted by Trinity College Dublin.

Introduction

This is a book about a brief moment in film history and one of the individuals responsible for it. For a few all-too-short years, as cinema developed from a turn-of-the-century fairground attraction and before it became a full-fledged corporate enterprise, Hollywood drew to it some of the most talented individuals of the day. Fired by the idea that the movies might just be the "seventh art," they determined to test the boundaries of this new medium and to create films that would be the artistic masterpieces of their generation.[1]

One of these visionaries was the Irishman Rex Ingram. At the height of his fame, he was ranked alongside D. W. Griffith, Marshall Neilan, and Erich von Stroheim among the greatest artists of the moving pictures. Another of his peers was French director Maurice Tourneur, whose dedication to pictorial compositions closely paralleled Rex's. His masterpiece of 1921, *The Four Horsemen of the Apocalypse,* made a star of Rodolfo Alfonso Raffaello Piero Filiberto Guglielmi di Valentina d'Antonguolla, better known as Valentino. Later he went on to discover Valentino's successor as "Latin lover" of the popular imagination, Ramón Novarro. As one extraordinary film followed the other, the name Rex Ingram on the opening titles of a release was a guarantee to his studio, Metro, of box office success and to audiences worldwide of breathtaking filmmaking. Today he is all but forgotten, revered by a handful of cineastes. (Many people, if you mention Rex Ingram, confuse him with the African American actor of the same name.) Only Neilan, who too started as an actor and migrated to behind the camera, could claim to be so neglected by film history. Neilan also came from Irish stock (although born in California) and, true to stereotype, wrought his own self-destruction through his excessive predilection to drink. An aversion to authority led to his often-repeated quip "An empty taxi cab drove up to the studio today and Louis B. Mayer got out." The same characteristics saw an end to his Hollywood career. Rex Ingram, as we shall see, left on his own terms, nor did he conform so disastrously to stereotype, but he did share Neilan's views on Mayer. He also shared

1

Neilan's matinee-idol features, and few people failed to comment on his extraordinary good looks.

Photographs show us a tall, vigorous, athletic man. Unless forced into a suit, he is dressed in an open-neck khaki shirt with a gold brace-let, sometimes two, on his wrist. He smiles into the camera somewhat self-consciously, looking as if he would rather be elsewhere; often he is a little too posed, as if too aware of the artificiality of the studio public-ity shot. "His expression was one of seriousness," the English writer Sewell Stokes observed, "though no one could have called him grave. He seemed all the time to be waiting for something to happen, a trifle apprehensive, yet one felt that no matter what surprising thing did hap-pen, he would be able to deal with it, coolly."[2] At his side, smiling sweetly, one cannot miss his wife of many years, Alice Terry, whom he made the star of his films and who became his partner in adventure. In Hollywood in the early 1920s, they were *the* glamour couple, their every movement reported and photographed.

More self-contained than Neilan, less controversial than Griffith, Rex Ingram was artistically closest to his good friend and admirer Erich von Stroheim. It was to Rex that von Stroheim turned when Metro-Goldwyn-Mayer Studios (MGM) rejected his four-hour masterwork *Greed,* secretly shipping him a copy of his film in New York for further cutting. Both men insisted on authenticity, which meant shooting on location for outdoor sequences and otherwise creating minutely detailed interiors. Yet there was a difference, for Rex was first and foremost an artist and secondly a storyteller. He was a man with a tirelessly enquiring mind, who loved travel and chance encounters, who walked down the streets of Hollywood always with an eye out for a face that might work in a film or an item in an old shop that could furnish just the kind of period detail he so loved to reproduce in his historical dramas. Later, as part of Rex's great North African adventure, his assistant then and lifelong admirer Michael Powell observed casting sessions with fascination: "Few of them were regular actors: he would bring them in off the street, from bars, from fairgrounds, from the mountains. He would coach them and costume them and insist that the cameraman light them for the effect he wanted. These flashes of human faces that belonged to people who had suffered and laboured and been through disappointment and degradation, were fascinating to this young Irish-American, with regular features and handsome as a god."[3] The grotesque and the beautiful appealed to Rex in equal measure, and so for every Latin lover he cast in a lead role, he also included a hunchback, a dwarf, or a leering drunkard as sideshow.

To create his visual masterpieces, this pioneering filmmaker had recourse to a book of tricks that he was writing as he went along, with John Seitz, his visionary cameraman, always alongside him refining his craft. Fantasy, escapism, and magic—those were what audiences sought on the screen, Rex believed, dismissing the tendency of studios to release reports from the set that let audiences in on the secret. "To acquaint audiences with the mechanics of motion picture technique," he pronounced, "breaks down the illusions of the screen as people go to the pictures for the emotional reaction from illusions it creates." Warming to his theme, he compared filmmaking to a piano recital. No one would expect the performer to take away the casing of the piano and throw a spotlight on the wires within. "So why reveal how rain is made to order for picture scenes: how railroad wrecks are simulated? Why destroy illusion when illusion is the prime desire of the audience?"[4]

James Joyce slipped a reference to his fellow exile into *Finnegans Wake,* where he appears as "Rex Ingram, pageant-master."[5] Both men left Ireland to pursue their art in more worldly cultures than their own; neither returned. Yet both bore the imprint of their Irishness on their personalities and in their work. In Rex's case it is hidden in a series of images that hark back to growing up in rural Ireland the son of a Protestant rector. To reclaim him as an Irish director, then, entails finding clues in his films that lead back to his childhood. In other ways he was a man of his time and class, a cosmopolitan European who fell in and out of love with America, an Orientalist, a restless traveler, a man of extraordinary intellect and vision but, equally, one who vividly demonstrated the prejudices of his day. He was also born of a generation that lost so many of its young men to the Great War, and that terrible catastrophe looms large over his own work.

Rex Ingram's films are populated by ghosts. This book too is about ghosts—ghosts of the cinema, of history, of the Irish past. As I was writing it, Thaddeus O'Sullivan released his tale of small-town, 1950s Ireland, *Stella Days* (2011). The film focuses on the struggle of the progressive, worldly priest Fr. Daniel Barry, played by Martin Sheen, to build a cinema in the face of hostility and suspicion from certain members of the community. In one sequence a panel of local office-holders interviews a young man for the position of village schoolteacher. Pressed on his interests, the hopeful candidate mentions cinemagoing and adds that he was impressed to find that Rex Ingram's people came from the area. The panel looks confused. "Who?" Brendan McSweeney (Stephen Rea) asks. "You know," his fellow interviewer Emmet Quinn (David Herlihy) prompts him. "The Protestant rector's son who went off to become a director." Father Barry quizzes the candidate on his favorite Rex Ingram film and proceeds to appoint him on the spot.

I asked the makers of *Stella Days* why they had included this sequence in their film. The screenwriter, Antoine O'Flatharta, replied:

> Ingram's connection with the area is mentioned in the original memoir [Michael Doorley's *Stella Days 1957–1967: The Life and Times of a Rural Irish Cinema*]. So I figured that the character Tim might know this and use it in the scene when he was being interviewed for the job. The fact that Ingram was Anglo Irish was also useful to rile Brendan and bring into focus his sectarianism and ignorance of film/art at an early point in the story. So poor old Rex ends up as a bit of a fleeting figurehead for suspect arthouse cinema and also for the "vanished" gentry![6]

To understand how Rex Ingram became a ghostly presence in cinema's history, one has to go back to the beginning, to Dublin, to the dying years of the British Empire. For this is where Reginald Ingram Montgomery Hitchcock started his life.

I

Childhood in Ireland

On a wet blustery winter's day in Dublin, Reginald Ingram Montgomery Hitchcock, later to be known as Rex Ingram, or Reggie by his family, entered the world. The new baby, born on Wednesday, 18 January 1893, was the first child of twenty-five-year-old Francis Ryan Montgomery Hitchcock and Kathleen Hitchcock (née Ingram), who was two years younger than her husband.

Number 58 Grosvenor Square, the Hitchcocks' home, was in Rathmines, Dublin's largest suburb. The house was a recent addition to this comfortable square of solid two-story red-bricked houses—a listing of the streets of Rathmines from 1891 indicates that in that year, numbers 53–59 were still a construction site.[1] Dublin center was a brisk walk away, and for those who preferred public transport, there was the city's first tramway, which carried passengers every three and a half minutes at peak time from Rathmines to the elegant shops of Grafton Street. It was a prosperous area, home to many Protestant and middle-class Catholic families who kept their distance from the overcrowded, damp, unsanitary housing of Dublin's notorious tenements, for this was a country sharply divided by social class and occupation.

It was also a country on the brink of massive change. Rex was born a citizen of the British Empire, as were all Irish children of his generation. Protestant families such as his were often assumed to be more English than Irish. But while many Protestants felt a strong allegiance to the British Crown, others were keenly aware that the time for change had come. One of these, the Irish poet, Protestant, and nationalist William Butler Yeats, created some of his greatest works in these years, pausing only later, in 1939, to worry: "Did that play of mine send out / Certain men the English shot?"[2] The play in question was *Cathleen Ni Houlihan*, which he wrote and infused with nationalist rhetoric in 1902. With Lady Gregory he founded the Abbey Theatre in 1904 to provide a stage, literally, for the Irish cultural revival. Of all the figures of the Irish revival, Yeats became most fascinated by the occult, by theosophy, and by mysticism. For him, as for others of his generation, the East offered an antidote to the pragmatism of modernity and of British colonial authority. Another alternative was to look back to the Celtic past of mythical warriors and dream of a moment when their deeds might inspire the Irish people to throw off the yoke of imperialism. Whether the Hitchcock family knew Yeats can only be conjectured, but what is certain is that Rex's father was a friend of the Trinity College classicist Louis Purser, and Purser was a great friend of the poet's, making it more than likely that they were acquainted. Rex grew up reading Yeats and in turn was to be inspired by this fusion of mysticism and romanticism and a love of the Orient.[3] Both too were to experience an intense ambivalence about war, in particular the necessity for armed insurrection.

The boy's first and fondest memories were of his mother. Tall and slender with gray eyes, she had long dark hair that when loosened fell to her waist. Brushing it emitted an electric crackle of static. In his unpublished memoirs, "A Long Way from Tipperary," Rex writes:

> When her hair was brushed and coiled on her neck or on the top of her head, my mother would take me on her knee and, rocking me gently, sing to me, her lips close to my ear:
>
> . . . a garden of roses with dew heavy-laden
> And thy mother's voice singing an old lullaby:
> Hu-ush thee, hu-ush thee, none shall harm thee
> dearest little child . . .
>
> And curled in her arms, my cheek against her breast, I would sleep.[4]

Kathleen Hitchcock was a gentle presence around the household. She played the piano and sang; she enjoyed carving in wood, creating panels for her husband's churches and ornate wooden frames for family pictures. She also painted in oils. By contrast, Francis Hitchcock was a formidable personality, intellectually and physically domineering. By the time of his first son's birth, he was already making a reputation for himself as a scholar of note. While still at Trinity College Dublin, he won the Berkeley Medal for Greek. He subsequently became a prolific author and by his death had published some fourteen works on ecclesiastical and historical topics, from the early Christian St. Irenaeus to studies of Celtic life and art to treatises on St. Patrick. A towering figure—he stood well over six feet tall and was shaped in proportion—Francis Hitchcock held firm opinions on many different subjects. When he was not engaged in writing his books and later when he had a parish of his own, the Reverend was a lover of the outdoors. He was also a boxing fanatic who enjoyed nothing more than settling in for a few rounds with a punching bag.

Kathleen shared none of her husband's robust good health. When Rex was six years old, she fell so ill with typhoid fever that he was sent to stay with his paternal grandmother and two aunts on Leinster Road in Rathmines. By now the family had moved to 11 Rathdown Road, off North Circular Road in the parish of St. Mary's Church where, on 15 March 1896, Rex was joined by a younger brother, Francis Clere, or Frank to the family.

On Leinster Road, Rex shared a room with his kindly Aunt Edith. His grandmother was a more formidable figure, and his Aunt Cecilia was set to take after her. Unusually for a woman of her era, Cecilia Hitchcock had gained a degree in classics and now spent hours seated in front of the dining room fire with a rug over her knees, reading and marking texts in Greek and Latin with a blue pencil. The small boy followed her example, marking his own books with a blue pencil and then embellishing the margins with caricatures of Aunt Cecilia. Only the arrival of Rex's father bearing a large, vividly drawn cardboard cutout of Richard Coeur-de-Lion was enough to distract him. That night, his Aunt Edith read to him from Joseph François Michaud's *History of the Crusades* with its vivid Gustave Doré illustrations, and his imagination lit up. It was unfortunate that the next caller to announce himself from behind the bolted door of the tradesman's entrance also went by the name of Richard. Grandmother had been napping with a copy of the *Irish Times* when the excited child grabbed her arm with his grubby hand and announced that Richard Coeur-de-Lion was at the house. Her reading glasses flew off her head into the fireplace, shattering on impact. "Is this child completely out of his senses?" she gasped.[5] Punishment was swift.

According to the census of 1901, both Aunt Edith and Aunt Cecilia had learned to speak Irish, although their mother had not.[6] This suggests that the sisters' allegiances lay with the Irish nationalists, who sought freedom from British rule, rather than with the Unionists, who wished to remain part of the union with Britain, since the use of the Irish language was a strategic weapon in the cultural wars.

A Country Childhood

Their doctor advised the Hitchcocks that a move to the country would be the best for Kathleen, and in October 1898 the bishop of Killaloe appointed Reverend Hitchcock to the curacy of Nenagh in County Tipperary. From being a child of the suburbs, Rex was thrown into life in a small Irish village. The church was opposite the green, and the curate's house stood right on the street. From its windows Rex and Frank could look out at the village. On market day the place bustled with activity as local farmers and their families came to buy and sell sheep, cattle, and eggs. Traders set up stalls, selling clothes and trinkets, and as the day wore on the pubs filled. Fights were not long in breaking out. The two little boys gazed at it all in fascination.

Better even than market day was the day Cleary's Circus came to town. Posters announced, in addition to the usual performing elephants, bears, and horses, the inclusion of a cinematograph. Rex's father promised to take him to the afternoon performance. Rex consulted with his friends, Harry Lewis and Georgie Cooper, sons of two local bank managers. Could there be such a thing as moving life-size pictures? Bets were laid, and Georgie produced his trump card, a thick little book of drawings that when thumbed gave the appearance of moving images. The famous Corbett-Fitzsimmons fight of 1897 came to life.

Harry, Georgie, and Rex met at the big tent, paid their money, and took their places:

> I saw a flickering "rainy" cinematograph, very black and white, with men running a hurdle race at twice normal speed, and a train coming into a station and then scenes of Mr. Somebody in his record breaking though topheavy [*sic*] motorcar, which moved without them, but would, I thought, have looked better with horses.
>
> I was impressed enough to start production on my first motion-picture, a short. The subject, Richard Coeur-de-Lion cutting off a Saracen's head, had action enough; but the result—twenty draw-

ings, starting with Richard drawing his sword and ending when the Saracen's head and trunk parted company in a gush of red pencil—had technical flaws not apparent in the Corbett-Fitzsimmons production. The movement was jerky. A defect due partly to an oversight on my part; a slight variation in scale in all of the drawings, and partly to an uneven stitching job by Bridget [the family maid], who had sewed them together.[7]

In 1901 the Hitchcocks moved again, this time to Borrisokane just ten miles away in County Tipperary, where Reverend Hitchcock was appointed rector. It was a step up for the family. Now they lived in a rectory, a fine house with five acres of land running down through trees to a river:

We had a big garden that was more like an orchard, with all the apple, pear and plum trees in it; and there was a lawn with flower beds, bordered on the south by an avenue of pines and cypresses and on the north by copper beeches and chestnut trees. A gate under the trees led into a little grove hedged in with yew and box, and at the end of the grove stood an old thatched house that had once been the school, but for years had been used for laying out the apples in straw. On wet days my brother and I played in the house, and we had it to ourselves for nobody ever came there.[8]

In Borrisokane the Hitchcock boys continued to live the life of country children, with their father keeping a stern eye on their physical development. He and Rex set up goalposts in the field beside the rectory, and the two brothers practiced dropkicks and rugby passes together. Rex had a donkey too, named Bessie, that he rode to visit neighbors. Less enjoyable were lessons with Reverend Hitchcock. They took place in the morning from nine till twelve and in the afternoons from two till five, with Wednesday and Saturday afternoons free:

He did his best to teach me a lot of Latin and Greek, and not quite so much history and geography, and even less arithmetic, algebra and Euclid which he was not good at himself, and did not consider important anyway, believing that only classical scholarship really counted in fitting you for the battle of life. The fly-leaves and margins of all my lesson books were covered with drawings of horses and friends. My attention never stayed long on the text before me, and if my father was not there at my elbow, my pencil seemed to draw of its own accord; and though he would make me stay in after study hours rubbing these drawings out, in due time others took their place.[9]

The Irish midlands were still dotted with the "big houses" of the Protestant landed gentry, and as the rector's sons the boys were always welcome in those homes.[10] Indeed, although one local resident later remembered them as friendly children, she also remembered that Rex and Frank were not allowed to mix with the villagers.[11] Instead they played cricket and tennis with the neighboring big-house families. They were close friends with the Saunders family of Killavala, and it was Captain Saunders who gave Rex his first saddle and then, after Bessie died, his first pony: "When I got on that pony, I knew I would never want to get off her. She was rangy and had a long mane and tail and was high in the withers so the saddle did not slip forward like it did on the donkey, and needed no crupper to hold it in place. She had a way of her own too, of stepping out and tossing her head, and looked like a little racehorse, not like the potbellied Shetland ponies you saw other people with, and her name was Lady."[12] His other companions in those days were Cecil Saunders, the captain's son; the miller and the local priest, Father Maher, with whom he went crow-shooting. There were girls too, and kisses, and young love—first with Girlie, then with Norah.

A Reluctant Schoolboy

In 1903 when Rex was ten, his parents' thoughts turned to schooling. The salary at Borrisokane was not enough to send a boy to boarding school, and there was no suitable Protestant secondary school in the area. Kathleen Hitchcock accompanied her husband to the synod in Dublin to make sure he requested a move to a better-paying parish. They returned home with the news that the family would be relocating to Kinnitty in County Offaly on the Tipperary border, about twenty miles from Borrisokane, where the salary was £150 a year. Just before they left, Captain Saunders's stable boy put Lady to a fence without checking what was on the other side, and she landed in marsh, breaking her leg. The beloved pony had to be shot.

Although boarding school was imminent, Rex was still too young to attend. For his first two years in Kinnitty, once the torture of lessons in the classics was over he was free to roam the Irish countryside. His mother gave him a curly-haired, chocolate Irish water spaniel whom he named Towser, and boy and dog escaped the rectory classroom as soon as they could to run wild in the fields together. In summer he and Frank swam in the Brosna River near Kinnitty, and Rex and Towser would dive from the bank at Drumcullen Bridge. Reverend Hitchcock fixed himself up a punching bag in the coach house, and in the evening, after a day's writing and the torture of trying to teach his older son, he would go out and practice on it long into the night. Meanwhile the parishioners of Kinnitty were to grow accustomed to seeing the massive figure of their new rector jogging along the footpath to the village post office as part of his fitness regime.

The boys went on holidays to the West of Ireland, sometime visiting their cousins, the Lamberts in Galway, other times staying in Lahinch or Lisdoonvarna. A day's outing might be to Dublin to watch a rugby international or polo or go to the races. One of the families with which the Hitchcock boys were particularly friendly were the Darbys at Leap Castle, Roscrea. Leap Castle in those days was a familiar sight to passersby, rising out of the landscape menacingly, its appearance magnified by the faux-Gothic Elizabethan architecture added by previous generations of wealthy Darbys. From the outside, the first impression was of tall, gray turrets and castellations and tiny, deep-set windows. Once indoors, one stood in a vast entrance hall that had an ancient, polished slate and sandstone floor that shone like marble. The castle boasted in the region of twenty-eight rooms, including servants' quarters, schoolrooms for the children, and two kitchens. The formal rooms—the drawing room, the dining room, the study, the hall—gleamed with ornate mahogany and oak, and in the winter fires burned in vast fireplaces topped with marble mantelpieces. The furnishings all had their own history and included, among other family heirlooms, a fruit table that had once belonged to Napoleon Bonaparte. On the walls hung the portraits of the Darbys' ancestors.[13] Underneath the ancient oak flooring, it was rumored, lay a network of deep dungeons carved into the rock, where the bones of the ancient enemies of the original warrior-like O'Carroll family lay hidden. And there were ghosts. Overnight guests of the Darbys came down to breakfast trembling and telling of waking in the night with a horrifying feeling of cold around their hearts. When they had fallen back to sleep, they saw in front of them a tall woman dressed in a long, red gown, her hand raised threateningly above her, apparently glowing from within. Above the main hall stood the room where "one-eyed" Teige O'Carroll slew his brother and where other guests reported seeing strange lights glow at night. Rex was drawn over and again to the bloodstained bedchamber, lingering over its gory traces.

Like many of the Anglo-Irish of her day and earlier, Mildred Darby was fascinated by the supernatural. Living in these vast houses with their often violent histories, increasingly aware, as the new Catholic middle classes took control of politics, that public life held no place for them, the old Protestant families found themselves haunted by history. Bram Stoker's 1897 classic, *Dracula,* is perhaps the best-known eminence of the Anglo-Irish Gothic novel, but from Charles Robert Maturin through Lady Morgan to Sheridan Le Fanu, the tradition was constantly reinvigorated. Mildred Darby wrote articles for the journal *Occult Review* about the ghosts at Leap. She followed this with the popular tale of the Irish famine of the 1840s, *The Hunger,* published in 1909 under her nom de plume, Andrew Merry. That she spun a good yarn was brought home to Rex when he discovered to his fury that she had painted the bedchamber red as a joke.

In 1922, during the Irish Civil War, Leap Castle would be burned to the ground, as were others of the Protestant big houses that Rex and Frank played in as children. Many of the sons of those houses would die even before then, victims of the Great War, and become ghosts in another way, forgotten by history. In the new Ireland, there was no place for the old Protestant landed gentry or for any of those who had fought on the side of the British.

Ghosts were not only Rex's preoccupation. His father's own interests were eclectic and reflected the intellectual concerns of Irish life in the early years of the new century. The newly popularized theories of Sigmund Freud and Charles Darwin had made him rethink the question of evil, wondering if it was a product of nature or nurture. If such questions belonged firmly to the realm of theology or philosophy, his *Types of Celtic Life and Art,* published in 1906, is a celebration of earthiness and Irish superstitious practices, much of it drawn from the reverend's own travels around the country and from listening to folktales told locally in Kinnitty.

This book makes its author come alive in a way the theological treatises cannot, and one has an impression of a vigorous, curious, slightly hectoring personality cycling determinedly off to explore neolithic tombs or Norman castles, recreating as he goes scenes from the Celtic past. He writes of ghosts and specters, shape-shifters and magic. He tells of the stone fort that stands on a hill in the demesne of Castle Bernard in Kinnitty and of his visits to the *crannogs* (artificial islands) at Loughrea and Lough Derg, which once used to be the homes of the Celtic chiefs. Most of all, he celebrates the bravery of the ancient Celts of Ireland and their learning. Back at his desk at the rectory, he recreates with gusto scenes of ancient horse-racing and chariot-driving, imbuing them with a vividness that one may well imagine characterized his own bedtime tales to his children:

> Now the young men are preparing for the foot race. They are removing their cloak pins, and taking off their brilliantly-coloured capes. And now they unwind the broad scarf from their waist, the heavy kilt is thrown aside, and in their light silk tunics and hosen they bound lightly into the course, their great, muscular arms and throats, tattooed with quaint designs, exposed to the admiring crowd. The word is given, and the competitors bound forth at full speed, now clearing an iron bar, breast high with the greatest ease, and now gliding as rapidly beneath a two-foot rail. The race is keenly competed, and as keenly watched. It is over, and the victor is carried off by his friends in triumph.[14]

Later, shocked by the fate of so many of the old Protestant families at the hands of the IRA, Reverend Hitchcock became disillusioned with nationalist Ireland; in the 1920s, during the Irish Civil War, he carried around with him a revolver given to him by his son Frank. But when the boys were growing up, his viewpoint was firmly unsympathetic when it came to England's long history of invading and occupying their smaller neighbor. It wasn't until the reign of Elizabeth I, he reminded his readers, that capital punishment was introduced into Ireland.[15] Overall, his was a picture of an ancient society at once enlightened and fierce, ruled over by just lords and the "fair ladies of Erin," a society in its day infinitely more civilized than that of neighboring England.[16]

Rex, in his turn, was to embrace the supernatural, lacing his films with ghostly apparitions, tricksters, and unearthly premonitions. To the end of his days, he remained fascinated by battles and military adventure. Kinnitty is just six miles from Birr, and the boy rode his bike to and fro between the two towns, visiting friends at the Leinster Regiment stationed at Birr

Barracks. There he delighted in caricaturing the men in uniform, with their monocles and their upright bearing, and then gifting his drawings to his subjects. A day at the Baldoyle races produced a series of caricatures of the well-heeled race-goers; another was of a thin, monocled man in uniform holding a lighted cigarette between the fingers of one hand, with gloves and a cane in the other, standing on Grafton Street.

Drawn though he was to military life, Rex was also his mother's son, artistic and dreamy. Growing up in Kinnitty left him with happy memories of long days in the outdoors, where he was free of the troubling hand of authority. Formal education, however, beckoned. In September 1905 he duly arrived at St. Columba's College, a boarding school in the Dublin mountains for the sons of the Protestant gentry, where he remained for five years, until Easter 1909. The school had been founded in 1843 with the intention of offering English-style education to Irish children, a kind of Eton for Ireland. What made it distinctive was that the founders intended that the boys should also be educated to speak Irish so as to arm them, particularly when ordained to be Church of Ireland clergy, to be able to convert Roman Catholics to Protestantism. Boys wore gowns to class, attended chapel every day, slept at night in wood-paneled dormitories, and studied classics and mathematics (the teaching of Irish soon dwindled to nothing). Afternoons were spent playing cricket, rugby, and other character-building sports.

For Rex, St. Columba's was one long, sustained nightmare. The prefect system left him at the mercy of these older boys whose role it was to drill obedience into the new students. It was a structure of discipline designed to produce good citizens for the Empire, manly types who would toe the line when required and move into leadership positions when the need arose. For a dreamy, artistic, obstinate child with little interest in book-learning, St. Columba's meant the layering of punishment upon punishment. Rex wrote out lines for talking in chapel and then more lines for crossing the Quadrangle, a privilege reserved for the fifth and sixth forms. When writing lines broke down, the prefects punished him physically, sometime strapping him so harshly that welts rose from his buttocks and his hips bled. Being caught crying was cause for further punishment. He was bullied without respite.

As one of his school friends, Roderick Greer, recollected, "A rebel at heart he had a discomforting disdain for authority, and escapades brought him into close conflict with those responsible for discipline."[17] Rex's letters home to his mother put a brave face on a nightmare of loneliness. In one letter he wrote, seemingly cheerfully:

My Dear Mother

I am getting on very well I was third in weeks order this week and I shall soon be top I am getting next to Killingley in L [Latin] prose. But I think his pater [father] must do some of his for him as he never has any mistakes and always does the whole of the arithmetic papers.[18]

The young boy was happier on the playing fields, where he threw himself into rugby, representing St. Columba's on the first team for two seasons. He also broke the public schools' record in the 100-yard race, running it in eleven and a half seconds, and taking prizes in the high jump, the long jump, and hurdling.[19] The only class in which he excelled was art; everything else was a disaster.

Those who did think of Rex in later life remembered a loner: "I think of Reggy [sic] Hitchcock as a rather solitary and independent character not very popular with some of the other boys who had the herd instinct strongly developed."[20] Another old boy remembered Rex as a spoiled, irritating, tiresome boy, very frequently in trouble with authority and other boys.[21]

Still, Rex eventually made friends at St. Columba's. Besides Greer, whose mother, Matilda, was Rex's godmother, there was Osborne Burke, whose parents lived in Rathgar (at 1 Sunbury Gardens), not far from where Rex was born. Rex became a frequent visitor to their house, where he formed a long friendship, apparently platonic, with Burke's older sister, Cherrie. He and she would stroll down Grafton Street, with Rex always hopeful that she would be spotted on his arm by one of his tormentors from St. Columba's. The two shared a passion for collecting cards—pictures of the famous stage performers of the day—and ransacked the catalogs of those American companies who would mail to Ireland. If she saw a card she knew he wanted, Cherrie would quickly buy it; he always wanted more: "If you could get me any pretty actresses," he begged her, "Gabrielle Ray etc. I especially want one of Maud Allen."[22] One of his favorite illustrators was Charles Dana Gibson, creator of the iconic "Gibson Girl," a series of sketches that established an ideal of the young, independent American woman. Gibson also famously illustrated *The Prisoner of Zenda,* a novel that would feature large in Rex's life. To Cherrie, Rex spilled out his ambitions: maybe to go to Canada and work there in the advertising industry.[23] He tested out sketches and doggerel on her, always soliciting her opinion on his latest offering.

Holidays became precious, an escape from school into the countryside. Much of that time he spent with his mother, accompanying her as she made the visits expected of a rector's wife, calling in on the parishioners, wealthy or poor. Although he and she were intensely close, Rex was becoming distracted by other female company. In Kinnitty, a young woman named Joan caught his eye. She was as unconventional as he and shared his love of the outdoors. They started going shooting together, taking their guns out on the woodlands surrounding the rectory where birds and rabbits made easy prey.

Meanwhile Kathleen Hitchcock was growing frailer. One day, Rex and Joan pulled up the carpet in the hall and started the phonograph. As they danced, Kathleen looked on, until Reverend Hitchcock came home and said:

"Go and ask your mother to dance."

"She can't dance," I said starting the machine for another dance with Joan.

"Do as I tell you," he said.

I left Joan reluctantly and went into the drawing-room.

"Want to dance, Mumsy?" I asked in a voice that lacked enthusiasm.

She did not answer.

"Mumsy," I said again, "want to dance with me?"

She only shook her head and then I saw she was crying and knew at once she had overheard my thoughtless remark.[24]

Smitten with guilt and suddenly aware of just how poorly his mother was, Rex swore to her that he and she would spend the rest of the holiday together. Joan was soon put out of his thoughts. In the autumn term of 1908, he returned to school as reluctantly as ever. Not long after the start of term, he heard that Kathleen was to have an operation. The surgeons were hopeful. But on 8 October 1908, Rex's adored mother passed away.

By the time he was sixteen, it was obvious to all around him that Rex was a distracted student, only content when he was drawing. His father, however, had been appointed to the prestigious position of Donnellan Scholar at Trinity College and was determined that Rex would attend his old university. They sat together at the study in Kinnitty, with Francis Hitchcock trying to persuade his son to concentrate on mathematics and Latin. Rex had other ideas. Increasingly, he was drawn to the idea of travel abroad. The death of his mother had upset him deeply, and it was this as much as anything else that determined him to leave. For a while Latin America seemed like a good proposition, and so he took Spanish lessons. He found he had a facility for languages. Then, there was Canada. Working in the advertising industry continued to tempt him. He bombarded the magazines with offerings and had success with the new British magazine *Boxing*, which published some of his sketches.

In the village he sat outside the post office and listened to the returned emigrants talk of Chicago and New York City and of South America, of "the Bocca in Buenos Aires," he writes in his memoirs, "where the women of all nations are to be found, and about the white slave traffic, and about South American revolutions and Irishmen who took part in them, and about the Pampas and the great *estancias* with their *maté*-drinking gauchos and thousands of head of cattle and fullbosomed, whitetoothed, oliveskinned 'Chinas,' and, as that French song puts it, about 'autre choses aussi que je n'ose-e pas dire-e.'"[25]

At night, he escaped in his dreams, back to the Lamberts' home, Aggart, in Galway with a fair-haired girl who reminded him in some way of his mother. In his dream the Lamberts' wolfhound, Brian Boru, accompanied them:

> And we saw the family vault outside the windows where Uncle John and Aunt Anna were buried, and there were rabbit hutches beside them that I had never noticed before at Aggart. And then we passed the house where the miser my uncle John had told me about used to rock the cradle, and there was a light in one window, and Brian Boru began to bay, and his coat bristled, and we tried to look in through the window, but there were cobwebs on the other side of the panes and we could see nothing. But we could hear a sound like the slow tock-tock of a grandfather clock, only there was a creak to it, and occasionally the clink of something that hit the floor. And I knew it was the miser rocking the cradle full of gold coins. And, as can happen in dreams, the cobwebs disap-

peared suddenly and we saw in, and there was the miser on his knees rocking the cradle full of gold just as my uncle John had seen him. And as he rocked it the layer of coins on the top of the cradle began to undulate and two gold hands, that looked more like the claws of bats than hands, pushed up through the gold and seized the miser by the throat. Then the girl screamed and ran back, calling to me to come away. When I came to her she caught hold of me, but I was not feeling afraid myself, only a little creepy. So I pulled Brian Boru over by his collar and told her to hold him, and stepped up to the window. But when I looked through the window into the room there was nothing at all there, just the moonlight streaming in on the floor where a couple of mice were playing.[26]

During one holiday, Rex went to stay at Drumbawn, the estate of John O'Meara. For a while, he was distracted from his thoughts of death by meeting Sophie Rosa, the daughter of Carl Rosa, of the Carl Rosa Opera Company. It was Sophie who loaned him Robert Hichens's best-selling novel *The Garden of Allah,* set in North Africa. He began to imagine seeing the places so vividly described by Hichens and promised himself that when he had made his fortune in America, he would go to North Africa: "And it was one of those promises I made myself and kept, and never regretted."[27] Many years later he would meet Hichens in the very place, Staouli, where the Trappist monastery described in the book was located, when he was making his own version of *The Garden of Allah.* The two men were to find they had much in common, not least a love of the desert and the exotic. Hichens too was the son of a clergyman, a defiant figure who little resembled stereotypes of his profession, or that Hichens's own mother was Irish, from Westmeath.

Rex returned to St. Columba's to take the entrance exams to Trinity College but failed mathematics. His father was disgusted and tried to coach him in the subject himself, persevering through the summer until he was defeated by the effort. Meanwhile changes were taking place at St. Columba's. Its warden (school principal), the Reverend W. Parker, had broken his leg playing rugby and was in trouble for mismanaging the school finances, and so the Reverend R. M. Gwynn was appointed acting warden. He was much more sympathetic toward Rex's ambitions and persuaded him back to St. Columba's for one more term to play rugby. He also promised the boy special help with his correspondence course in advertising. Rex still irritated the other boys immensely, now because of an infuriating tendency to hum the recent music hall hit "If I Should Plant a Tiny Seed of Love" over and over again.

Most of those who were with Rex at St. Columba's remembered above all his last day at school. Fired with bravado, Rex stepped out and challenged a master to lay down his robes and come out behind the gym to see who was the better man. The school gathered in anticipation of the spectacle, but as the boys listened from behind the door, all they could hear was the future famous Hollywood director being caned.

Of the onlookers who watched Rex emerge from his inglorious defeat, most were to die later in World War I. Only a few remained to recall the tall, quiet, artistic boy who went on to direct one of the most vivid antiwar films of its day, *The Four Horsemen of the Apocalypse*. He too would soon slip away, never to return to Ireland. Still grieving for his mother and filled with wanderlust, Rex booked his passage to America.

With Reverend Hitchcock lecturing in Trinity, it fell to Frank to see off his brother: "At 6:30 am we left on a lovely morning from the rectory, Kinnitty, for Roscrea railway station across the Slieve Bloom Mountains, by a road called Boharaphuca—the way of the spirits. As we climbed the road, we always dismounted from the outside car as the gradients were too steep for the horse. We could see the Shannon glistening in the morning sun and the Devil's Bit Mountain, also the great keep of Leap castle." Little did he know then that he would not see his brother for another fifteen years, when Frank himself was in a Swiss hospital near Davos recuperating from the damage inflicted on his lungs in the trenches. "I returned home very, very miserable, I remember, for he had always been such a kind and gay brother to me, particularly since the death of our mother in 1908."[28] Rex sailed from Queenstown (now Cobh) on the SS *Celtic* on 25 June 1911, registering his profession on the ship's manifest as "artist" and his age as nineteen (he was eighteen). He too was filled with a sense of loss:

I felt my confidence leaving me, and leaving me, also, the longing to see far-off lands and the men and women who lived in them. And I wondered what was going to become of me, and if I had not been a fool. And I turned so I would not see the Irish coast any more, for I was beginning to feel a tightening in my throat. I walked forward, bent against the wind, and crossed the deck to the starboard rail where I could see the open sea. The wind was higher on the starboard side, whipping spray from the wave-crests, and everything was grey on this side too, but there was menace as well, the black sky, waves breaking high over the bow. And suddenly, as I looked, the sun broke through the clouds and three great shafts of sunlight lit up the sea ahead.[29]

His final destination was New Haven, Connecticut. He arrived in New York on 3 July 1911.

2

New York Bohemia and the Lure of the Movies

Although he had a younger brother in the United States, Rex's father had not kept in touch with his family. The man who greeted Rex as the *Celtic* berthed was Bert Gordon Hitchcock, a director of the New Haven Railroad. He had made contact many years previously with the Reverend Francis Hitchcock, wondering if they were related. They weren't, they agreed, but the correspondence between the two continued. On hearing of Rex's plans, Bert Hitchcock insisted that the young man stay with him and his wife. Reverend Hitchcock, who had been dreading the idea of his older son arriving a stranger in a strange land, was delighted. Rex was to wear a red or white rose in his lapel, and Bert would recognize him and take him to his home in Connecticut. Amused by this, Rex took a photograph of himself on the *Celtic* wearing his rose and sent it to his brother, Frank.

Bert Hitchcock had arranged a job for Rex at the New Haven dockyard as night messenger, collecting the waybills from the steamers that plied their way carrying freight between New York and New Haven. Rex recalls in "A Long Way from Tipperary":

> I went to work those days at 6:00 p.m., upstairs in the frame office building across the road from the docks, where I helped the night clerks in the record office copy waybills until midnight, which was dinnertime. Some of the clerks brought their food in dinner pails like the yardmen. I brought mine in my pocket as I only ate sandwiches. Next door to the freight office was the Dutchman's saloon, where a nickel got you a beer and free lunch of pretzels, sausage and sauerkraut; and if you felt that way, for twenty-five cents more

21

you could have the Dutchman's daughter as well in the little room behind the bar.[1]

The work was long and cold and hard, and Rex was surrounded by people from all the world's nations, some who spoke English, most who did not. The police were Irish, and he came to know them, as he came to know the prostitutes who sat out on the doorsteps on warm summer evenings. One of them had eyes like his mother, was older than he was, and called herself Daisy. He fell in love with her straightaway. She refused to contemplate his marriage proposals, and he managed to blind himself to the reality of her occupation. When it came to the point when the unspoken truth had to be acknowledged, Rex flew into a rage, and Daisy left the dockyards.

Throughout his memoirs, Rex draws on his mother's presence/absence in descriptions such as this. Soon the girl of his dreams of childhood will reappear, first as a brunette and then made over as a blonde and later as his wife. His was a Victorian imagination in many ways, a world of virgins and whores, fallen women waiting to be rescued. His fascination with slums and working-class life has a Dickensian ring to it, though later this would be replaced by a similar fascination with North African tribespeople. For now he was drinking in the colorful life that formed his new surroundings and that shortly would feed into his first films.

He wrote home with news of how he was getting on. Reverend Hitchcock was horrified. Had Rex lost his grip on the little grammar and syntax he had learned? What was a "broad"? And a "cinch"? Did he mean "clinch"? As for the loose women in his neighborhood, this was regrettable: "I hope you keep your thoughts clean, and your body as well. *Mens Sana in Corporo Sano:* this is my motto." Rex's mother, the reverend continued, had been spared the shame of her eldest son failing his Trinity entrance, but he had been doing some research and discovered that there were universities in America bigger than Oxford, Cambridge, and Trinity put together. One called Harvard was apparently good. He believed that New Haven had a university. Kathleen had left behind a small amount of money, and he would be happy to put that toward the cost of acquiring a university education in America. Could Rex please look into this and mail him copies of the entrance exams, mathematics in particular, for his father to look at?: "I am quite sure you would have more chance of passing your examinations, as the standard of scholarship in America is undoubtedly below that of T.C.D. [Trinity College Dublin]."[2]

There was indeed a university in New Haven. It was called Yale, and on 2 January 1912 Rex enrolled at the Yale School of the Fine Arts. In September he joined the sculpture classes taught by the renowned artist Lee Lawrie, who later would become most famous for his bronze statue of Atlas at New York City's Rockefeller Center. Lawrie took quickly to his new student, and the two remained close friends to the end of Rex's life. During his first summer vacation at Yale, Rex asked Lawrie for a job as his assistant and put in many fruitful hours learning the practical basics of sculpture—building armatures, casting, making glue molds, and so on.

At Yale, Rex discovered an environment that suited his individualist temperament, and he was more popular here than he had ever found himself at school: "He seemed to us to be a gay, happily balanced young man with a sparkle to his personality which won friends and opened doors," another former Yale student, Margaret Harmon Graves, remembered. "Once in a while, while working in the studio, he would sit on a stool by my modelling stand and spend the whole afternoon regaling me with the wildest and most varied tales, all stories created on the spur of the moment. He seemed quite carried away with the pouring out of all his creative imaginings. It was fun listening to him."[3]

Rex joined the staff of the *Yale Record*, the university's humor magazine. The issue of 18 June 1912 contains a number of his pencil sketches—including a page of caricatures of the suffragette movement. In one a battered-looking man is sitting on the pavement reciting a lament:

Put me upon an Island where the girls are few
Put me among the most ferocious lions in the zoo
Put me upon a treadmill and I'll never fret
But for Pity's sake don't put me near a suffragette.[4]

Other satirical sketches were captioned "Sketches of Yale" and covered college sports, the freshmen's art studio, and two seniors taking a tumble on roller skates. In another issue, Rex was allocated a page, which was titled "A few British Sketches from one of our Foreign Contributors." Here the caricatures included a couple of Irish topics—"An Irish Colleen" was transformed into an old woman smoking a pipe, while a portly gentleman in black was depicted as "An Irish Mimber [Member of Parliament]."[5] The style is swift, assured, and satirical, with the same subversive take on his subjects that had characterized his schoolboy sketches. Not as mainstream as the sketches of the widely admired Alban Bernard Butler, Rex's contributions prefigure his films in one way, in that their humor is highly idiosyncratic. Even when he tried, Rex could never quite manage to be populist. Still, he was rewarded with the job of associate editor and then with election to the magazine's editorial board. Yet, when it came time to take up his position, Rex had dropped out of Yale. A listing of Yale nongraduates of 1914 notes that Reginald I. M. Hitchcock was now to be found care of T. Edison & Co., 2826 Decatur St., New York, NY.[6]

The Lure of the Movies

On days off from sculpting classes and the *Yale Record,* Rex discovered D. W. Griffith. First, he and his friends took to patronizing the nickelodeons, learning the names of the regular stars of the one-reelers—John Bunny, Norma Talmadge, Maurice Costello. "The Kalem company had sloe-eyed slender Alice Joyce, who wept without provocation and without screwing her face up," he recalled years later. "I envied the dark young man in whose arms she climaxed every film while round punctured holes appeared all over the screen, stamped there by an unfeeling censor."[7] But it was his first D. W. Griffith picture that overwhelmed Rex. The film, *Man's Genesis* (1912), with its Stone Age setting, was hardly vintage Griffith, but it convinced Rex and his friends to return over and again to the nickelodeon, catching each new Griffith film as it came out. They went back for the Pearl White serials and kept on going. One film that they all admired was William J. Humphrey's *A Tale of Two Cities,* made for the Vitagraph company in 1911 and starring Florence Turner and Maurice Costello: "I did not go to this picture with an open mind, for I had seen the stage version, *The Only Way,* at the Theatre Royal in Dublin with Martin Harvey as the star. It was the first play I had seen and was still my favourite. But after the Vitagraph version got underway I found myself liking Costello in spite of my prejudice."[8]

One of the friends that Rex made at Yale, and who also worked with him on the *Record,* was Horace Frederick Newsome. In summer of 1913 Newsome invited Rex to vacation with his family on Long Island, New York. There Rex met Charles Edison, son of the inventor and moving picture pioneer Thomas Edison. The younger Edison introduced Rex to his father, but the old man was stone deaf and couldn't understand a word his son's guest said. Next Charlie invited Rex and Horace to visit the Edison studios at 198th Street and Decatur Avenue in the Bronx. Charles Sumner Williams, a friend of Charles Edison's at the Massachusetts Institute of Technology, was working there (later he would become vice president of Edison Industries), looking after stories and checking titles. Rex assured Sumner Williams that he had a list of ideas and had written a couple of scenarios if he would like to see them. Williams agreed to look at them, so Rex sent them round the next day.

When he discovered that the Newsomes were leaving home for a month, Rex began to worry. He had eight dollars and thirty-five cents to his name. Accordingly, armed with the address of a magazine artist he had met in New Haven and who had promised to introduce him to his agent, he moved to New York City. The magazine artist's name was Rollin Crampton, and later he would become famous for his abstracts and geometric shapes. But then he was living in the most bohemian of New York locations, the Lincoln Arcade. Now the site of the Lincoln Center, this was a six-story loft dedicated to artists, an "erratic maze of tunnels in a building afflicted with makeshift architecture and arthritis, where muscle builders and fortune-tellers and astrologers rented space cheaply."[9] In 1909 Robert Henri, the painter and famed art teacher, set up the Henri School of Art on the sixth floor, down the hall from the room taken by his illustrious pupil George Bellows and the artist Edward R. Keefe. Another occupant of the building was Marcel Duchamp, who arrived in New York in June 1915 and shared loft space with his French colleague Jean Crotti, who too had just moved to America. Duchamp kept his "ready-mades"—*Bicycle Wheel, Snow Shovel, Trap,* and *Hat Rack*—suspended from the ceiling of his studio. From 1917 the white porcelain urinal he had purchased and submitted for exhibition as *Fountain* hung above a doorframe. The Lincoln Square Theater was in the same building, and a block away stood Tom Sharkey's athletic club, immortalized by Bellows in his 1909 painting *Stag at Sharkey's.* Boxing was still outlawed in New York when Rex moved to live there, and so for fans the only legitimate way to watch the sport was at a private-membership athletic club. One may guess that Rex was to be found in the clamorous crowd at Sharkey's when fights were being staged, just as he may have enjoyed a drink across the street at Healy's Saloon, where, in the winter of 1909, Eugene O'Neill conceived the idea for *The Iceman Cometh.*

Rex ascended the shabby building to Crampton's apartment, where Crampton's roommate Worth Brehm let him in. As he waited for his friend to arrive, a man appeared at the door. He was short, with a little black moustache, and in spite of the heat he was wearing a long black cape that trailed to the ground. This was topped with a wide-brimmed black hat and accompanied by a silver-topped cane:

> "Crampton isn't here," he stated rather than inquired.
>
> Then he came in closing the door after him.
>
> "Hello, Benton," said Brehm.
>
> "That bastard," said Benton, "that bastard Ralph Barton has gone out and locked the door of his studio."
>
> "Wise boy," said Brehm.
>
> "Told him I was going to work in it this afternoon, and left a new canvas there," Benton said.
>
> "Why not work in your own?" Brehm said without looking up.
>
> "Light's better in his," said Benton. "Got to start another abstract composition today . . . Thought Crampton might have a spare canvas I could borrow."
>
> Brehm shook his head. Benton poked the curtains apart with his cane and pulled out a couple of canvases from the stack next to the stove. One of them was a study of a girl's head.
>
> "Crampton's?" said Benton, observing the back of it with interest.
>
> "No, mine," said Brehm, looking at it.
>
> "Size I need," said Benton. Brehm went on working.
>
> "Got no unused canvases," he said.
>
> "This one will do fine," said Benton.
>
> "There's a portrait on the other side of it," Brehm said.
>
> "I'll paint it out," said Benton.
>
> "The hell you will," said Brehm.
>
> Benton looked at him in mild surprise.
>
> "You mean you want to keep this?"[10]

Despite this inauspicious beginning described in Rex's memoirs, Thomas Hart Benton was to become one of Rex's closest friends in New York and to remain in touch with him for the rest of his life. Born in Neosho, Missouri, in 1889, Benton came from a distinguished family. He was named after his great-uncle, also Thomas Hart Benton, one of the first two US senators elected in Missouri and one of the great champions of

Manifest Destiny, a concept of American exceptionalism. The younger Benton's father, Maecenas Benton, was a lawyer and congressman and devoted his political career to tackling, as Erika Doss writes, "the unbridled greed of corporate capitalism in the Gilded Age."[11] Rebelling against the family tradition of Republicanism, Benton decided to study art; according to Doss, "his generational rebellion led him, as it did others, to search for a new vision to correspond with the changed world of the twentieth century, a vision which he eventually found in modern art."[12] And in cinema, it might be added. After studying at the School of the Art Institute of Chicago, Benton departed for Paris in 1908 to continue his education at the Académie Julian. In 1913 he moved to New York City, where he met up with Ralph Barton. An awkward, abrasive man, Benton was also a homophobe; he had been sexually molested as a student, and "his adult friends were mostly of the heavy-drinking, boot-stomping, he-man variety."[13]

This description hardly fits Rex or the other young man who was to form the third member of the friendship, Ralph Barton. Born in 1891, Barton had grown up a lonely child in Missouri, the youngest son of eccentric parents who, despite their professional vocations of lawyer and artist, devoted their lives to what Ralph's mother, Catherine, termed "metaphysics or mental science."[14] Their house was given over to healing, often literally, as Catherine and Ralph's father, Abraham, took in penniless patients whom they would treat through prayer and who would roam the house freely. A childhood talent, by 1910 Barton was publishing his illustrations in the *Kansas City Star,* where he was then employed. Sometime in late 1911 or early 1912, he moved with his equally young wife, Marie, and their daughter, Natalie, to a small apartment in the Washington Heights neighborhood of New York City. As his work spiraled upward, he took a studio in the Lincoln Arcade. Ralph Barton shared Rex's habit of executing lightning sketches of friends and family. One such sketch from this period is of his new friend; the accompanying text reads: "Rex Hitchcock of Oxford— Dublin and Yale! Sculptor who has seen 'a very good friend of mine at Oxford get the nastiest sort of a spill at polo—breaking the pony's leg—and still keep his monocle in his eye!' Hitchcock wears one." Sure enough the drawing depicts a very austere, angular Rex complete with monocle, an unlikely prop. Rex moved in with Benton and slept on a mattress on his studio floor. With piecemeal commercial illustration work, he might just about scrape by.

In 1913, the year Rex moved in to the Lincoln Arcade, an exhibition took place in New York City that was to rock the artistic world. This was the International Exhibition of Modern Art, or the Armory Show. Held at the armory of the 69th Regiment, it aimed to introduce New Yorkers to the best of their own American avant-gardists and to the new generation of European artists. A slow burner, the event received little attention in the beginning, but when descriptions of pieces such as Duchamp's *Nude Descending a Staircase* and Henri Matisse's voluptuous, exotic naked islanders began to circulate, the crowds started to arrive. In four weeks, a hundred thousand visitors attended the show, turning up in such vast numbers in the evenings that the entry price had to be raised from twenty-five cents to a dollar to control attendance. The overall response was one of outrage, but among Rex's circle of friends this was an eye-opener—an exposure to a kind of art that few had seen before. Ralph Barton returned several times, we know, and it may be assumed that his friend Reginald Hitchcock did too.[15] According to Barton's biographer, it was, however, his discovery of the Egyptian wing of the Metropolitan Museum of Art in 1914 that was his major epiphany.[16] Again, one cannot know whether he dragged his friend from Ireland with him, but given that all three young men were spending so much time together, it is reasonable to suppose that, in New York City, in this artistic environment, Rex too was able to develop the fascination with the ancient world he had inherited from his father and to take it in new directions, as he shortly would in his films.

Edison

Meanwhile, Rex urgently needed to make some money. Rollin Crampton walked Rex around the offices of the leading New York publishing companies—*Life, Vanity Fair,* the *Christian Herald.* On each occasion Rex was disappointed. The editors he met acknowledged his talent but advised that he needed experience. Without independent means, how could he achieve that?

Horace Newsome suggested he go back to the Edison studio and remind them of his scenarios. Rex strolled in and, according to his account, became swiftly involved in coaching Eddie O'Connor in rudimentary golf for a scene in *Seth's Sweetheart* (Charles Ransom, 1914). He then pressed Sumner Williams for a response to his scenarios. "One of our directors, Mr. Ridgely, likes that Cuban story you sent in, *Family Honor*," Sumner

Williams replied, "but there appears to be a scene that bothers him—a girl falling off a horse or something. Why don't you go down and have a talk with him? He's on the set."[17]

Richard Ridgely was encouraging about the scenario, for which he said he was prepared to pay twenty-five dollars, but the safety aspects of the sequence in which the female lead fell off her horse when riding disguised as a man worried him. Rex volunteered for an extra ten dollars to carry out the stunt himself. Ridgely agreed to a trial, and, if it went well, he would buy the scenario. The crew found a suitable cliff, and Rex mounted the horse. Now feeling somewhat anxious, he rode the horse around the cliff a few times to get him used to it: "I unbuckled the stirrup leather next to the precipice and held the strap in my hand. When the whistle blew I started the horse at a gallop, leaning all my weight in that stirrup intending to let go of the leather the minute they fired the shot so that the fall would look natural, and not as if I was throwing myself off. But when they fired, the horse swerved, reared and dumped me right over the cliff. I came near breaking my neck on the way down." But Ridgely was happy and offered Rex a small part in the film, provided he help him with the script. This meant an extra thirty dollars: "Prosperity was beckoning me!"[18]

Exactly at what point Rex finally gave up on the idea of becoming a sculptor and threw in his lot with motion pictures is not quite clear. In September of 1913 he was back in New Haven, at 16 Woolsey Street. On 9 September he wrote to his Aunt Lizzie, enthusing about his work on the *Record* and the thrill of studying under Lee Lawrie. Yet, in a postscript, he slips in the warning that "if I can't make good at sketching or sculpture, I might try the moving-picture acting which is the best paying thing in America in that line."[19]

Although, at first glance, it seems inexplicable that the man who described himself as an "artist" on the ship's manifest just two years earlier should abandon his studies at Yale and fling himself into the already shocking milieu of early film production, one needs to remember that cinema was the most exciting new art form to capture the American imagination. It was dynamic, protean, and open to all comers, a beacon of opportunity for con men and talented artists alike. As much as great pioneers such as D. W. Griffith attempted to lure the middle classes to the pictures with adaptations of the kind of novels they so favored, so too were city slum dwellers thronging to the nickelodeons to see the tales of murder, melodrama, and mystery that were the lifeblood of early cinema. At this moment, films were in transition as well, developing from the earlier "primitive" model of sketches and gags to lengthier and more sophisticated plots and forms of storytelling, more akin to the cinema of today.[20]

Studios were also unregulated places, with employees as likely to appear in front of as behind the camera. In the early days of filmmaking, stage actors shunned the movies, only looking for a job on screen when all else failed, so anyone with a face that fit a role was as likely to be cast as a seasoned performer. Rex was to find himself painting sets one day and contributing to a script the next. With his good looks, he was also quickly appropriated for minor parts.

He started as he was to continue—bringing his obstinate perfectionism to bear on his colleagues: "When *Family Honor* was screened Mr. Ridgely thought it was the best picture he had made. He asked me my opinion and I said what I had said all along, that the players were too old for their parts and Richard Tucker who played the cowardly younger brother of the heroine was so much bigger than his sister that his uniform would have made her look like a scarecrow, and anyone could see they were not his clothes she wore." In one fell swoop, he thus alienated Ridgely and the rest of the cast and crew.[21]

The Family's Honor (as the film ended up being named), a drama of the Spanish-American War, was released in 1913 and starred Charles Sutton and Charles Ogle. It is startling to see the name "Rex Hitchcock" appearing in large letters (unlike the name of the director, Richard Ridgely, which was nowhere to be seen) on the publicity sheet. Edison was promoting their picture via an unknown writer.

In the film, Alva Bellina (Mabel Trunnelle) is the daughter of a Spanish army general, General Bellina (Charles Sutton), who is killed in battle with his son José (Richard Tucker), Alva's twin brother, at his side. As he dies he entrusts José with an important secret mission, but José panics and flees the battlefield. Alva dons José's uniform and sets off herself with the dispatches. On her way, she is attacked by American soldiers and taken, fainting, to Lieutenant Adams (Charles Ogle), who realizes who she is. They hear shots, and the body of a soldier is brought into the tent—it is José, who has found out about the sacrifice his sister has made and tried to avenge the family honor. With his arm around the weeping Alva, Adams promises that José will have a soldier's funeral and the blot on their family name will be removed. Adams and Alva fall in love. War story, melodrama, love affair—one can see why Edison was happy to put Rex's first scenario on the screen. Soon he was plunged into life at the studio.

This easy-come, easy-go atmosphere renders it impossible now to produce a fully accurate picture of who worked on what picture. On-screen credits were generally limited to the names of the lead actors, and the trade press was often little more informative. Thus, putting together a list of the films on which Rex worked can only be partial. He collaborated again with the forgiving Ridgely for his next script, the three-reel *Hard Cash,* landing the assignment by promising to write to one of his aunts for an authentic account of life in a "lunatic asylum." The fact that she had died many years previously was an incidental detail, compensated for by reading up on the inhumane treatment of inmates and composing a heart-rending account written to him by the "aunt." Ridgely was impressed: "He gave me two $5 paychecks and, when the picture started, made me his assistant."[22] Rex happily launched himself into his soon-to-be favorite habit of scouring antique stores for props in order to create a set that looked as close to the setting of the story as he could achieve. On location with the shoot, Rex found some fine camera angles under arches in an old stone fort and through barred windows where beams of light streamed in from a broken roof. He determined to use those images when he could start making his own films. According to his memoirs, he also offered Ridgely copious unsolicited, and evidently unwelcome, advice on how to achieve a sculptural, three-dimensional effect through lighting. For extra money, he played various inmates of the asylum. Fed up with the young neophyte and his relentless criticism, Ridgely put his foot down and refused to work with Rex again. *Hard Cash* was released on 26 September 1913.

Somewhat surprisingly, in another letter to his Aunt Lizzie, this time on Christmas Day 1913, Rex did not mention his move into screenwriting but insisted that he was working on becoming what he had always dreamed of, an actor: "You are disappointed that I gave up sculpture," Rex writes, "but . . . I simply could not live and keep it up—I should require about ten more years of study—here and abroad—to get the *grounding* that a sculptor must have, if he is to do good work. And while acting is placed[d] second to none of the arts—you can see that with a good director a juvenile man who is an earnest student stands a better chance of making a living— *especially on the screen*—as they say in the picture game. . . . I can make enough to live in a kind of a way at this business—I could not at sculpture." Later, when it was his turn to direct juvenile men, Rex would conveniently forget his assessment of the artistic qualities of acting and insist that it was the director alone whose vision must count. For now, however, he advised his aunt to look out for him in *The Necklace of Rameses* (Charles Brabin, 1914), due out shortly and in which he played the chief of the diamond crook gang.[23]

Although he does not mention them in his memoirs, Rex also acted in a number of other Edison films, probably including *Beau Brummel* (James Young), *The Artist's Great Madonna* (Van Dyke Brooke), *The Witness to the Will* (George Lessey), *The Price of the Necklace* (Charles Brabin), *The Borrowed Finery* (director unknown), *The Spirit and the Clay* (Harry Lambart), and *The Southerners* (Richard Ridgely and John H. Collins), all released from 1913 to 1914. These were thrilling yarns and often hugely ambitious in scale. Take for instance *The Necklace of Rameses*. The jewelry of the title first appears in ancient Egypt on the neck of a princess who has just died. Cut to the present, where it resurfaces in a New York museum and is now worn by a mummy. Enter the daring Diamond Mary (Miriam Nesbitt), who steals the necklace and gives the filmmakers the opportunity to indulge in a global-heist thriller, with the thieves escaping from one glamour spot of Europe to the next before meeting their inevitable end. Edison's pictures did not just tell fantastical stories with swift-moving plots—they have come to enjoy a reputation for detailed, often striking art direction. Rex, in common with his silent-era contemporaries, was learning on the spot. However, he was also building up a reputation for being troublesome. He worked on the scenario of the comedy *Why Girls Leave Home* (1913) with its director and former vaudeville performer, C. J. Williams. Before long they fell out, and Williams paid Rex off. Then Horace Plimpton, the studio manager, barred him from the studio. Rex's fledgling career at Edison was over.

Dismayed but not completely discouraged, he went straight to the Biograph Studios. There, he claims, he conducted a long conversation with a stranger to whom he gave a light in the foyer about how second-rate Edison was and how the only person worth working with was D. W. Griffith. This stranger was, of course, Griffith, and he left the highly opinionated young man with a reference that read: "Bill: make a test of this boy with Irma when you finish on number 1. D.W.G."[24] Later Griffith, whom Rex admired to the end of his days, referred to Rex as "one of my boys," presumably as a consequence of his influence on Rex's films, since the two never worked together.[25] Even that influence is questionable, since Rex was never to show the same interest as Griffith in the mechanics of film production.

Vitagraph

While he was waiting for the call back from Griffith, Rex met with Albert E. Smith. Smith was one of the founders of Vitagraph, an entrepreneur with a reputation for ruthless business acumen. The older man tossed Griffith's reference letter to one side dismissively but promised to give Rex a trial starting that Monday. Later he would remember his protégé as being "blessed with ability and cursed with impatience."[26] The move to Vitagraph was a good way to put this ability to the test—many of Vitagraph's releases were historical dramas and adaptations of well-known novels or of operas, an area that particularly interested Rex. Their production values were equally ambitious, and the studio is now considered one of the most innovative of the era.[27] As the biggest film company in America, Vitagraph was a magnet for expatriates of all hues and for the milling talents who washed in and out of the film studios of New York in search of a break. Rex recalls meeting the Russian playwright and actor Nicholas Dunaev on his first day at work. Aside from his literary fame, Dunaev also boasted the reputation of being able to bend a dime between his fingers. He was accompanied by a silent man whom he introduced as Mr. Bronstein and who obliged with some assistance as Dunaev performed his dime-bending trick. Later Dunaev told Rex that his friend was in fact Leon Trotsky.[28]

At Vitagraph, Rex played in routine melodramas, comedies, and crime films such as *Goodbye Summer* (Van Dyke Brooke), *Her Great Scoop* (Maurice Costello, Robert Gaillard), *The Crime of Cain* (Theodore Marston), *The Circus and the Boy* (Tefft Johnson), and *David Garrick* (James Young), all released in 1914. Mostly this acting work was anonymous and unexceptional. One picture, *The Moonshine and the Maid* (released on 7 December 1914 and directed by Charles L. Gaskill), in which he is credited as supporting actor, was, however, reviewed as "quite thrilling and very melodramatic with some emotional scenes." Happily, the critic continued on to comment that "the acting is well done."[29]

By night, Rex was writing verse, a new interpretation of the *Rubaiyat of Omar Khayyam*, which he intended to illustrate himself:

Across the turrets from the clouds on high
A figure flashes with a joyous cry.
The Herald of the Dawn is on his way
To drive the shadows from the morning sky!

"I am going to illustrate it in a rather unique way," he wrote to his "Aunt Cissie" (presumably Aunt Cecilia) back in Ireland, "illustrating the underlying thought, rather than the literal verse." As a young artist, Rex was evidently developing; no longer was his art to be representational but conceptual. He would never be a modernist, but the ideas to which he was being exposed in New York City were taking shape. He was also beginning to indulge in a practice that was to last throughout his life—collecting artifacts not just for his sets but for himself. "Are you leaving Leinster Road?" he enquired of Aunt Cissie. "If you do sell your things at auction—which I hope you won't—because old furniture and old paintings have associations that make them priceless, let me know before the auction what the things are. I remember (I think I do) a four poster bed—a spinning wheel—and old bits of furniture and a wonderful picture over the drawing room mantel—don't sell that whatever you do." He planned to buy a castle, he continued, and to make it a home for artists to work in, and to furnish it with antiques; maybe even to marry a rich American heiress. He had already purchased "some swords, Japanese prints, a Buddha—Chinese, and a drapery since I wrote to you last. I'm getting some old Peruvian pottery soon—too—wait till I get that old castle. I'm going to have a room entirely Chinese—a room Gothic, a room Persian and one big junk shop—to use as a study and library."[30]

What is most remarkable about this is that these are the words of a twenty-two-year-old, for if one were to look around the rooms of his villa in Nice in the late twenties or his final home in Studio City, it would be to realize that, with their clutter and paraphernalia from around the world, their books, paintings, and antique swords, he was living his life exactly as he had planned to back then as a young man starting out.

The only miscalculation was to believe that he had acting talent. At least in Wilfrid North's *Eve's Daughter,* Rex played a sculptor. He brought some of Lee Lawrie's plaster models onto the set and roped in Thomas Hart Benton to supply canvases for background material. Over the next five years, he found Benton regular employment behind the scenes on set design, carpentry, scene painting, historical research, and advertising.

"Rex Ingram," Benton later wrote, "was in those days a highly temperamental young Irishman. He was full of theatrical romance and was always writing scenarios and trying them out on me. He used to get me in a corner, mess his hair up, roll his eyes and recite concoctions in the most dramatic manner he could think of."[31]

Working in the moving picture business convinced Benton, as it would Rex, that this was a truly democratic art form, one that might effortlessly influence public taste and educate people in a way that modernism never could. As Benton scholar Henry Adams argues, his paintings from these years, particularly his vast mural, *The American Historical Epic,* which he created throughout the twenties, reflect the narrative sweep, as well as the shorthand of casting to type, of the films on which he had worked:

> Benton's murals are fast-paced, modern, and film-like, in their pace, their cutting from scene to scene, their grand vision of life. Even the use of stereotypes in filmmaking—the glamour girl, the cowboy, the farmer, the city slicker—taught him to create figures whom one can read at a glance in a large, complicated composition. In a stroke Benton had completely shifted the nature of American painting by producing a work that was larger, more powerful, more exciting that anything yet made by an American—more modern in its visual form, more controversial in its subject matter. He made the work of most previous American realists seem small and limited in its expressive ambition; he made most modernist painting seem weak and irrelevant, divorced from real life.[32]

Rex apparently even tried to persuade Benton onto the screen: "One time Rex got it into his head that I might be made into an actor and gave me a part in a bar-room scene with Paddy Sullivan and Jimmy Kelly and a lot of other pugs of those days who put on fights for the movies. When that picture came out it went into theaters in Missouri and some friends of my father saw it, recognised me and told him about it. The old man was outraged and wrote me a scathing letter about where my artistic ambitions were leading me." The story has a ring of truth to it that makes it hard to ignore, though equally hard to prove correct.[33]

At Vitagraph, Rex acted for his hero from *A Tale of Two Cities,* William Humphrey, who was now directing an unexceptional social problem film, *Fine Feathers Make Fine Birds.* He could do nothing right: "I was over-anxious to please him. He had seen the play I had made with Lillian Walker, and started off by telling me I knew nothing about acting. He played all the scenes for me himself and expected me to play them exactly the way he did. . . . At the end of the first day's work I was a wreck, and when I got to my dressing room, which I shared with 400-lb comedian Hughy [Hughie] Mack, I felt so discouraged that I cried, for I would have rather pleased Mr Humphrey than any director on the lot."[34] At home in Dublin, Rex's godmother, Matilda Greer, took Rex's father to the Grafton cinema where one of his errant son's films was playing. The two old friends sat in the dark, in tears—at the sentiment and at the sight of their beloved Rex on screen.

Fox

With the outbreak of war in Europe and the loss of their overseas markets, Vitagraph contracted swiftly. Albert E. Smith put many of the weekly-paid staff on notice. Rex was one such casualty, and in 1915 he moved studio again, this time to the recently formed Fox Film Corporation. Around him the talk was of the war, particularly among the European expatriates: "A letter came from my father. My brother had been at Campbell College, but when war broke out had gone to Sandhurst at once. He was now in Belgium with the 3rd Leinster regiment. My old friend Captain Montgomery had been killed at Mons. Things were looking pretty bad for the Allies, but my father placed a lot of faith in the British navy and the Irish regiments. . . . From time to time, I got cards from the trenches. They never said very much, but at least my brother was still alive."[35] On 16 May 1915 Frank left home for the front. As he arrived in Queenstown in the pouring rain, even the sight of a whole platform stacked with coffins prepared for the victims of the *Lusitania* did not deter the young man, and three days later he took his leave of his father, giving him a gift of his sword and his Sam Browne. In the gathering darkness, his ship weighed anchor and sailed for Holyhead in Wales and thence to France. We know about Frank Hitchcock's wartime experiences from his highly regarded memoirs, *Stand To: A Diary of the Trenches 1915–1918*, published in 1937. They tell of a nightmare world of freezing temperatures alternating with searing heat, rain falling in deluges, flooded dugouts, dirt, vermin, food covered in flies, constant and unpredictable death, and the ever-present stench of dead bodies. Most of his men were Irish, many from his own and neighboring counties. One, Willy McBride, was an old friend from Kinnitty.

Frank's book resounds with tales of the bravery and good spirits of his men, all volunteers. Like Rex, he enjoyed sketching, and *Stand To* is illustrated with his own drawings. In early February of 1917, while out exploring no-man's-land, he came upon a rusty Webley revolver lying beside a skeleton. As he was to return home on leave the next day, he held on to it as a memento for his father. This was the weapon that Reverend Hitchcock took to carrying under his clerical garb for protection during the Irish Civil War. It also fell to Frank to write to Rex and break the news that his beloved spaniel Towser had died.

In 1915 Rex made another significant change in his life, now taking his mother's name and becoming Rex Ingram. He was working with even greater focus and a sure sense that he had a future in motion pictures. As the writer Edward Montagne remembered of those days: "Rex insisted upon writing then what is put on today with difficulty. It is perhaps unnecessary to say that he was not a howling success as a scenario writer, but this did not daunt him. 'Art for art's sake' was his motto, even though he was opposed by the entire industry."[36] Changing his name was another statement of intent, not just an homage to his mother but a firm break with his father's ambitions for him.

Rex's task at Fox was to transform scenarios of Canadian director J. Gordon Edwards into workable screenplays and to help the veteran director make the shift from short films to feature-length productions. Edwards, in the opinion of William Fox, founder of the Fox Film Corporation, was still filming staged plays. He had to adapt to producing features that brought Fox's output closer to Griffith's, dramas created in the new language of cinema. Nor did scenarios necessarily have to be adaptations of existing stage plays or novels—he needed writers who could turn out original works, written specifically for the screen. Standing over Rex and Edwards, Fox insisted on the importance of building up suspense so that each "act" ended with a climax that was slightly more intense than the last, with the dip slightly less each time, thus carrying the audience through the film with the action. Films were to be swiftly paced and emotionally wrenching. An audience should never lose its attention. Other Fox directors—Herbert Brenon, Edgar Lewis, Will S. Davis, Frank Powell, and later Frederick A. Thompson and Raoul Walsh—were all drilled in the same techniques. Rex not only learned quickly from his mentor, he was also closely watching the films made by his contemporaries. Irish American

Walsh's Bowery gangster drama *Regeneration,* released in 1915, anticipated many Ingram traits, notably the loving close-ups of grotesques and bawdy underworld figures, but also the playful introduction of domestic animals whose naturalness of movement adds to the film's realism. Later, in a nod to Walsh's earlier film, Rex would include a sequence in *The Four Horsemen of the Apocalypse* that is a direct steal from *Regeneration.*

Fox had just signed the Danish actor Betty Nansen, and Rex's first assignment was writing the five-reel *Should a Mother Tell?* for her. The result, directed by J. Gordon Edwards, was a racy melodrama set in France during the Revolution and revolving around a miserly innkeeper who insists on sending his young daughter to work. Her mother instead sends her to a sympathetic family, where she grows up, eventually falling in love with their son. A sequence of nasty events ensues, including blackmail, murder, and a last-minute confession on the steps to the guillotine. The trade journal *Moving Picture World* was impressed: "Mr. Ingram is to be congratulated upon the remarkable skill with which he has copied the methods of Eugene Sue, Zola and the Elder Dumas. Not for an instant does the story lose its Gallic atmosphere, and it is constructed after the most approved rules of the French drama. The successive steps by which the climax is reached have all the mechanical perfection of plays by Scribe, or Sardou, and it is a decidedly vigorous and sensationally effective photoplay."[37] As well as sensationalism, the scenario already contains several signature Ingram touches—the waif, Raul, who doesn't speak; the inclusion of various domestic animals in key scenes; a double exposure that signals the beginnings of the innkeeper's madness; and a ghostly apparition—many of which would later reappear in his 1921 film *The Conquering Power.*

Rex followed this with a succession of equally full-blooded melodramas, including *The Wonderful Adventure* (directed by Frederick A. Thompson) and *The Song of Hate* (again directed by J. Gordon Edwards). The two films were released in 1915, with *The Song of Hate* to be his first adaptation of *La Tosca. Variety* labeled it "one of the finest features ever released."[38] His next writing assignment was on *The Blindness of Devotion* (J. Gordon Edwards, 1915), another melodrama whose story, the *Los Angeles Times* reported, was of "society's sins, combining love, beauty, hatred, revenge and action."[39] So torrid was the tale that *Variety* was convinced that it must have been adapted from an old French play since "nobody but a Frenchman could have conceived such a plot."[40]

The film concerns a wealthy French count who is entrusted with the charge of an adolescent boy, Pierre Cavereaux (Stuart Holmes). After a chance encounter in a restaurant, the count weds a much younger beauty. She in turn lures Cavereaux into her grasp. Only when he discovers whose wife she now is does he comprehend what he has done. Still he cannot resist the siren. To save her uncle's dignity, the count's niece marries Cavereaux, but his jealous adoptive stepmother attempts to chase her off. Meanwhile the count faces down the young man and hands him a revolver with the words, "If you have a spark of manhood, there is only one thing to do." Cavereaux does indeed shoot himself. The count then switches a poisoned demitasse that his young wife had laid out for him so that she drinks from it. He flings her dead body down the stairs onto that of the young man so that both may be reunited in death.

This was indeed heady material—vigorous, action-packed, and melodramatic. Rex moved on swiftly to his next project, *A Woman's Past* (directed by Frank Powell and released in November 1915), yet again teasing audiences with adultery, mistaken identities, and a last-minute courtroom drama. His scenarios demonstrate an ease with cinematic language, short, fast-paced scenes, elaborate camera and lighting instructions, and directions to cast secondary characters according to their looks. The counsel for the prosecution in *A Woman's Past*, for instance, is described as a "hard faced, cynical looking man."[41] His final film of 1915, *The Galley Slave*, which he cowrote and which J. Gordon Edwards directed, saw Rex maintaining his form with a Theda Bara vehicle that had the screen's newest and most exotic (if American) vamp married to an artist against her father's advice and forced by her uncle-in-law to have sex with him in return for money. Again, multiple misunderstandings occur, a child is born, more misjudged alliances are formed, and Francesca, Theda Bara's character, ends up shooting her conniving husband.

In 1915, Rex found success in another field. His short story "The Criminal" was published in the leading socialist newspaper of the day, the *New York Call*. With illustrations by its author, it is a tale of a miscarriage of justice and its consequences. An innocent man convicted by a corrupt jury has been imprisoned for six years when he catches sight of his image in a piece of tinware that he picks up and polishes. He becomes obsessed with this image and determined to escape by ripping the stones out of his cell wall. Two wardens come upon him as he is working on his plan. The scene that follows presages many of the later films: "As he stood there firmly, the moonbeams from the opening in the wall throwing a strange mottled light on his striped suit, from his face every vestige of his former self disappeared. He became the lowering animal, the beast that had stared at him from the canister, waiting to strike, once and with terrible effectiveness before the end." And so he strikes the warden, crushing the man's head like a rotten apple, and he laughs as they put him in chains, later to be electrocuted.[42] This is social injustice fiction Dickens-style; the tone of the writing is also very much the tone of early cinema, at once exploitative and moralistic. Rex was at one with his peers in realizing that lurid tales of hardship appealed to tenement immigrants and liberals alike, and in common with many of his fellow practitioners he would proceed to make this the platform for his own entrée into film.

Writing scenarios was making the young man a living, but he itched to direct. William Fox promised him that if he wrote an original story for Robert B. Mantell or Theda Bara that was good enough to produce, he could direct it. Rex swiftly returned with the scenario he had written at Vitagraph, *Black Orchids*. Bara scoffed at the notion that she would read anything but pronounced herself enthusiastic about the title. Fox did read Rex's proposal and was equally positive, encouraging Rex to develop the scenario with Bara in mind and dangling the promise of a seat in the director's chair in front of him. Then he called Rex into his office. He loved what he had read, he told Rex, but he needed him to keep working on scenarios. J. Gordon Edwards would direct *Black Orchids*. Rex was enraged and refused to agree to this. Fox threatened that he would have Edwards direct a picture so similar that Rex would be unable to make *Black Orchids*. Rex still would not consent to having anyone else direct his scenario. Fox took the script from his desk and brought it to the door. He handed it to Rex without a word. Then he walked back to his chair. Rex recalled: "And so ended one of the happiest associations of my life. One from which I learned more than from any other in my motion picture career. Lee Lawrie and William Fox gave me the grounding in sculpture and drama that helped me get ahead of others that had been less fortunate in their apprenticeships. William Fox gave me, too, my first real chance in life and taught me enough to enable me to make the most of opportunities that came my way when I left his company."[43]

With this, Rex declared his apprenticeship over and launched himself as a film director.

3

Rex Ingram, Director

On leaving Fox, Rex made his way across the Hudson River to Fort Lee, New Jersey, where the World Film Company was based. He had his eye on working with Clara Kimball, who had just decamped from Vitagraph to Jules Brulatour's Peerless Pictures, the jewel in World Film's crown and home to numerous expatriate filmmakers, including Maurice Tourneur. It may have been that hint of European cosmopolitanism that attracted him, or it may just have been opportunism. He knew that Kimball's husband, Jimmy Young, was unhappy with watching Tourneur work with his wife, and so he was proposing that they consider one of his scenarios, either *Black Orchids,* or another, then called *Yellow and White.* Rex, of course, would direct.

Everything looked like it was going well. Rex signed for a salary of $200 per week to direct Kimball in *Yellow and White,* though she insisted that he play the artist, rather than Nicholas Dunaev, for whom Rex had written the part. He immediately set to work on creating a set that would reproduce the atmosphere of Chinatown as accurately as possible. Once the shoot started, matters began to go awry, and as soon as Young saw Rex kiss his wife on set (as part of the filming), he closed down the production. Rex demanded that he at least be allowed to keep the footage he had shot. He processed it and then walked across the Fort Lee lot to Universal Studios, where he screened the incomplete film for Julius Stern, cofounder of Universal.

Universal

At this juncture Universal was swiftly rising to become a major force in film production. The company was a conglomerate of independents, including the New York Motion Picture Company, the Powers Motion

Picture Company, the Independent Moving Pictures Company (IMP), and various smaller companies. At the head of the organization was Carl Laemmle. In 1914 Universal had split its operations, building one studio in North Hollywood and the other in Fort Lee. Julius Stern had been head of IMP and Victor Studios in New York City and relocated with Laemmle to Fort Lee. One of his functions in Fort Lee was to interview potential new employees. This was where Rex found himself. Stern watched his footage with him and told him he would show it to Laemmle. They were looking, Rex heard on the lot, for a vehicle and a leading man for their star, Violet Mersereau, who was currently on payroll with nothing to play in. With her blonde, childlike looks, she best fitted ingénue roles, but none was forthcoming.

Rex assured Stern that he was not acting material but that *Yellow and White* would be perfect for Mersereau. He would direct, as Rex recalls in his memoirs:

> "Listen," said Julius. "I give you a hundred bucks a week to direct Mersereau, and I give you two hundred bucks for the story, which is a lot of dough."
>
> I put on my hat and started out.
>
> "Hey, where you going, what's your hurry?" said Julius. "I raise you to a hundred and fifty bucks, and you give me the story for nothing."
>
> "Tell your secretary to give me back those bobbins of film," I said.
>
> "How much do you want anyway?" said Julius.
>
> "I told you," I said. "Five and two."
>
> "Didn't I tell you Mersereau's already cashed four hundred and fifty bucks without turning a crank?"
>
> "No fault of mine," I said.
>
> "It's charged up to her next picture," said Julius.
>
> "Two hundred is my salary," I said.
>
> "And if you make a lousy picture?" said Julius.
>
> "If I do, you can have back every nickel I get for story and production," I said.[1]

And on that basis, Rex received his first major directing assignment.

No sooner was the contract signed than the first threat to Rex's new career struck. The World Film Company made it clear that they were in no hurry to release the rights to *Yellow and White*. Fearing that Violet Mersereau's long-awaited start in front of the camera would be further delayed, Stern demanded that Rex come up with an alternative scenario. Improvising hurriedly, Rex responded with a new plot. If anyone noticed that it bore a distinct resemblance to George Bernard Shaw's 1912 play *Pygmalion*, they didn't pause to mention it. The new work concerned a slum child, a district attorney who vowed he could reshape her socially, the threat of a loveless marriage, a gunshot, and a happy resolution. Mersereau and Stern were convinced, and so *The Great Problem* went into production. It was to be a Bluebird film.

Bluebird was a new unit set up by Universal to cater specifically to mainstream audiences. They soon built up a reputation for making films of superior visual quality, a reputation to which Rex certainly contributed, making seven films for the company. As a Bluebird director, he was at once part of a wider organization of cost and labor—with choices regarding expenditure, casting, and editing the responsibility of other departments—but at the same time the creative head of the film, particularly once production was under way, and most especially when he also wrote the scenario, as he liked to do.[2]

At once Rex threw himself into creating an authentic Bowery set. With his assistant, William "Big Bill" Dyer, who also played Skinny McGee, he toured tenements, bars, and dives, plundering them for details. Rex wanted extras with faces that looked authentic, a practice to which he would return over and again to the end of his career. One of them was an old friend from the New Haven dockyards, a run-down boxer named Buffalo, whom he immediately put on payroll with instructions to mess up the set: "I put Buffalo to breaking windows and repairing them with putty and brown paper. Bill and I strung clotheslines outside them that gave an authentic air to the vista of tenement fire escapes beyond them. In the hall we stuck a garbage can with garbage in it and around it, salvaged from the restaurant and everywhere else we could find any. A couple of half starved cats were in a cage off-stage ready to be used when the moment came."[3]

Carl Laemmle swung by to see how his new director was faring and was intrigued by what he saw, if alarmed at the stench from the garbage. He had with him Pat Powers of the Powers Motion Picture Company, an Irishman from Waterford, with whom Rex struck up an easy friendship. If any other of Universal's management team were concerned by the state of the set, they had even more to worry about when the reviews of Rex's first film as director appeared after its release in April 1916. *Variety* was at its excoriating best when it came to pronouncing the second-rateness of *The Great Problem*. The plot particularly drew the critic's fire: "How in the name of goodness," the writer fulminated, "anybody could have written such a consistently commonplace scenario is difficult to imagine." Indeed, the final story was more redolent of the Victorian penny-dreadful than *Pygmalion*: A crook steals medicine for his dying wife and is jailed. His young daughter is left all on her own and is caught picking a pocket. The district attorney takes her in and tries to educate her. Just as she is about to marry well, she runs away attired in her street urchin clothing and sells newspapers. After several more plot twists, she stops a bullet her father intends for the district attorney. She and the attorney marry: "'One Year Later,' when you naturally look for a junior dist. Atty. you are shown instead a telegram stating the dis. atty's reform bill has passed. Oh you Rex Ingram," the review concluded.[4]

If the words are harsh, they point to a problem that was to dog Rex's career; in truth, writing was not his strongest point. To the end of his days, as his unpublished short stories show, he tended to overwrite, inserting detail where it was unnecessary. Still, *Variety* might have recognized the visual richness of the Bowery dive and its Rabelaisian inhabitants, including, alongside the half-starved cats, another future Ingram signature motif—the appearance of a dwarf waiting tables, whom the rowdy drinkers take pleasure in kicking around. Low ceilings add to the dense use of space here, while by contrast the district attorney's home is designed to look elegant and expansive. Views through windows to exterior objects add a sense of three-dimensionality. In one scene, light shining on a Chinese vase in the DA's hallway reflects the rest of the interior, opening up space, rather than confining it with clutter as the Bowery scenes do. Violet Mersereau too produces a performance worth waiting for, at once ingénue and adventurer.

Within two months, Rex had redeemed his critical reputation. *Broken Fetters*, as *Yellow and White* had become, was released on 3 July 1916. It was equally melodramatic, revolving around an orphaned child who is adopted after the murder of her father. Only now the film opens in Shanghai, and the child is the daughter of the American consul. She is kidnapped by white slave traders who carry her off to New York, where a young American artist purchases her. He has been disinherited by his father and plans to make her his model. Inevitably they fall in love. In the end, after many melodramatic twists and turns, the artist is reunited with his fortune and marries the girl. This time *Variety* found much to praise in the film, particularly its exotic Oriental atmosphere.[5] This was also what particularly pleased Rex about his picture:

> We visited hop joints and gambling dens where solemn Chinese smoked opium, or played Fan-Tan and Twenty-One with grave recklessness. We had a camera with us and made some time exposures of the hop joint. We took measurements of the bunks, and arranged with my patrolman friend [a policeman on the Chinatown squad] to rent the real pipes and *layouts* for the picture. We bought a dab of opium smeared on a playing card and I tried it out, cooking it over the little oil lamp as I held it in the bowl of the pope with a skewer-like *yen-hawk,* my neck resting on one of those cube-shaped *suey-bows* covered with finely woven matting that serve the smoker for a pillow.[6]

The *Moving Picture World* critic agreed with *Variety,* adding that "well-timed suspense, natural action, good photography, and rich and appropriate costuming are other attributes worthy of mention."[7] Rex was swiftly becoming a director to be noticed, most particularly one whose visual style was defined by its proliferation of detail.

Sunshine and Orange Groves

Until now most film production had taken place on the East Coast. However, by the mid-1910s, a shift was occurring. Lured by the sunlight and the exoticism of the surrounding scenery, film producers were relocating to the Los Angeles area. Although the film industry would soon became known as "Hollywood," the name was vaguely applied to an area on the outskirts of Los Angeles whose center was Hollywood Boulevard and Highland Avenue (home to the Hollywood Hotel), but it could also equally vaguely mean any number of locations that the moving picture business gradually occupied across Southern California. Few members of the movie colony actually lived in Hollywood, which was considered a small town (a pedestrian could cross the street without looking both ways).

But they were happy to raid the area for location shooting, taking over streets and even private homes at a moment's notice, while the wide-open spaces of Beverly Hills provided the perfect location for the popular horse operas, as the early Westerns were called. Residents became used to finding cowboys lounging in bars and top-hatted villains dining in restaurants on their way to and from work and resigned to streets being closed at a moment's notice to facilitate shooting. Indeed, they had every reason to put up with the new visitors, who were already elevating real estate values to previously unheard-of heights.

Universal began to divest itself of its New Jersey production base, as other companies also decamped from New York City. Laemmle approached Rex and urged him to move too. Although he was loath to leave New York City with its bohemian, artistic milieu, Rex knew that if he was to pursue a career as a director he needed to relocate. He sublet his apartment to Theda Bara and took a train to Los Angeles. He was particularly eager to see the Californian missions, those pioneering outposts established by the Spanish Catholic orders in the eighteenth and nineteenth centuries to convert Native Americans. As soon as he arrived, he made several visits to them, marveling at their apparent age, at the cracked, fading colors of the plasterwork, and the simple beauty of the buildings such as those in San Juan Capistrano. His next picture, he concluded, would be set in one such mission.

Rex describes in his memoirs the scale of the new Universal studio, which was like nothing he had encountered before,

> with its acres of outdoor sets—towns and villages of all conceivable and inconceivable countries crowded together against a background of purple hills. . . . The plaster work on some of these streets had cracked and fallen away, and their shells of houses had been patined by rain and sun. Among them I found a Latin-American market place with barred windows and colonnaded façades and a church at one end of it. I saw that only a few repairs would be needed to make it shootable, and the missions were waiting for me. We decided on a Latin-American version of La Tosca, with Universal's most talented dramatic star, Miss Cleo Madison, in the leading role.[8]

Rex, Cleo Madison recalled, "was very young but he was an eager and a good director . . . and our work was always harmonious and pleasant."[9]

Madison was a very different star from either Theda Bara or Violet Mersereau. She had started as an actor but moved quickly into production, directing at least nine films for Universal and then heading up her own company. According to a profile published in *Moving Picture Stories,* she gave up film direction in order to appear in this new picture. The language of the report reflects a curious sense of Madison passing on the baton to a new talent (in reality it seems that she had given up directing as a result of her marriage to an abusive drunk): "She [Cleo Madison] feels that she must concentrate all her powers on the interpretation of this great part, so she has resigned the reins of direction in favor of Rex Ingram, who is already known for his splendid work in the Mersereau pictures, 'The Great Problem' and 'Broken Fetters.'"[10]

The Chalice of Sorrow, as the version of *La Tosca* would become, tells the story of Lorelei (Cleo Madison), an American prima donna who captivates the Mexican governor, Sarpina (Wedgwood Nowell). She promises to give herself to him in order to save her lover, who is his prisoner, but then she stabs the governor to death. The film was released on 9 October 1916.

Variety's reviewer was enthralled by the film's atmosphere, particularly its visual artistry and its use of light: "A fine painter could not have managed his shadow effects better." For this they gave credit to the film's photographer, Duke Hayward, and there is no need to doubt that Hayward, who was a talented cinematographer, did influence the look of the film. Yet *The Chalice of Sorrow* is unmistakably a Rex Ingram production: "We got some beautiful shots in the mission; and a prison love scene, photographed in the damp cellars of San Fernando mission with the aid of a mirror, the light streaming through a small barred window onto an aluminum reflector in front of the camera, was pretty effective."[11] Opening out onto the Southern California desert, the film has a much greater sense of space than the New York pictures, while Sarpina's quarters, as Rex recollects, were shot through with moody lighting. There is a real menace to the exchanges between Nowell and Madison, as there is in the sequences where Sarpina's lover, the artist Marion Leslie (Charles Cummings), is tortured.

Indeed, with its dark, untidy interiors lit by candelabras and hung with crucifixes, torn curtains blowing in the wind, and its searing, empty "Mexican" vistas and mustachioed bandits, the film seems very modern, a precursor to so many such films, particularly Sergio Leone's spaghetti

Westerns. In an article on Rex's contribution to early industry ambitions to foster an art cinema, Kaveh Askari has suggested that Rex's production was influenced by Cecil B. DeMille's *Carmen* of the previous year. DeMille, like Rex, had positioned himself at this point in his career as a director of art films, making claims for his use of lighting and invoking the influence of Rembrandt as Rex would, particularly in his future collaborations with John Seitz. *Carmen* too had its origins in opera, and both films make a deliberate play for that section of the audience familiar with high-brow culture. Both films are very evidently staged, with dramatic lighting effects and compositions, and it is very credible that Rex did have DeMille's successful production in mind when it came to making his own cinematic opera.[12]

The Chalice of Sorrow's surprise ending (because of a missed message, Lorelei's lover dies anyway), not unjustifiably irked the *Variety* critic, who thought it inspired by a "'misguided' effort to 'be different.'"[13] Already Rex was torn—between the lure of mass entertainment, with its shocks and its thrills and its manipulation of the audience's emotions, to which he had been drawn since childhood, and his own suspicion of mainstream culture, coupled with an embedded reluctance to conform. He could imitate the idiom of contemporary America and stamp his mark on his films' visual style, but the banality of the happy ending was a step too far. An unexpectedly unhappy ending, or an open ending, was to become another Ingram trademark. A trademark of a very different kind is to be found in the film's casting. *The Chalice of Sorrow* includes an extra whose face would become most familiar to viewers of Rex Ingram productions—that of John George. Swarthy, hunchbacked, and a dwarf, the Syrian-born George went on to feature in a further ten films for Rex and become part of his legendary retinue of dwarfs, little people, crazies, and eccentrics.

For his next release, *Black Orchids,* he took the plunge, creating an original story that shocked the critics. The script was the same one that he had initially planned for Theda Bara; now Cleo Madison would take the lead. She played Marie de Severac, a young woman who is engaged to the celebrated artist George Renoir (Francis McDonald). Her father, Emile (Richard Le Reno), observes her flirtatious behavior and decides to tell her a cautionary tale borrowed from the novel *Black Orchids,* which he is currently writing. This story-within-a-story forms the main part of the film and portrays its protagonist, Zoraida (also played by Cleo Madison), as a serial seductress who attracts the amorous attentions of father Sebastian de Maupin (Howard Crampton) and son Ivan (Francis McDonald). Duels, rivalries, and accidental poisonings ensue, with another of Zoraida's lovers, the Marquis de Chantal (Wedgwood Nowell), finally locking her in a dungeon and leaving her to perish alongside the slain Ivan. A major plot twist turned on the intervention of an ape, played by one of Hollywood's established animal thespians, a thoroughly bad-tempered animal named Joe Martin.

This was potent material and more than enough of a morality tale to persuade Marie to mend her ways and *Variety* to opine disapprovingly that "it is possible that a French writer might have handled such a situation with sufficient subtlety to save it from offense, but the screen is not subtle. The thing [the father-son love rivalry] is quite uncalled for." Yet the same critic was full of praise for the look of the film, hailing *Black Orchids* as "an almost perfect example of all that moving backgrounds should be." The handling of light and shadow and the overall compositions were all adjudged to be exemplary.[14] Other reviews echoed a real sense that this was a breakthrough picture for the industry, bringing new levels of artistry and composition to popular fare. *Black Orchids* was released on 1 January 1917 and was an immediate hit. The public was enchanted by its heated melodramatic atmosphere, as were Rex's peers in the film business. Overnight he went from being a modestly familiar industry figure to a bankable name and one, it was suggested, capable of much more.

In the making of the film, Rex had increasingly been experimenting with light: "We had learned a lot from *The Chalice of Sorrow*, particularly about the rapidity with which the sun moved from the mirrors. So instead of rehearsing and shooting, we rehearsed all day and shot what we had rehearsed the next day."[15] He knew that the story was ordinary enough—it was the visual treatment that was so outstanding. So did Universal, who signed him on a year's contract at $300 per week.[16]

Doris Pawn

It was Cleo Madison who introduced Rex and Doris Pawn. Pawn was born in Nebraska, the baby of a large family. Her acting career began with her cousin when both were around seven years old. The two ransacked the plays printed in the Sunday magazines of the day and divided the roles between them: "We understood nothing of the sex-triangle stuff, and the family used to sit convulsed with laughter at our declamations about our 'pas-shun' and our denunciations of 'the other woman, vile rep-tile!'"[17]

School productions followed and work with a local stock company. When Pawn was seventeen, she and her family visited California. Her mother returned home, but her brother agreed to stay with her for three months to allow her to try her luck with the studios. She landed a part as an extra with Universal, which was when Madison introduced her and Rex. "She was very pretty and young," Madison remembered.[18] Photos show a cheerful, blonde young woman but give little else away.

Pawn appeared in Fox's *Blue Blood and Red,* made a few pictures for Universal, and then signed to Fox, where she regularly partnered with George Walsh. When Rex met her, she reminded him of "the head of the Victory figure that leads Saint Gaudens' bronze General Sherman to the sea in front of the Plaza Hotel in New York." She had slightly heavy features which also led him to consider that "a life mask of her would need practically no retouching to make a pretty swell fragment of sculpture."[19] Such sentiments are a credit to Rex's observational skills but less suggestive of a capacity for falling head over heels in love. His memoirs, by this stage, had also detailed a number of encounters where he falls for and instantly proposes to women whom he values for certain qualities but not because he is overwhelmed by irrational and all-consuming passion. In keeping with this trend, he invited Pawn to dinner at his Pinehurst Road bungalow to be served by his Japanese cook. So successful was the dinner that he concluded it with an awkwardly phrased proposal, recalled in his memoirs: "Before she left, I asked her if she was married, had ever been married, or ever intended getting married. She said no to the first two, and to the third, that she had never given it a thought. I said if she ever did give it a thought, and the idea appealed to her, to let me know."[20]

After a second delicious dinner, again courtesy of the Japanese cook, Rex took matters to the next level:

> "I've often wondered how it feels to be married," I said. "It can't be so bad about this time when you come home after a tough day's work. I don't like being alone in the evenings. Don't you ever get bored being alone?"
>
> "Sometimes I do," she said.
>
> "Listen," I said. "I'm stopping by for you in the morning and we'll go down and get a marriage licence."

"My goodness, what on earth for?" she asked.

"It's not a bad thing to have in the house," I said. "And if you ever did decide you'd like to be married we'd only have to drive over to Santa Ana and see the judge."[21]

This is pretty much how matters proceeded until, on 15 March 1917, the underwhelmingly romantic couple tied the knot.

Rex continued to work with Bluebird through 1917, writing and directing films (*The Reward of the Faithless, The Pulse of Life, The Flower of Doom, The Little Terror*) that offered their audiences the vicarious pleasures of a world of vice and fallen women, glamorous dancers, and doomed love. With *The Little Terror* he made a foray into comedy, setting his story among circus performers and having Violet Mersereau play both mother and (after she dies) daughter of the circus family.

Fragments of two of these films survive. *The Reward of the Faithless*—another outing for a story of star-crossed lovers, mysterious deaths, and ghostly apparitions—displays many of what were now recognizable motifs. There is a sequence in a low-ceilinged pub where swarthy men down pints of beer and watch a young woman dancer until their attention is distracted by a dwarf (John George) springing onto the top of a barrel, cavorting dementedly. A moment of kindness to a poverty-stricken woman comes from a crippled man played by Rex's friend, the hunchback Bill Rathbone. This is contrasted with the home of the wealthy Guido Campanelli (Wedgwood Nowell), with its sense of space and light. *The Flower of Doom* returns the audience to these contrasting worlds of poverty and glamor. The story now is of a reporter, Harvey Pearson (M. K. Wilson), who falls for a cabaret dancer, Neva Sacon, played by Gypsy Hart. He unwittingly pins a flower on her costume that is the symbol of the Chinese Tong, and as a result she is kidnapped. Turning to his old acquaintance Charley Sing (Frank Tokunaga), Pearson makes a visit to the opium den of Tong leader Ah Wong (Gordo Keeno) and kidnaps the beautiful Tea Rose (Yvette Mitchell), planning to swap her for Neva Sacon. Matters become increasingly complicated when the bohemian sculptor, played by Rex's old friend, the lumbering Nicholas Dunaev (who also appeared in *The Reward of the Faithless*), falls for Tea Rose. In the closing sequences, Ah Wong grabs Tea Rose as she is about to run off with the sculptor, and we leave the latter sitting, dreaming of her.

The existing fragment contains exquisite blue-tinted sequences, and overall the film appears more confident and more sophisticated than Rex's work of a year earlier. The "Rat Hole," a low-life bar, is the setting for a sequence of highly choreographed fights, while Gypsy Hart's dancing provides equivalent entertainment for the better-heeled metropolitan sophisticates. Increasingly Rex was adding to the atmosphere by casting interesting faces, and his fascination with criminality and immigrant street culture showed no signs of diminishing. Although he was not inhibited by the invisible proscenium arch of the stage set and regularly placed his camera at angles to the action for effect, these early films establish another signature stylistic trait—setting up elaborate scenes and playing them out in front of the camera with little or no camera movement. Indebted as he may have been to D. W. Griffith, Rex was uninterested in developing this aspect of filmmaking in his own work, leaving that to the other pioneers. Instead, he increasingly experimented with movement within the frame, and his later films are remarkable for dynamic lines of action that crisscross the set.

Although Rex had no choice in his stars, he did have considerable leeway in casting extras. For him, this meant bringing in dwarfs, hunchbacks, and all manner of disabled and disfigured actors. Such performers included John George, Bill Rathbone, and countless other uncredited names as background players. Word trickled down that Carl Laemmle was unhappy with this practice and that the censors had decided that seeing such persons was dangerous to pregnant women. A telegram arrived from Pat Powers, who was still based in New York: "HQ says you have put all the hunchbacks in California in stock, and the production department can't keep track of what you're doing because you don't follow the script. There appears to be only one copy of it, and the scene numbers you gave them and those you shoot don't coincide. Make an effort to cooperate with the boys. Remember you're not the only director out there. There are thirty-nine other units on the lot."[22]

The reluctance to conform to authority that Rex's peers had detected in him in his time at St. Columba's was no temporary adolescent phase. If anything, it became more entrenched with age. He proceeded to ignore Laemmle and Powers. Matters simmered and then threatened to erupt. Rex wrote to Powers; the latter responded with a telegram: "Do nothing and say nothing till I get there. Leaving Sunday night."[23] Powers managed to smooth over the problems between Rex and the production department temporarily, but now another break loomed. At home, Rex and Doris Pawn were not hitting it off. She had banned "Humpty" Bill Rathbone from the house, and Rex was furious with himself for indulging her horror of deformity. Nor could he tolerate the feeling that she was limiting his personal freedom. More fundamentally, "we had little in common. Often two or three days would pass without our addressing a word to each other. She was beautiful to look at but I could not just sit and admire her all evening."[24]

Back in Europe, Frank Hitchcock was distinguishing himself on the front. On 10 January 1917 he commanded and led the first large-scale daylight raid at the Double Crassier—two enormous slagheaps rising over the flat landscape at Loos in France. He and his men entered and held The Triangle, an enemy stronghold that had been believed to be impregnable. So stealthy was their approach that of the eight German prisoners they took, one had been standing next to his periscope reading a newspaper when Frank sprang on him. For this mission, he and two of his subalterns were awarded the Military Cross.

Rex too resolved to join up. America had entered the war in April 1917, and he wanted to be part of it like his brother. He visited the recruitment offices of the Aviation Section, US Signal Corps, completed his application for pilot training, and awaited his call-up.

Paralta

Meanwhile the inevitable break with Universal came. Rex, however, was not long out of work. The celebrated actor Henry B. Walthall was seeking to reestablish his career after the high point of playing Ben Cameron, "the little colonel" in D.W. Griffith's *The Birth of a Nation* (1915), and had set up his own production company, which would release its films through Paralta Studios and guarantee him a return to starring roles. He now invited Rex to direct his first two productions, *His Robe of Honor* and *Humdrum Brown*. Ever restless, Rex was quick to seize the opportunity, one that held out the lure of more control. He set up his own office at Paralta, decorating it with three of his sculpted heads, Venus, Hamlet, and a Chinese opium smoker.

Both films were released in 1918. In the first, Walthall starred as the crooked judge who is returned to the path of righteousness through the love of a virtuous woman. In the second, he is the put-upon bank clerk who must undergo many trials and tribulations and melodramatic misunderstandings before being reunited with his small-town true love. Walthall, John Ford later said, "was one of the greatest actors of all time—a personality that just leaped out from the screen," but neither of his films with Rex returned him to the glory days of working with D. W. Griffith.[25] Both received respectful reviews, without suggesting that they amounted to anything other than slightly above-average melodramas. The only one that has survived, *Humdrum Brown,* is indeed unexceptional, though with some identifiable humorous Ingram flourishes, such as the sequence where Humdrum Brown (Walthall) passes a blind man and drops money into his outstretched cup. In the next scene the old codger swiftly places the bills into a well-stuffed roll of notes before returning to begging. The film is fast-moving, building up to a breathless finale where Brown tackles Tanner (Howard Crampton) on board ship as he tries to make off with the inheritance, and the police race to the rescue in a speeding launch that zigzags through the harbor leaving a visible wake.

The only light on the horizon for Rex was meeting "a very young girl whose cameo face was rendered more striking by the placement and beauty of her eyes."[26] Alice Taaffe was playing in a minor role and at noon used to sit outside the studio lunch counter and strum the ukulele. Apparently she did not mind being assessed on the basis of her sculptural potential, and the two struck up a friendship. Rex began to look forward to seeing her.

Finally the response came from the Signal Corps. Now Rex discovered that he had never fully completed his citizenship application—and to enlist in the Signal Corps, one had to be a citizen. The alternative was to join Great Britain's newly formed Royal Flying Corps Canada (RFC Canada), which had been set up to train Canadian volunteers. Canada, as part of the British Empire, had joined the war in 1914. As Rex still had British citizenship, enlistment was not a problem.

He had a few farewells to make before leaving:

When I said goodbye to little Miss Taaffe on the bench outside the studio lunchroom she wept charmingly.

"If you give me your address I'll send you a picture postcard," I said.

Reginald Ingram Montgomery Hitchcock in his mother's arms. *Courtesy of Library of Congress*

Early sketch, "Grafton Street" (1910). *Courtesy of the National Library of Ireland*

"In the Paddock" (1910). *Courtesy of the National Library of Ireland*

Rex Ingram as a schoolboy.
Courtesy of Trinity College Dublin Archives

Rex Ingram as a young man.
Courtesy of Trinity College Dublin Archives

Ingram sketches from the *Yale Record,* circa 1912. *Courtesy of the National Library of Ireland*

(Above) With Earl Williams and Lillian Walker in *The Artist's Great Madonna* (Van Dyke Brooke, 1913). *Courtesy of the National Library of Ireland (Below)* Ingram (as Rex Hitchcock, top left) in *The Southerners* (Richard Ridgely, John H. Collins, 1914), with Sally Crute, Richard Tucker, and Mabel Trunnelle. *Courtesy of the National Library of Ireland*

(*Above*) Lillian Walker, Earle Williams, and Ingram (as Rex Hitchcock) in *Eve's Daughter* (Wilfred North, 1914). *Courtesy of the National Library of Ireland* (*Below*) Ingram (as Rex Hitchcock) with Charles Ogle (extreme right). Although the film is identified as *The Ironmaster* in the Liam O'Leary Archives, that is almost certainly incorrect. *Courtesy of the National Library of Ireland*

(Above) Ingram (as Rex Hitchcock) in *The Borrowed Finery* (1914), standing behind Sally Crute. *Courtesy of the National Library of Ireland (Below)* Ingram (as Rex Hitchcock) with Helen Gardner in *The Moonshine Maid and the Man* (Charles L. Gaskill, 1914). *Courtesy of the National Library of Ireland*

(Above) Violet Mersereau and Charles Francis in *Broken Fetters* (1916). *Courtesy of the National Library of Ireland (Below)* Wedgewood Nowell and Cleo Madison in *The Chalice of Sorrow* (1916). *Courtesy of the National Library of Ireland*

Cleo Madison in *Black Orchids* (1916). *Courtesy of the National Library of Ireland*

Claire du Brey and John George in *Reward of the Faithless* (1917). *Courtesy of the National Library of Ireland*

In the uniform of the Royal Flying Corps Canada during World War I. *Courtesy of the National Library of Ireland*

Alice Terry (as Alice Taaffe, third from left) in *The Day She Paid,* 1919. *Courtesy of the National Library of Ireland*

L-R: Elmo Lincoln, Harry von Meter, Nancy Caswell, and Mabel Ballin in *Under Crimson Skies* (1919). *Courtesy of the National Library of Ireland*

(Above) L-R: Rudolph Valentino, June Mathis, and Ingram, with feet resting on Pomeroy Cannon. *The Four Horsemen of the Apocalypse* (1921). *Courtesy of Bill Grantham (Below) L-R:* Brodwitch Turner, Nigel de Brulier, and Valentino in *The Four Horsemen of the Apocalypse. Courtesy of the National Library of Ireland*

(Above) Ingram directing *The Four Horsemen of the Apocalypse. Courtesy of the National Library of Ireland (Below)* Valentino and Alice Terry in *The Four Horsemen of the Apocalypse. Courtesy of the National Library of Ireland*

(Above) Valentino and Alice Terry in *The Four Horsemen of the Apocalypse.*
Courtesy of the National Library of Ireland (Below) Rex Ingram, Ralph Barton, and
Alice Terry in 1921. *Courtesy of the National Library of Ireland*

Sketch for *The Four Horsemen of the Apocalypse* by Ingram. *Courtesy of the National Library of Ireland*

"From a Harp to a Harp," 1922. *Courtesy of Bill Grantham*

(Above) Ralph Lewis in *The Conquering Power* (1921). *Courtesy of the National Library of Ireland (Below) Ingram (fourth from left) on the set of *The Conquering Power* with Lewis Stone, Valentino, Alice Terry, prop man Mike Fitzgerald (squatting), and John Seitz on camera. *Courtesy of the National Library of Ireland*

(Above) Valentino and Alice Terry in *The Conquering Power. Courtesy of the National Library of Ireland (Below)* Lewis Stone and ghost in *The Conquering Power. Courtesy of the National Library of Ireland*

(*Above*) Barbara La Marr, Lewis Stone, and Ramón Novarro rehearsing a sequence in *The Prisoner of Zenda* (1922). *Courtesy of the National Library of Ireland (Below)* Rex Ingram and Alice Terry. *Courtesy of Trinity College Dublin Archives*

ALICE TERRY

As Princess Flavia in "The Prisoner of Zenda"

A Metro - Rex Ingram Production

Alice Terry in *The Prisoner of Zenda. Courtesy of Bill Grantham*

(*Above*) Alice Terry, Rex Ingram. *Courtesy of Academy of Motion Picture Arts and Sciences (Below)* Terry and Ingram at the time of their marriage (1921). *Courtesy of the National Library of Ireland*

Alice Terry in *Scaramouche* (1923). *Courtesy of Trinity College Dublin Archives*

"Send it here," she said not looking at me for fear her eyes were red. I put my hand under her chin and tilted her head up. She closed her eyes and a couple of mascara tears trickled down her cheeks. Perhaps that is why I kissed her again.

I was gone before she had time to protest or acclaim my action.[27]

This delightful wartime-hero departure narrative has a counternarrative. Alice remembered meeting Rex before he left: "He asked me to walk over to the set, and we went across the street, and it was all dark," she told Liam O'Leary, "and I thought 'this is a little bit leery, and I don't think he's over here to show me where the set is.'" Maybe, she warned herself, he was one of those directors who was always after everybody. He told her he was leaving shortly for the Canadian air force and promised to give her a call one day. Then she heard him calling his wife and talking to her, and thought, "'That's that, I'll never see him again.'"[28]

Pilot

In March 1918 Rex Ingram left Los Angeles to start life as a cadet in the RFC. In preparation, he wrote to his brother and asked him to procure for him a pair of riding breeches and a pair of Fox's puttees (a specific type of leggings). Already a stickler for detail, he insisted that Frank use a tailor in an Irish hunting district or county as only they could cut hunting breeches. Frank agreed and went straight to his favorite tailor, a man called Joe Molloy in Kinnitty, whom he said cut breeches for the master of the fox hounds and was far superior to any tailor in London's West End.[29]

Pleased with the outcome, Rex later sent home a photograph of himself in his uniform. In it he is standing on the wing of a plane, his goggles perched on his forehead, his leather coat tightly belted, his Irish puttees without a wrinkle. He smiles as he always does, with that faint air of self-consciousness. According to a scribbled note on the back of the photo from Frank to Liam O'Leary, the photograph was sent from Toronto, where Rex was said to be a flying instructor.[30]

Just what part Rex actually played in the war has always been something of a mystery. After his return to civilian life, it was widely understood that he had been injured in a flying accident. However, the Royal Air Force (of which the RFC was a part) has no record of him either being a flying instructor or being involved in a flying accident.[31] In an interview carried out in 1966, the pioneering Canadian filmmaker James Booth Scott told Gordon Sparling:

> In the spring of 1916, much to the relief of my teachers, my formal education ended. My father got me a job in the Union Bank (now defunct) where I sat at a high desk and tried to look like a banker without much success. Toward the end of 1917 I couldn't stand it any longer and joined the Royal Flying Corps where I spent the following year learning to fly Curtis [sic] Jennys. It was slow going as my instructors spent most of their time in the hospital or the morgue while I ran a projector in the camp theatre. There I met Rex Ingram (producer of the Four Horsemen with Rudolph Valentino) who was busy decorating the officers' club rooms. He was quite handy with the paint brush and wasn't especially crazy about flying.[32]

Rex certainly commenced his wartime career far from the airfields. He was posted to Jesse Ketchum High School in Toronto, a wartime depot where his task was to scrub floors. Spotted executing a quick sketch of one of the officers, he was soon elevated from floor scrubbing to drawing maps. He attended flying lessons and basic training, learning to dismantle and reassemble a machine gun. Such practical aspects of becoming a pilot appealed to him, particularly when it involved working with equipment. However, as soon as it came to taking the required examination, the old weaknesses that had seen Rex fail the Trinity College entrance reappeared. He failed the exam. He took the exam again and failed again. He took it a third time: "Motors stumped me again. It is one thing to change a spark plug, swing a propeller, blow the dirt out of a carburetor or unscrew the top of the magneto to see if anything is disconnected, but ask me how all these parts function, or why they function together, today I cannot tell you."[33] He failed.

Finally, on his fourth attempt, Rex passed his exam. He was posted to the camp at Deseronto, a small town on Lake Ontario. Learning to fly solo was the next challenge. After witnessing his pupil destroy two undercarriages and come close to taking the bottom off a third, Rex's instructor declared his task impossible. He recommended that Rex fly as an observer. Rex persuaded him instead to let him take up the aircraft, a Curtiss JN-4

"Jenny," on his own. The instructor, for some obscure reason, acceded to his plan and watched as Rex took off.

Once up in the sky, Rex forgot every instruction he had been given. Soon the airfield was far in the distance. Once looking down, he saw two other planes flying toward each other. Unable to fathom why they were so close, he looked again, only to see them crash and both drop, one in flames, to the ground. He felt so nauseated that he lost control of his own aircraft and only miraculously escaped the same fate. He flew on. Suddenly he realized he had been up in the air for over forty-five minutes, when a first solo flight was supposed to last no more than five. He was also considerably higher than was permitted. Spotting a stretch of water, he concluded that he ought to land, reckoning that he must still be near the aerodrome. He eased the plane down only for it to start backfiring. It was beginning to get dark. At last he spotted the camp's water tower and the deserted aerodrome. He dropped lower. All that was in his way was a damaged aircraft that some mechanics were fixing. Seeing the plane approach, they scattered. Rex landed, colliding with the other aircraft and destroying it. The following morning, he was up for orders on three charges.[34]

Soon after, he received a telegram from Doris Pawn. They had parted on better terms than they had enjoyed for some while and had kept corresponding while Rex was in Canada. Then the letters stopped. He asked his friends in Los Angeles to check on her, and they reported that she seemed fine. Next the telegram arrived. It read: "NO USE WRITING STOP FINISHED."[35] His marriage was over.

It was at Desoronto that Rex was put to decorating the officers' mess. Still, he continued to fly, with one mishap following another. On one occasion he took off in an untested aircraft and failed to clear the trees at the aerodrome: "I saw I was going to crash and switched off, shoving the stick forward and hard over on the right—with opposite rudder. We took it on the side. My belt snapped and I was thrown clear. . . . When I got to my feet, I was bleeding from the mouth."[36]

From there, he was transferred to Beamsville aerodrome in Ontario. It was bitterly cold, and pilots had to fly without windshields. The food was maggoty, and Rex had no leather flying jacket. He began spitting blood again. Still, he was now considered fully trained. He readied himself to sail to Europe, only sorry to leave behind the friends he had made in Toronto: "I had sat at a mother's table in the place of a fallen son; at a sister's in the place of a brother. Canada had been hard hit by the war, and smiled through it all. In these brave hospitable people I had found the virtues of British and American combined."[37]

Before Rex's ship left for Europe, the news came through: the war was over; the armistice had been signed. Suddenly, he had nowhere to go and no money. He was still spitting blood, and the camp doctor told him his intestines were damaged. On 19 December 1918, Rex was discharged and granted an honorary commission as second lieutenant, with effect from 1 January 1919. He left Canada and returned to Los Angeles.

Crisis

On his return from the service, Rex immediately went to see his wife. Doris was staying in a hotel and at first refused to see him. When he in turn refused to leave, she came downstairs. She was distant and reluctant to talk. She was leaving, she told him, the next day for Nebraska.

Rex followed her there, turning up at her mother's home. Mrs. Pawn was welcoming, and Doris a little less frosty. That evening, he dined with them and slept on a divan in the sitting room. If he could get a job, Rex wanted to know of Doris, could they retrieve their marriage? She was reluctant to commit herself: "On the porch I held her very tightly in my arms, hating to part from her. Feeling now, more, perhaps than at any other time in my life, the need of sympathy and affection. But as I walked down the steps I had an idea that it was with a sense of relief she closed the door behind me."[38]

Rex now began to trek around his old studios. At Universal he was greeted by a young Irving Thalberg, now secretary to Carl Laemmle. Thalberg promised to pass on the word to Laemmle that Rex was waiting to see him. Universal's former star director and bête noire waited from ten in the morning to five o'clock. In the end, another assistant handed him some continuity work on a Western, but no pay was forthcoming. People who recognized him and remembered *Black Orchids* gave him the occasional loan, among them Allen Holubar, whom Rex had once briefly met when they both worked on the East Coast. But the message was always the same: he was out of touch, and there was no work.

It is a measure of how quickly the industry was developing in this period that studios were now wary of Rex. After all, he had barely been out of films any time. One change was that features were now the standard. Another was that the studios had invested heavily during the war years and were more averse to risk-taking. A further difference was that the old melodramatic acting styles were being replaced by a more naturalistic, restrained manner of presentation.

Rex sold his dress suit for ten dollars. Day-to-day, he stayed in his uniform. He returned to Universal and demanded that he be paid for his continuity work. As he was standing there, a striking-looking man entered the room. Rex remembered having seen him on his last visit. Then he thought he must be a German officer, but now he learned that his name was Erich von Stroheim. He was wearing a camel-hair overcoat, yellow gloves, and spats and carrying a Malacca cane. Swigstrom, Laemmle's assistant, leapt to his feet and stretched out his hand. Rex's memoirs describe the scene:

> Herr von Stroheim uncovered his shaven head, removed his gloves and laid them with his cap and cane on the executive desk before taking it. But as he shook hands he did not bow.
>
> "I am starting *The Pinnacle* [later released as *Blind Husbands*, 1918] on Monday," he said with a slight German accent. "I need a comfortable office and script girl."
>
> "Sit down, sit down, Mr. Stroheim," said Swigstrom.
>
> "Von Stroheim," corrected Mr. von Stroheim.
>
> "Von Stroheim," said Swigstrom, and to me, dismissing me with a nod: "See me Monday morning."[39]

Von Stroheim recalled the encounter differently. He was then, he told Liam O'Leary, shooting *The Devil's Passkey* (1920). In walked a man in a khaki overcoat. He was extraordinarily good-looking—"I mean good-looking isn't the word, he looked like a Greek god. And he looked rather provokingly at me, challengingly, kept his eyes without blinking, looking at me and it made me nervous." Von Stroheim assumed that the good-looking man was treating him with hostility because he mistook him for a German (he was Austrian).

But Rex had other reasons: "Ingram said, 'What is this son of a bitch doing here? He's got my job.'" Von Stroheim now understood what had happened and went over to Rex, not clicking his heels as usual but making an attempt to seem friendly. Rex explained to him that "'it's very difficult for a man who comes back. I was a director here and now I'm through the war. I've been in the air force and I have no money and I've no civilian clothes, it's kind of tough to see the ex-enemy having, so as to say, my job.'"

In the end, according to von Stroheim, they shared one, then two, then about ten or twelve bottles of whiskey and became friends or, in his own words, "palsy-walsy."[40] The friendship was to last many years, through the debacle over the editing of *Greed* in 1924. Maybe both men immediately recognized in each other the autocratic habits that allowed them to create works that were brilliantly individualistic. It would be Laemmle's young secretary, Irving Thalberg, who would change all that and establish a new model of production where the producer's word was final, in the process eliminating mavericks such as the two men standing in the office near his, morosely assessing each other.

The Monday morning meeting never materialized, and Rex was now unwell and bitterly poor. According to Alice Terry, when he fell so ill, Bessie Lasky (wife of Jesse Lasky, cofounder with Adolph Zukor of Famous Players–Lasky Corporation) rescued him. Finally, in late 1919, Bessie asked Elizabeth Waggoner, an art teacher at Hollywood High School, to take him into her home at 2041 Pinehurst Road, just down from where Rex and Doris had lived before the war. There he slept on the porch, and for the next three months these two kindly women nursed him back to health. Elizabeth made a small studio for him, and with the help of Anna de Mille they secured him a position as set director on an Irish film (*Peg o' My Heart*) being directed by Anna's husband, William C. de Mille at Famous Players–Lasky. Rex always believed that de Mille paid his salary out of his own pocket.[41] In any case, even before the film started, Rex fell ill again and was too unwell to work.

Alice Terry

Alice Taaffe was born on 24 July 1899, the youngest of three children. Her father, Matthew Taaffe, was of Irish origin, from County Kildare. Her mother, Ella, was widowed young, and the family—Alice, her sister Edna, and brother Robert—moved to California. She started her career in 1914 at Inceville, the pioneering studio created two years earlier in the Palisades Highlands (between Santa Monica and Malibu; now the Pacific Palisades) by Thomas Ince to make his popular two-reelers. Alice shared a house with Enid Markey, one of the stars at Inceville. One day Enid asked her if she would like to work in a picture in which she had the lead role. It would take about a week. Alice needed the money and accepted the offer.

Being a bit player at Inceville wasn't a glamorous job. In one picture (*Civilization*), she told Liam O'Leary, she was a French peasant chased by the Germans, and the next day she was a German chasing herself. To finish off the picture, they all had to put on German uniforms and ride horses in the background. Such was the lot of stock players, interchangeable as they were.[42] She continued as an extra until 1916, when director Charles Giblyn spotted her and with remarkable prescience cast her as the innocent Ruth Tyler, who is seduced by a handsome sculptor played by the Dublin-born William Desmond in *Not My Sister.* Her next role was in an Ireland-set film, *A Corner in Colleens,* directed by Charles Miller (also in 1916), in which she played one of four orphaned Irish sisters who become embroiled in the revolution. Since this is a lost film, one is reliant on synopses to flesh out the plot, but it is possible that it was set during the Easter Rising of 1916. In any case, it was one of many romances whose background of Irish rebel activity was designed to pull in the vast Irish American audience. Certainly it was more likely to do so under its final title, rather than its working title, *The Pig's Sister.*

Alice suffered intensely from low self-confidence, and when Reginald Barker fired her from the set of one of his films, she found it hard to pick herself up again. Still, she did, continuing for a few more pictures at Inceville before joining Universal. There she made another handful of films, in both minor roles and as an extra. It was when playing in one of these that she first met another aspirant performer. The picture was titled *Alimony* (Emmett J. Flynn, 1917). The young man made a brief, uncredited appearance as a dancer. Neither she nor Valentino could have imagined the circumstances of their next professional encounter.

By 1918 Alice's career was going nowhere. She was battling with her weight, her looks were neither vamp nor ingénue, and she hated being an actor. To her relief, she landed a job in the editing room at Famous Players–Lasky. However, the ether that constantly hung in the air from the equipment affected her lungs, and she had to quit. She was forced to return to screen roles, now bizarrely cast as a mother to Wallace Reed's Bryce Cardigan in *The Valley of the Giants* (James Cruze, 1919). That Reed was in fact only a few years her junior apparently made no difference.

One day the phone rang at Alice's home—she was now living with her mother, her sister Edna, and her husband, Gerald—and a voice said, "This is Rex." They arranged to meet at Highland and Hollywood Boulevard.

When Alice stepped off the streetcar, "there he stood in this little cap and a trench coat that I saw from there on, you know, and it was that coat Marcus Lowe offered him $10,000 to get rid of."[43]

"'What do you want to see me about?' asked Miss Taaffe, getting off the street car," Rex recollected. "'If you weren't sure, why did you come?' I asked. 'I thought it would be nice to see how you had changed,' she said. "And you have. That uniform is cute.'"[44]

He wondered if she would like to pose for a head that he was sculpting. "But after a look at my drawing, she glanced in the mirror and decided she preferred her reflection."[45] Rex was so sick that she only posed two or three times and then didn't see him again for several months.[46]

Around this time, Rex met Allen Holubar, who told him that he should contact Pat Powers again. Rex called over to the studio and watched a young juvenile in rehearsal—still Valentino was only being cast in minor roles. Thanks to the intervention of Holubar and Powers, Rex was called a few days later to go to Universal. They offered him a job directing Elmo Lincoln, better known to the public as Tarzan, for $300 per week.[47]

According to Rex, he and Valentino struck up a conversation shortly afterward, and Valentino, or Rodolfo Guglielmi as he was then called, asked him if he would have a job for him on his next film. When Rex informed him that it was not the kind of film that would suit his looks, he asked instead if he could buy Rex's breeches as he liked the inside-knee button. There followed an amicable discussion about the optimum placement of buttons, and they parted with Rex promising that he would loan them to the young man when he had a spare pair, which currently he could not afford.[48] Given the relationship that was to follow between the two men, and their widely opposed sartorial tastes, the incident seems improbable, though not impossible.

The Elmo Lincoln film excited Rex, for its story—of gunrunning and Mexican rebels—reminded him of the stories of his favorite writer, Jack London. Most of all, creating the atmosphere offered possibilities. With his crew, he moved into the old Laguna Beach Hotel. Noble Johnson, the African American actor, played the "Man Friday" character "Baltimore Bucko," and Beatrice Dominguez the "Island Girl." Although her name has not gone down in film history, it perhaps ought to have, as Rex would shortly cast her to dance the tango opposite Rodolfo Guglielmi in a very different film. But by the time that film was released, she had died on the operating table, aged only twenty-three.

Another minor member of the cast was supposed to be Alice Taaffe. Rex raged at his assistant when a request to have her play an extra was unsuccessful. The assistant assured him that when he phoned her number, Alice told him that her mother disapproved of her doing location shooting "under certain conditions."[49] One may guess that a handsome young male director constituted the majority of those conditions.

Unfortunately for Rex's ambitions, *Under Crimson Skies* ended up a far cry from Jack London, and Universal put its release on hold when they realized that Famous Players–Lasky would shortly release the genuine article in *The Sea Wolf* (George Melford, 1920). The production was only to become significant insofar as it provided the first occasion for Rex to work with one of Universal's editors, Grant Whytock. The latter had been working on von Stroheim's *The Devil's Passkey*, a project that infuriated him so much that he asked Universal to give him another film to work on while he waited for the fanatical director to select the perfect take. That film was *Under Crimson Skies*.

Editing in the early 1920s was accomplished by hand and eye. Whytock explained to researcher Paul Kozak: "When I tell some of these young fellows who never worked in the silent days that I never had a moviola until 1928, and that we used to go through this enormous amount of film by hand, they look at you as if, well 'I don't believe it.' Editors then had to rely on holding the film up to the window or a box light to see where to cut. I had jeweler's glasses. I've still got them around somewhere. Most editors became so adept at running the film through their fingers that it was almost like having a projector."[50] Whytock had started out in Inceville and was already experienced in his craft when the two men met. They took to each other immediately. "Rex was awfully good about letting me have my way pretty well," Whytock told Kevin Brownlow. "We would discuss things, and then I'd say well now, I've got to do it, you never know completely how it's going to look—our pictures were always so much overlength. So we'd discuss it and he'd be worn out [by the] time we'd finished the picture, and I'd say now you go away for a little vacation and I'll send for you."[51] On set Rex was increasingly demanding complete authority, yet for such a controlling man he was also surprisingly trusting. All he needed was a group of people whom he could rely on to share his vision so completely that even in his absence they were working as if he were there. Now he was gradually building up that group; Grant Whytock and his wife, Ota, were to become two of its core members.

The next assignment for Universal was an unusual one—directing Francelia Billington in *The Day She Paid,* an adaptation of the short story "Oats for the Woman," by the popular women's writer Fannie Hurst. With its glamorous New York setting and its narrative of love among the well-heeled classes, it was a far cry from Chinatown melodramas and racy French period pieces. This time he managed to ensure that Alice was cast as an extra. "Miss Taaffe was unsmilingly polite to me," Rex writes in his memoirs. "I realized at once that she had come without knowing I was the director. Her aloofness, or indifference, annoyed me. I made a few caustic remarks of a personal nature. She began to weep."[52] "Rex bawled me out, unmercifully, and I walked off the set, I wouldn't go back," Alice remembered.[53]

The Day She Paid appeared on 21 December 1919. On 5 July 1920, Universal released *Under Crimson Skies.* The critical response to the latter was less than warm. The *Film Daily* considered the story "very unconvincing," only finding space to praise the storm sequence.[54] Other trade papers agreed.

With his health restored and the money from Universal in his pocket, Rex left the care of Elizabeth Waggoner and moved into the Hollywood Hotel. He was in the right place to meet people, and he soon did. The Englishman J. Frank Brockliss, who was one of the chief suppliers of American films to Britain and continental Europe, claimed he owned the rights to certain of Jack London's short stories, including *The Mutiny of the Elsinore.* Rex pressed Brockliss to sell the rights to him. Brockliss told him to speak to Richard Rowland, the head of Metro Pictures, as he had made a deal with him to produce them. Rowland—"lovable, careless, prodigal Richard Rowland," as Jesse Lasky said of him—was elusive; if it was all right with Maxwell Karger, Metro's general manager (and Valentino's best man at his ill-fated marriage with Jean Acker), then it was all right with him.[55] Karger refused to give Rex the stories but instead offered to put him on the Metro payroll. After much haggling, Rex pushed the salary up to $600 and then waited around for a week.[56] He had other conditions too, and these included no interference from Metro. Karger came back to him and told him that the title for the London stories was not yet cleared, asking him to direct *Shore Acres* in the meantime. The move to Metro, where Rex would stay for his greatest films, was agreed.

Shore Acres (1920)

Rex's first picture for Metro was a shameless attempt to cash in on the success of D. W. Griffith's *Way Down East* (1920). Griffith's film told the tale of a poor country girl, Anna (played by Lillian Gish), who is tricked into a relationship by an unscrupulous man-about-town and bears him a child, who shortly afterward dies. When she falls in love with the local squire's son, her past comes back to haunt her, and the film winds up in a famous finale with Anna fleeing to her near death on the ice floes of the local river. It was a traditional portrayal of American womanhood, one that resolutely ignored the modern city girl who would define the 1920s. *Shore Acres* was based on the play of the same name by James A. Herne. The story tells of Martin Berry's opposition to his daughter Helen's marriage in favor of a moneyed suitor and the crisis that ensues when Martin loses all his wealth in a property deal that goes wrong. Only the intervention of his brother, Nathaniel, saves him, but the cost of Nathaniel's help is that Martin sign over his farm to his wife.

Shore Acres was first performed in 1892 and had since made a millionaire of its author. Metro was hoping that Rex would ensure the same success for them. Alice Lake was cast as Helen, Edward Connelly, who had played Nathaniel Berry in a London production of the play in 1901, reprised his role on screen, and Frank Brownlee played Martin Berry. It looked like it would be easy to run off a new version, particularly since a previous screen production (directed by John H. Pratt) had appeared in 1914. Rex ensured that it was nothing of the sort.

Soon after shooting started, the rising cinematographer John F. Seitz received a phone call from a Mr. Butler at Metro: "I got a very eccentric director, Rex Ingram," Butler told Seitz. "After viewing the rushes from his new film, Mr. Ingram hasn't seen one foot of the film that he liked." Butler introduced the cinematographer to his troublesome director, and Seitz found himself face-to-face with a handsome young Irishman in a temper. Rex informed Seitz that he liked the work he had done photographing *The Westerners* (Edward Sloman, 1919), especially the shadows; the next day, they shot some scenes of *Shore Acres* together and sent them to the lab to be developed. When they came back, Rex was still not happy. The contrast on the image was too high. "I can fix the contrast," Seitz assured him, "but tell me something. You must have stills from your older, earlier films. Can I see some of those?" This was in the morning, and they were due to shoot more exteriors that afternoon. Rex looked through all his pictures and couldn't find a single one he liked. They went out together again, and this time shot some sequences around the Point Fermin lighthouse at San Pedro. This was where *Shore Acres'* climactic set piece—its equivalent of Griffith's river floes—was filmed. Helen Berry takes to the sea in a fishing smack to escape with the young doctor, Sam Warren (Robert Walker). When a storm rises, their lives are threatened, and her father, who is at the lighthouse with his brother, refuses to intervene to save them. Finally Uncle Nat overpowers Martin, and the fugitives are saved. The sequence was shot in a large wooden tank on the wharf with a life-size smack that they dragged through the waves, pumping jets of water over it. Back at Metro, Seitz spoke with Tom Storey, in the lab: "Listen, Tom, I don't want you to develop for eight minutes. I want you to develop for six minutes. And everything else exactly the same." The result was much more to his liking, with far less contrast. Still, he knew he could achieve more. He cut the development time down to five minutes. When Rex saw the result, he said it was the first time he had ever seen an image on the screen he liked.[57]

And so a relationship between director and cinematographer was launched that was to produce eleven more films, many of them extraordinary. If D. W. Griffith had his Billy Bitzer, Rex had his Johnny Seitz; the two men collaborated together over the years and over continents with mutual respect—luckily, since so few other cameramen could bear to work with a man widely referred to in their circle as the "crazy Irishman." From then on, both men read the scripts. Seitz read carefully to get the feeling of the story, then planned the lighting and created the setups. Rex inspected them and looked for changes, Seitz made them, and the two would keep at it, two perfectionists, until they were satisfied. What Rex saw in Seitz was initiative. What Seitz saw in Rex was a visual artist whose training in sculpture never left him and who was making his films for just one audience member—Lee Lawrie. For Rex, if what he created might please Lawrie, then it was worth it.[58] Between the two men, they developed a manner of lighting a set that was inspired by Rembrandt's use of light and was widely referred to as "north light."

Shore Acres was mostly shot on location at Laguna Beach in Orange County, since it reminded Rex of Ireland. Alice had now agreed to be an extra. The day after Rex called her, she got on the bus from Los Angeles with all the other extras to go to Laguna Beach. They stopped on the way for something to eat, arriving only after dark, at eleven o'clock. When Alice stepped off the bus, Rex was there waiting for her. "And he took my case and carried it to the house and I thought 'Here we go again, uh oh.' When we got to the room, we were staying in this beautiful house right next to the beach, I said 'where's your room?' and he said 'I'm next door.' He left and I tried the door and it was locked from my side but not from the other side and I stayed up all night and he never bothered me. I was exhausted and he had had a good night's sleep."[59] During the production of *Shore Acres,* Doris filed a petition for divorce, and Rex did not oppose it. The marriage was now officially over.

By the time of its release in May 1920, *Shore Acres* was too familiar and too Victorian to make the kind of impact that *Way Down East* had. Rex never cared for the film or what he called "Drury Lane melos," but it had at least given him the opportunity to establish his terms at Metro (no interference with a Rex Ingram project) and to commence the process of assembling a stock company, with John Seitz as his cameraman, Grant Whytock (who had moved with him) as his editor, and Edward Connelly and Alice on screen. Metro still chose his projects and attempted to control their casting and budgets, which he adhered to tightly anyway, but once on set he was king. If Metro did not like his pictures, they could lay him off.

One response to his latest release must have delighted him, and that was Lee Lawrie's. In a letter preserved in Rex's scrapbook, Lawrie writes:

Dear Ingram

I have just seen Shore Acres. I think that it is a splendid thing. You know, as an artist, that to handle realism or the true to nature stuff, keeping it on the grand scale is a difficult thing to do. The finest thing, I thought, about Shore Acres, is this: that the story itself is the interesting thing, so unlike many picture plays where the more or less interesting scenes are disconnecting features of the story.

There is another thing about it that it seems to me is important in producing a play. Shore Acres is a compliment to the audience in that it is not over played to bring out the intention. In some plays the point is driven in with a hammer.

The choice of the scenes made beautiful pictures, especially the scene showing the return of the boy and the girl.

It is a fine thing. It is being run all of this week in New York's largest and finest theatre.

Let me know when I can see another.

Yours,
Lee Lawrie.[60]

Hearts Are Trumps (1920)

Rex moved on swiftly, still determined to put Alice in front of the camera—his camera—and not just as an extra. All accounts agree that she was loath to return to acting. She would have preferred, she told him, to work as an assistant editor. However, Whytock's assistant was Ota, and according to Rex she was the boss. To replace his wife was to lose Whytock. Alice tried for script girl, and Rex refused to consider it. He cast her as the ingénue in *Hearts Are Trumps,* his next film for Metro, offering her seventy-five dollars per week for five weeks.[61] He now changed her look: "I was putting on some make-up one day, and there was a blonde wig and I put it on and it looked so silly and just then Rex came in and said 'Leave that on' and I thought 'Oh no, I can't do this part,' but I kept it on. And it felt so silly.'" Because they were on location, they did not see the rushes for three days. When they finally went into the projection room, Alice was feeling terrible, with a bad headache, and a sense of foreboding that she would be thrown off the picture. Instead, when she saw how she looked as a blonde, she realized that she was completely different, even her freckles seemed to have gone, and from then on, even in rehearsal, she always wore the wig on screen.[62] Only in *The Arab* did she revert to being a brunette: "I had always been very self-conscious," she remembered later, "and somehow with the blond hair I felt like I was someone else and so I had a little more confidence."[63]

Rex's faith in Alice's potential to be his screen star didn't prevent him from tormenting her—over her looks, her weight, her attitude to acting. He made her fix her teeth. Then, he changed her name from Taaffe to Terry, telling her that his mother's mother played Shakespeare when she was young and her stage name was Terry.[64] He wasn't just controlling on set but off. On one occasion, taken by a pretty young woman on the film, he vanished off to dinner with his new discovery. When he came back, he found Alice in her room showing Walter Mayo, their assistant director, some chords on the ukulele. Rex was outraged and announced that he didn't want Walter in Alice's room. Alice was left wondering what business it was of his.

In the end Alice played the female lead in all his films bar *Trifling Women* (1922), when Barbara La Marr took her place, and his final film, *Baroud* (1933). She also rose to become an acclaimed star whose evident good nature, both on and off the screen, made her a favorite with the public. She was never quite beautiful but always sweet; reviewers were prone to call her wooden, and her range was certainly limited. Without Rex's intervention in her career at that moment, it is hard to imagine that she would have stayed in moving pictures, but it is also undeniable that Rex needed Alice as much as she needed him, professionally and, soon, personally. Her work behind the scenes, regrettably, has been far less acknowledged and now, since her interviewers didn't think to ask her about it, is hard to reconstruct. In 1924 Rex explained just how important Alice was to him: "Miss Terry's nicely balanced sense of judgment at all times makes her advice to me invaluable, not only in the work of directing, but also in business. Her instinctive knowledge of the fitness of things convinces me that she would make a good director. In fact, it is to her I have always gone when in a quandary over some ticklish point in a production. And her advice, given in an unassuming way, has solved many a problem that seemed insurmountable."[65]

It was Alice, for instance, who reminded Rex of a scene he had shot in a much earlier Bowery film, *The Pulse of Life,* that he would shortly transpose to the Boca, the Buenos Aires barrio, to create the famous tango sequence with Valentino in *The Four Horsemen of the Apocalypse*. But more than this, one can readily speculate that in Alice, Rex recreated his image of his own mother. If she was now the fair-haired girl who reminded him in his dreams of Kathleen, she was also always the embodiment of purity on screen, only abandoning her angelic demeanor to play the spy, Freya in *Mare Nostrum,* many years hence.

Hearts Are Trumps, an adaptation of the popular stage melodrama by Cecil Raleigh, was Alice's first picture in a major role. The story was unexceptional—a tale of love, intrigue, and a moral message to do with the values of happiness over wealth. But with John Seitz behind the camera and Grant Whytock in the editing room, Rex's production rose easily above its predictable story line. The press recognized what they saw, commenting on his latest venture with enthusiasm, especially praising the casting and scenery. Only one or two small comments about slow pacing sounded a warning note.

For the first time, a new name appeared on the credits of a Rex Ingram film, one that would make a decisive difference to the career of the swiftly rising director. That name was June Mathis. It was their next film together that was to transform the fortunes not only of Rex Ingram and Alice Terry, but of everyone associated with it—not least that of Alice's old dancing partner on *Alimony,* Rudolph Valentino. The film was *The Four Horsemen of the Apocalypse.*

4

Apocalypse at Metro

In January of 1920, Rex celebrated his twenty-seventh birthday. For the first time since his return from the military service, he was in secure employment and, although he never wasted an opportunity to mention how his heart really lay in sculpting, he was fast making a name for himself in the film industry. He was making money too; after *Shore Acres,* Metro raised his salary to $1,000 weekly.[1] Still, there was little in his career to suggest that he would soon be hailed as one of the foremost directors of the decade, if not of the silent era.

It began with a novel. Richard Rowland, the president of Metro, was following with fascination the mounting circulation figures for Vicente Blasco Ibáñez's latest book, *The Four Horsemen of the Apocalypse.*[2] It was, in today's language, a literary blockbuster. The story is of an Argentinian family and its philandering patriarch, Don Julio Madariaga, whose two daughters marry, respectively, a Frenchman, Marcelo Desnoyers, and a German, Karl Hartrott. As his grandchildren are born, Madariaga favors one over all the others, Julio Desnoyers, the son of Marcelo. Julio grows up elegant and spoiled; his German-Argentinian cousins are trained to be goose-stepping little patriots from birth. The book opens in Paris with Julio, who loves nothing more than to dance, squiring the beautiful though married Marguerite. World War I is threatening, but Julio is uninterested. In his apartment block lives a mysterious Russian, a socialist in dirty clothing named Tchernoff, whose visions tell of an impending disaster—the arrival of the Beast in all its hideousness, who will attempt to govern the world and force mankind to render him homage and whose presence will be heralded by the Four Horsemen of the Apocalypse: "God is asleep, forgetting the world," continued the Russian. "It will be a long time before he awakes, and while he sleeps the four feudal horsemen of the Beast will course through the land as its only lords."[3]

Laurier, Marguerite's husband, enlists and serves bravely. Marguerite trains as a nurse, and when she hears that Laurier is wounded—blinded in one eye—she too goes to war to nurse her husband and serve the cause of the French. Meanwhile, Marcelo Desnoyers has rushed to his ancestral village of Villeblanche to save his property and his castle, only to find himself drawn into the war, no more so than when the Germans invade and occupy the village, killing all they see. Their leader is Desnoyers's nephew, Otto von Hartrott. At last Julio joins up. The war transforms him from the indifferent ne'er-do-well of his Paris days to a brave soldier, much praised by his fellows and the pride of his father. Desnoyers Sr. is sure that this son is charmed and will never die, but, toward the end of the war, he learns of his own boy's death. The family travel to the battlefields to find Julio's grave, and as his father sobs over it, he too feels the presence of the Four Horsemen of the Apocalypse.

Author, Adventurer

The author of this antiwar bestseller, Vicente Blasco Ibáñez, was as colorful a character as any of the many books he wrote.[4] Born in 1867 in the Mediterranean city of Valencia, he grew up above his parents' corner grocery, not far from the bustling marketplace where he would often set his early stories. He started writing when he was just fourteen and had his first story, "The Boatella Tower" (La Torre de la Boatella), published in November 1882. Fired by this success and only sixteen, he left home to seek fame in Madrid. He brought with him the manuscript for a historical novel that, to his surprise, was rejected by the publishing houses in the capital. His response was to set up his own publishing house, Editorial Prometeo. He also launched himself onto the political scene, making inflammatory public addresses that soon landed him in jail. At this point his parents intervened, and the young Vicente was hauled home.

Valencia did nothing to quell his spirit, however, and Ibáñez divided his time there between making increasingly pro-Republican, anticlerical speeches and taking a degree in law. In 1890 he was forced to flee to Paris, where he quickly immersed himself in the bohemian life of the city. An amnesty provided the opportunity to return to Valencia, where he wrote a three-volume history of the Spanish Revolution. He plunged himself further into left-wing agitation and founded his own newspaper, El Pueblo (The People). Now a familiar sight on street corners and in working men's clubs, the fiery, heavy-set orator gunned himself into a fury as he churned out column inches for *El Pueblo* and set about forming his own political party. In 1896 he was forced to flee to Italy, where he passed his days writing a book on his host country, *In the Land of Art* (En el País de Arte). On returning to Valencia, he was arrested and sentenced to two years of hard labor in the prison of San Gregorio. Over the next few years, his life was punctuated by prison sentences and political engagement; by now he had been elected to the National Congress. Until 1904, when he became disenchanted with politics, Ibáñez accompanied his public appearances with the writing of a series of novels, many of them drawing on the life and traditions of his native city.

In 1904 the now infamous author and agitator left Valencia, first for Madrid and then for several years of travel. He dreamed of establishing a city high in Patagonia, which he would call Cervantes and would boast the best aspects of European architecture and civilization. But nothing came of Ibáñez's ambitions, and in 1913 he returned to Europe and became a journalist in Paris. In France, President Raymond Poincaré requested him to write a novel that would be a testament to the war, and so *The Four Horsemen of the Apocalypse* saw the light of day. The book was published in the United States to coincide with the end of World War I and was an instant bestseller, running into many editions.

This then was the book that had caught Richard Rowland's eye. Received wisdom insisted that the public was weary of war pictures, yet sales of *The Four Horsemen* suggested otherwise. Ibáñez's writing promised to translate easily to screen: his chapters cut between characters and places in the manner of film editing, his descriptions were vivid, and apart from some lengthy digressions on the moral and ideological villainy of the entire German race, his writing style was pacey. Rowland didn't waste his time reading the book but, following a hunch, made an offer for the rights. When it emerged that William Fox was hot on his heels and had offered Ibáñez $75,000, Rowland upped Metro's offer to an advance of $20,000 against 10 percent of the royalties.[5] The deal was struck (and Ibáñez was made a wealthy man for life).

June Mathis: A Maker of Young Men

Next, Rowland called in June Mathis: "'Take this book and make a continuity. When you get one you like bring it to me. You've got to make good on this for me. Everybody in the world thinks I'm crazy.'"[6] According to Terry Ramsaye's verbatim account of the behind-the-scenes negotiations (and other sources agree), it was Mathis, who had worked with Rex on *Hearts Are Trumps,* who proposed that he direct this film. In fact, it is more than likely that she first suggested that Metro acquire the rights. Certainly she read the novel. If Vicente Blasco Ibáñez constitutes the absent father of Rex's new fortunes, with Richard Rowland as a sort of haphazard godparent, then June Mathis must take much of the credit for ensuring that the picture was made, and who made it.

June Mathis enjoyed a brief but exceptional career in Hollywood. Born June Beulah Hughes in 1889 and reared in Salt Lake City, she left home at the age of fourteen with her heart set on making it in vaudeville. For the next twelve years, she slogged her way through a series of minor roles and a trade that regarded young women as little other than cheap fodder for men's sexual appetites. By 1913 she had enrolled in a writing course in New York and followed this with a job in one of Metro's subsidiary companies. In 1919 she moved to Los Angeles and swiftly rose to head of Metro's story department, a much more influential position then than now. She was a prolific screenwriter herself and took a hand in many other scripts, reworking them and fashioning them for the market. All this led her to be declared in 1923 "the most powerful woman in the motion picture industry."[7]

Photographs show a short, blowsy, dark-haired woman who looks impervious to the glamour swirling around her. She was, above all, focused on ensuring that any project she worked on saw the light of day in a manner that reflected the professionalism by which she lived. Yet the down-to-earth appearance belied a personality that was far from mundane, for Mathis was a spiritualist with a strong leaning toward Orientalism. Like Rex, she was fascinated by the exotic qualities of ancient civilizations, although she took this further than he did, believing that she had once been an Egyptian and that Rex, along with her other new discovery, Rudolph Valentino, had in this previous life been her sons.[8] While they remained on good terms, Rex responded with a gift of a scarab brooch.

In this life, or the other, one of June Mathis's most admired skills was her ability to discover talent, particularly that of young men. "To be a maker of young men," Gladys Hall declared in a profile of her, "is a position greatly to be envied and never to be deplored, [as] will be admitted by any woman over the dead line of thirty-five in these United States."[9] As both women recognized, it might not have been a glamorous vocation, but it offered remarkable opportunities to wield authority. "'They [young men] assure me,' laughed Miss Mathis, 'that they will do whatever I may require of them, *no matter what it is.*'"[10] As innuendo goes, this was a far from subtle hint at life in the new studios.

Out of this entanglement of conspiracy, ambition, and talent, another name now emerged, that of Rudolph Valentino. The story of the young man from Castellaneta in southern Italy is so familiar as to need little reminder.[11] Born in 1895, just two years younger than Rex, and six years the junior of Mathis, Valentino had thus far made his career as a dancer, seizing his opportunity during the dance craze that swept New York in the war years. Light of foot, with a sensitivity of expression that enthralled his partners, he was particularly adept at the latest fashion from Latin America—the tango. At "tango teas" women hired male escorts to teach them to dance, a financial transaction that sorely tested what society deemed to be appropriate behavior. Worse still, the routines were highly suggestive, liberating the senses, and threatening to overturn America's lingering Victorian standards. Any man who danced such a dance was surely not a real man—but he could be a film star.

Valentino's first success came in a small but widely noticed role in the hit *Eyes of Youth,* directed by Albert Parker and released in 1919. Hearing that *Four Horsemen* was being cast, he wondered if there might be a dancing part for him on the production. He already had an ally on the Metro lot, Maxwell Karger, who informed him that Mathis was looking for him. Not expecting much, Valentino made an appointment. To his astonishment, he found that she was considering him for Julio Desnoyers. Against all advice, Mathis insisted on hiring the young unknown, Metro's only compensation being the minuscule salary—$350 per week—they were to pay their leading man.[12]

To Samuel Goldwyn, Rex was to claim that he had discovered Valentino: "There's a fellow, I thought, who would be great in pictures, and if I get my job of directing back I'm going to use him. . . . When *The Four Horsemen* came along I thought of him immediately."[13] He repeats the assertion in his memoirs, saying that he had Allen Holubar screen Valentino's existing performances and that Rex himself tracked Valentino down to New York. Both Rex and Alice had certainly met Valentino professionally but, given Mathis's seniority at Metro, it is more likely that the casting decision was hers (interestingly, her salary at $750 per week was lower than Rex's).[14] In fact, Rex told Robert Florey that he watched Valentino in *The Delicious Little Devil* (Robert Z. Leonard, 1919), where he played an Irishman, Jimmy Calhoun, and thought he pulled too many faces. In his opinion, the part of Julio called for someone more powerful, more sober, more French, and he had been considering importing a star from France. Mathis, he told Florey, insisted, and pointed out that "she had pleaded Valentino's cause with Rowland just as she had pleaded mine with him."[15]

It was, however, certainly Rex who cast Alice as Marguerite and against the better judgment of Metro, which wanted to balance Valentino's inexperience with a seasoned screen performer. Rex consulted with John Seitz, who agreed with him. Alice gained the role and a salary of $250 per week.[16] For Madariaga, Rex cast his mind back to Raoul Walsh's *The Honor System* (1917) and Pomeroy Cannon's performance as the deputy sheriff, James Phelan. The book gave no clues as to Madariaga's appearance. Rex made a drawing of how the character appeared to him and mailed it express to Ibáñez. The telegram came winging back with his response: "PERFECTO."[17] Cannon was in.

A Terrible Beauty

June Mathis was sensitive to the differences between American and European culture, telling one interviewer that Americans were essentially optimistic and liked this sensibility to be affirmed by the movies, with happy endings to their films: "We will probably never be able to appreciate the terrible beauty of a great tragedy as the Europeans do because we can't understand it. For you see we do not feel the great hatreds and the great loves which call forth tragedy. We refuse to play on our emotions."[18] The use of the phrase "terrible beauty" recalls W. B. Yeats's famous poem "Easter, 1916," which had been published in 1921 and includes the celebrated lines:

> All changed, changed utterly:
> A terrible beauty is born.[19]

There is every reason to believe that Mathis, with her mystical turn, was familiar with the poetry of Yeats, as was Rex, and although their execution of Ibáñez's novel predates "Easter, 1916," the film was to reflect that romantic-apocalyptic vision that had gripped Yeats's imagination. His earlier and equally celebrated "The Second Coming" (composed in 1919 and published in the same volume as "Easter, 1916") is, with its vision of the apocalypse, uncannily similar in theme to *The Four Horsemen:*

> Things fall apart; the centre cannot hold;
> Mere anarchy is loosed upon the world,
> The blood-dimmed tide is loosed, and everywhere
> The ceremony of innocence is drowned;
> The best lack all conviction, while the worst
> Are full of passionate intensity.[20]

Easter 1916 was the date of the Irish rebellion against British rule, while "The Second Coming" is a horrified response to World War I. Rex must surely have had both events in mind as he was filming *Four Horsemen,* just as he must have reflected on his own brother's experiences in the trenches and the terrible loss of life experienced by his generation of young men during the war. Destined always to be a bystander and not a participant in the wars of the twentieth century, he was to be drawn back to images of conflict over and again, visualizing, as did Yeats, this remorseless human drama with both fascination and revulsion.

Behind the Scenes of *Four Horsemen*

Rex and June Mathis worked closely together on the screen adaptation, adding in a number of significant changes, including toning down some of the more unforgiving anti-German components. Even afterward in the edit, they deleted scenes that would be unduly offensive, including one of an orgy in the German officers' mess, with the solders sitting around a table cheering on one of their men who is dancing on the tabletop in drag. (This sequence was reinserted for later releases and appears in Kevin Brownlow and David Gill's restoration.) Mathis recognized that scenes such as this would resonate most of all with those who had had direct experience of the war: "In the German banquet scene in the 'Four Horsemen of the Apocalypse,' I had the German officers coming down the stairs with women's clothing on. Now to hundreds of people all over the country, that meant nothing more than a masquerade party. To those who had lived and read, and those who understood life, that scene stood out as one of the most terrific things in the picture."[21]

At Metro the production was viewed with alarm. Marcus Loew, with his showman's instinct, sensed that there might be a hit in the offing; still, he was desperate to keep costs, and therefore the potential financial loss, to a minimum. "June, Johnnie Seitz and I were the only enthusiasts—always excepting Dick Rowland, whose flair for making big deals and fortunes, and then losing the fortunes was traditional," Rex remembered.[22] As a precaution, Mathis wrote, and Rex filmed, an alternative happy ending, in which Julio recovers, Marguerite's husband dies, and the couple is united at a joyful wedding and fiesta at Old Madariaga's plantation. Maybe they never planned to use it. In any case, she and Rex held their nerves and proceeded with the original tragic conclusion.

Confirming the misgivings of management, *Four Horsemen* ended up as Metro's most expensive production to date, costing in the region of $640,000.[23] The transition from the small-scale melodramas Rex had been directing prior to this vast production, the forerunner of today's blockbusters, was staggering. Yet he never gave the impression that he might lack the experience to take it on. On the contrary, the twenty-seven-year-old occupied the director's chair as a general might take to his command. He was confident that his tried and trusted technical staff would rise to the challenge with him, and throughout he relied heavily on Seitz and Grant Whytock. Rex would film the open-air set pieces often with twelve or fourteen cameras running simultaneously (Griffith, by contrast, was using five in his setups).[24] Faced with hundreds of feet of footage to view every night, Rex called on Whytock to select the most striking shots for the rushes. Years later Whytock confessed that he only managed to do this by ignoring all but two or three of the master cameras. Since duplicating a negative eventually resulted in poor-quality copies, he also assembled a second negative for overseas markets, often using different takes or takes from cameras placed near the first-choice viewpoint. Indeed, so popular was *Four Horsemen* on release that the original print wore out, and Whytock had to assemble a third print from third-best material, resulting in a version that lacked certain shots and sequences. As Whytock told Richard Koszarski, he considered himself lucky that "it all made sense."[25] It also means that different audiences across the globe saw quite different versions of the film.

If the technical setups were testing, dealing with armies of performers and assistants tried Rex's patience to its limits. His obsession with fidelity to detail saw him hire ex-officers from both the French and German armies to assist him on set. They started off treating each other politely but soon fell out; it took little for national differences to be ferociously aired. "The new litany," the weary director commented to a journalist, "should include the exhortation, 'From war experts the good lord deliver me!'"[26] The assistant director, Curt Rehfeld, was German and took delight in spending eight to nine hours a day training the extras and cast to goose-step.[27] Fights continued to break out as the experts vied with each other, with issues such as whether or not the butler in the Desnoyers' Paris home should be wearing gloves while serving tea causing near warfare.

Fidelity also meant having the actors in speaking roles talking in the appropriate language to outwit the lip readers who loved to divulge what silent actors were really saying in pictures. This only added to Alice Terry's anxiety, and she took to getting up at five in the morning to study French and continuing her studies on board the streetcar on the way to the studio. It was still a struggle, and the young star decided to cut a corner or two by learning just one title and repeating it each time she was on camera. Only Valentino could speak French, but he was quickly driven crazy hearing Alice repeat the same line of dialogue interminably: "'If you say that one more time, I'm going to——'" he finally threatened. Rex was summoned to restrain his lead and insist that Alice work harder on her French.[28]

Then there were the extras. The crowd scenes required legions of participants. However, unlike real soldiers, extras knocked off for the evening. It infuriated Rex to find that, after a long day meticulously setting up a scene, his "regiment" of five hundred soldiers had gone home for the evening. Time off was not a concept that amused him. Nor were matters much easier behind the scenes among the principals and the production team. Speculation has added spice to rumor. In Mathis's case, Emily Leider has concluded that there is no evidence that she and Valentino were lovers, writing instead that they truly loved one another "as friends."[29] Liam O'Leary, on the other hand, stated, with just a hint of contempt, that Mathis was "undoubtedly" in love with Valentino. He also considered that "it is not at all impossible that she was also in love with Ingram himself, but received small encouragement from that direction."[30]

Hala Pickford, the editor of the memoirs of Valentino's second wife, Natacha Rambova, has echoed this opinion.[31] She goes one further in deciding that Mathis couldn't have been anything other than motherly toward Valentino because she was so enamored of Rex: "June didn't fall in love with him [Valentino]. She had already given her heart as well as her brains to Rex Ingram."[32] Pickford based her deductions in part on the fact that Rex divorced Doris Pawn in 1920 at the time he met Mathis. His subsequent marriage to Alice Terry, in this account, "rocked Hollywood," and in a further aside Pickford remarks with some accuracy, if equal acerbity, that "before being spotted by Ingram, Terry had indeed been nothing more than an extra girl."[33] Both Valentino and Rex were fresh from marital disasters, which made them available; Valentino had more errors to make, but Rex would find a life companion in Alice. We know that Mathis was comfortable in the company of gay men, as was Alice, and both women may equally have simply enjoyed the presence of two attractive males who, if not gay (and Valentino was not, even if certain section of the media hinted otherwise), saw more in them than prospective sexual partners. Alice had worked with Valentino before, and both got on well on set, laughing at the days when they were extras and hardly daring to believe that this film might be a success. Rex managed to act with civility toward Valentino for much of the duration of the shoot, recognizing the qualities that drove him. He confided presciently to Samuel Goldwyn afterward that "he's very ambitious and earnest, and if he doesn't take what the fans say too seriously, he will live a long time as a picture idol provided, of course, that he is kept in good stories and has a capable director."[34] Whether Rex and Mathis ever did have an affair remains in the realm of speculation; if they did it was short-lived. Later, after the *Ben Hur* debacle (Fred Niblo, 1925), he refused to speak to her.

From the outset, both Rex and June Mathis were determined that this film should be not just an epic war story but an artistic triumph. "I wanted to get away from the hard, crisp effect of the photograph," Rex explained, "and get something of the mellow mezzotint of the painting; to get the fidelity of photography, but the softness of the old master; to picture not only the dramatic action, but to give it some of the merit of art."[35] To this end, he and John Seitz deployed lighting to create effects that would be visually and dramatically startling. Frame after frame is composed like a painting—in Julio's French atelier, for instance, a dusty light filters down the stairwell to right of frame, throwing shadows of grilled windows across the wall. To the left of the room, and left of frame, a group of models pose in a cluster, their cigarette smoke curling above them, drawing the eye upward into the room's corners.

Dancing the Tango

One of the most striking scenes, and the one that most people remember from *Four Horsemen,* precedes this, marking Valentino's arrival into the story. To shoot the Buenos Aires sequences (an addition to the original novel and scantily sketched out in the scenario), Rex assembled two hundred extras to play the various representatives of the Argentinean lowlife who peopled the Boca—buxom women, drunken sailors on shore leave, and squint-eyed drinkers. He drew on earlier work to create the atmosphere he needed: "When we came to rehearsing the tango, Rudy did so well that I made up my mind to expand this phase of the story. I did this by means of a sequence in a Universal picture I had made several years before [*The Pulse of Life*]. The sequence showed an adventurous youth going into a Bowery dive and taking the dancer after he had first floored her partner. Bones and marrow, I transposed this action to South America—yet only a few of my wise Universal friends recognized it."[36]

Rex rehearsed the tango sequence for three days, while Seitz worked on the lighting so that the background almost disappeared in a soft haze, literally leaving the floor to the dancers. Valentino's entry—dressed as an elegant, posturing gaucho—instantly recalls his earlier years as a tango-tea gigolo. As the film frames his face, he draws deeply on a cigarette, gives a boyish grin, and eyes the two dancers on the floor, exhaling languidly through his nostrils. Within minutes, he strolls over to them, watches them for a second or two more, cradling his whip in his hand, and then interrupts the dance. The young woman (Beatrice Dominguez) is quick to suggest that she would be open to a new partner, but her male companion needs to be thrown across the room before Julio can proceed. Rex framed the sequence with entry arches, and while looking up at street level one can just glimpse the legs of the pedestrians up high walking past. The camera cuts back and forth between the local band, old Madariaga seated at a table, the leery onlookers—one, in Rex's homage to *Regeneration,* eyes his glass unsteadily, just as Raoul Walsh's did, only to glimpse a fish swimming inside it—and the elegant dancer and his partner on the floor.[37] Seitz lit Valentino so softly that his features seem rounded and youthful and almost feminine, before teasing the viewer with cigarette smoke that drifts across the set, temporarily obscuring them. Now the camera cuts in closer, first to Julio's face as he pulls the young woman in to him, then to his shoes, their heels glittering with sharp spurs, a suggestive complement to the whip, and to the hint of femininity. Finally, the dance ends, and Julio reaches in and in close-up kisses his partner with proprietorial vigor, as if she were his prize, before leading her back to her table and seating her on his lap as he draws on his glass. In the final version, this sequence was tinted, as were a number of others.[38] As Alexander Walker writes of this scene in his notes from an early screening of *Four Horsemen,* "It is a very deliberately 'staged' debut—nothing leads up to it, but V[alentino] is *there* in all his gaucho aggressiveness, perhaps reacting to director—one seems to hear Ingram calling out guidance—a shade too deliberately, but nonetheless making instantaneous impact."[39]

It was indeed a showstopper. Valentino was to be just one in a long line of male Ingram leads who had in common an easy disregard for the conventions of machismo. Sold to a willing female public as Latin lovers, these types were the opposite of the frontiersmen heroes of conventional mainstream fiction. It is perhaps surprising that where Valentino's sexuality was always regarded with suspicion by the media, no whispers about Rex's sexual orientation appeared by association. He seemed to be able to "get away" with his casting choices by seeming to be a regular guy, with a film star wife (two, in fact) and a penchant for "macho" military clothing. He could wear a bracelet on his wrist without the press considering it worth the comment, but when Valentino flaunted his "slave bracelet," it confirmed his effeminacy. Even the profession of director (manly) was less suggestive than that of actor (a dubious occupation for a guy). With no evidence to suggest that Rex was a gay man, he nonetheless demonstrated a disinclination in his films, as in aspects of his life, to pander to conformity. It was this disinclination, then, one may guess, that gives us a Valentino that was much praised by the press and without any of the accompanying sneering—most notoriously the "pink powder puff" description—that was to mark his later career, from *The Sheik* (George Melford, 1921) onward.[40]

Indeed, there was never any suggestion in reviews of *Four Horsemen* that this was a film for a female audience, even though so much of it takes place in drawing rooms and interiors, and so little of it on the battlefield. Nor does the film revolve around the sensuous display of Valentino's body in the way that his later star vehicles would. Here, instead, Valentino, beautiful as he undoubtedly is, startling as his performance was, is part of a larger story of war and world affairs. In terms of the story line, Julio has to be sacrificed in the war to make a man of him. But it also suggests that the man that he was, was just as attractive.

Another bravura sequence was the destruction of the village of Villeblanche, which had been built in the hills behind Griffith Park. John Seitz set fourteen cameras running and waited for the light to be just right. It had to be completed in just one take. Finally, at four o'clock on a Sunday afternoon, everyone was ready. The cameras ran, and the take was perfect. Cannon shots rain down on the village, and from every angle blasts of smoke and debris erupt. Later Grant Whytock intercut the attack with a sequence of the Four Horsemen charging across the heavens. The advancing columns of soldiers pour into the ruined village and break into Desnoyers Sr.'s castle of treasures. Lest there should be any doubt about their brutality, they line up the villagers against a wall and gun them down.

Even without musical accompaniment, the film has a rhythm and narrative drive that is achieved by interspersing action and reflection. Moving from the pampas to Paris, scenes alternate between the outdoors and interiors, between the vast and the intimate. The love affair between Julio and Marguerite takes place indoors, in drawing rooms, in Julio's studio, and at the infamous tango teas, where, under the eye of the disapproving Paris matrons, Julio dances with Marguerite, abandoning his usual partners for this married woman. Only toward the conclusion does the story relocate itself to the battlefield and the trenches, where rain sweeps across the screen and a blue light bathes the earth. Tinted frames add to the drama, with color bursting on the screen in flashes of patriotic red and blue in the sequence where a singer performs "La Marseillaise" after war is declared. One brief subsequent scene, of the battlefield, is shot in the new, experimental Prizma Color.

Four Horsemen is threaded through with tiny motifs that give it a visual unity—a parakeet on a perch, a dancing monkey, crossed swords on a wall, children playing—and leaven the narrative. Sequence after sequence is set up with Rex's love for detailed interiors, and one can be certain that no item of furniture is ever placed at random but is there to draw the eye forward and backward and across the frame. As the mood of the film darkens, so the weather deteriorates, and in another striking composition, Julio stands looking out into the obscurity of the rain-splattered glass where he receives the news of the assassination of Franz Ferdinand.

The sequences in which the Four Horsemen ride across the sky were as extraordinary as anything that the early pioneers of cinema had imagined. In the original novel, Tchernoff explains that his vision of the Four Horsemen was inspired by Albrecht Dürer. Rex in turn recreates Dürer's famous woodcut of the mid-fifteenth century, intercutting between Tchernoff's impassioned look and a brilliant, red-tinted vision of the horsemen riding out of the mist and fog as if out of the screen and into the auditorium.[41] It is a bold sequence, coming as it does midway into the film, and shifts the action decisively from the drawing room into the streets and the battlefield. Indeed, it is this bravura quality that renders *Four Horsemen* so distinctive. Its technological innovations are few, but its execution is extraordinary. It was as if Rex and his youthful companions in adventure had taken the tools crafted by their elders and determined that everything they wrought was to be more beautiful, more brilliant, more moving that anything that had come before.

Rex, Mathis, Seitz, and Whytock (assisted by a friend of Rex's from Ireland, Pat O'Brien) worked round the clock, Rex says in his memoirs. "An early release date had obliged us to start shooting with an only partially finished script, which meant night work for June, my cutter, Grant Whytock, and myself. Grant cut each sequence as soon as the film came through the laboratory, and my takes had been picked. Ten cameras were grinding on the war scenes, so it was often midnight before we left the studio. John Seitz would go straight from the set to the laboratory. I believe there were nights he slept there." The costs escalated, and for an anxious three days the team had to wait for the all-clear from Metro's New York office to increase the budget for a film that many expected to fail.[42]

Once permission to continue came through, Metro pulled out all the publicity stops. Newsrooms were flooded with ever more hyperbolic descriptions of the vast resources that had been poured into the forthcoming release. More building materials had been used in the making of the film than in the erection of the world's greatest skyscraper (then the Woolworth Building in New York); a total of 12,500 men and women, or the adult population of a city of 60,000, had participated in the filming of the picture, either before the camera or as workers on the big sets; a complete telephone system, involving the use of a corps of electricians, operators, and a small fortune in cable and other materials, had been erected on the mountain ranch where the big exterior scenes for the picture were filmed.[43] If descriptions of the scale of the production were designed to impress, so was its cost—the film was routinely described as one of the most expensive ever made (though its budget would soon be trumped by the most expensive film of the silent era, 1925's *Ben Hur*). Just as today, this was an unashamed pitch for audiences. *The Four Horsemen of the Apocalypse* was to be a blockbuster like no other.

How to Market Art

Metro may have thrown themselves behind their new picture, but in the background many of the executives remained concerned. Ibáñez's novel could be counted on to bring in its own fans, but how was the studio to position Rex's film? It could not be sold on its stars (minor) or its director (emerging). Nor were most of the regular filmgoers guaranteed to be readers of translated fiction. An article by Grace Kingsley in 29 August 1920's *Los Angeles Times* reflects these anxieties. "There are a lot of film fans who aren't going to be excited over the title, 'The Four Horsemen of the Apocalypse,'" the article opens. "Maybe the soda jerker and the truck driver and the waiter never even heard of the Ibanez novel, and don't know a thing about it." Fatty Arbuckle, she continues, "remarked the other day, 'Those guys will probably think the four horsemen mean Tom Mix, Bill Russell, Bill Hart, and Harry Carey [all regular Western heroes].'" The solution was to target the upmarket audience and to impress on it that this film was Art. More than that, its director was an Artist: "Perhaps no director in the country could be better fitted than Rex Ingram for the task of filming the story inasmuch as he is an artist and a scholar, as well as a director and actor." A further source of worry was that audiences would be weary of war pictures. Kingsley, who might as well have been writing a press release as an independent piece of journalism, dances around the identity of the film: "While the story is a story of the war, it's not, for the most part, about the war, if you recognize the distinction."[44]

Finally Metro's executives decided to throw caution to the wind. They already had guaranteed access to the chain of upmarket movie theaters that Marcus Loew had brought with him to his purchase of Metro. Now they reasoned they would make a nationwide event of the film's release that would persuade audiences that this was no run-of-the-mill production. To that end, they formed the Four Horsemen Exhibition Corporation, which in turn trained technicians and provided support for over a hundred road companies that toured the film around America. The screenings were planned to reflect the magnificence of the movie; audiences were to be treated to a spoken foreword, a prologue, and an overture. All road-show screenings had orchestras, and many provided actors trained to perform the prologue. Viewers across the country would thus experience something similar to the big-city filmgoers. The most resplendent of all presentations was to be the premiere in New York's Lyric Theatre on 6 March 1921, followed soon after by the Los Angeles opening at the Mission Theater on 9 March. No detail of the premiere was neglected. For the release at the Mission, Louis Gottschalk composed an original score that he wrote in collaboration with Mathis and Rex. The illustrious Austrian émigré Dr. Hugo Reisenfeld was to conduct.

Rex, meanwhile, contacted Lee Lawrie. Would his old teacher consider a special commission? He would like a bronze made of the Four Horsemen as a gift for Vicente Blasco Ibáñez. Normally Lawrie only created pieces for public exhibition, believing that was the true purpose of art. But as a favor to his gifted student, and because the subject was so important, he would make an exception. In the end, he seems to have struck at least two statues, one for Ibáñez and another to be exhibited on the opening night in New York.

Still trepidatious, Metro organized a preview on 10 February 1921 for the great and the good of the film industry in New York's Ritz Carlton. This was as tough an audience as anyone could assemble, one with a natural tendency toward cynicism. At the end of the evening's entertainment, the response was instantaneous. All rose to their feet and applauded, completely captivated by what they had seen. Gradually a sense of hope began to accompany the planned release.

The official opening followed a month later. From the parterre to the boxes to the upper circle, New York's Lyric Theatre was filled; word had gone around that this was an evening not to be missed. The prologue struck up and the lights dimmed. A figure stepped into the spotlight on the stage dressed as John the Baptist and introduced the film's religious references. As he left, the screening began. An intermission broke the tension, only for it to return when a single musician took up a snare drum and played the haunting sounds of the military burial salute. Offstage a drummer dressed as Death picked up the rhythm and slowly advanced in front of the screen. As he passed across the stage, the orchestra in turn took up the beat, and the screening recommenced. When a singer, draping herself in the French flag, appears on screen and the orchestra strikes up "La

Marseillaise," a soprano was heard offscreen singing the words. Finally the nearly three-hour performance came to its tragic conclusion. As the last strains of the orchestra died away, applause filled the auditorium. The Metro executives must have let out a collective sigh of relief, for Rex's film was a triumph—one that would soon exceed anyone's wildest expectations.

As the guests and critics filed out, many stopped to congratulate the director. "Kinda young to turn out a big trick like this," the *Film Daily* observed. "Modest too. His appreciation shows in his handclasp."[45] The reception in Los Angeles was equally enthusiastic, and the film repeated its success a few days later when it opened at the La Salle in Chicago. After the run at the Lyric, *Four Horsemen* moved in April to New York's Astor Theater, where its takings broke the house record.[46] The critics were in awe, praising the film's cinematography, its use of composition, and its success in rendering a war story immediate and tragic. It was, the *New York Times* concluded, "an exceptionally well done adaption of a novel, and an extraordinary motion picture work to boot."[47] For Edwin Schallert in the *Los Angeles Times*, the scenes in Argentina and Paris "positively take you to those places," and the film overall bore the stamp of "excellent work."[48] *Variety* unhesitatingly placed the film in the pantheon not just of American but world masterpieces: "For it this young director, hardly more than a boy in years, must be accorded a place alongside Griffith. His production is to the picture of today what 'The Birth of a Nation' was. For a clear understanding of its artistic and pictorial superiority, comparison with the best of its predecessors becomes necessary. Therefore, be it said that 'The Four Horsemen' is the equal of everything that was great in 'Intolerance,' 'Cabiria,' 'Passion,' 'Hearts of the World' and 'The Birth of a Nation.'"[49]

The first person Rex saw when coming out of the theater the night the picture opened in New York was William Fox. Rex recalled in his memoirs:

> He took me in his arms and kissed me on both cheeks.
> "My boy, I'm proud of you!" he said.
> His was one of the tributes that touched me most. In a way I was sorry that it had not been for him I had made the picture.[50]

Praise was lavished equally on *Four Horsemen*'s pictorial qualities and its performances. Schallert noted presciently that "in the interpretation of

Julio, Valentino has assumed a place among the most dominant romantic actors of the screen."[51] And Alice Terry was greeted as a major star. In the multitude of interviews that followed the film's successful release, Rex was always careful to credit June Mathis for keeping a tight grip on the story and for overseeing continuity.

Not only was Rex's film an unqualified critical success—it was also a massive financial earner for Metro. By 1925 the gross earnings on *The Four Horsemen of the Apocalypse* had mounted to about $4 million.[52] The studio's hitherto faltering financial situation was transformed. The impact of *Four Horsemen* was not just confined to America but made the film a global phenomenon. In Paris it opened at the Vaudeville Theatre on 19 March 1922, where President Alexandre Millerand, Marshal Ferdinand Foch, Premier Raymond Poincaré, and the American ambassador, Myron T. Herrick, attended the first night. It premiered in Madrid a month later and across Europe.

In London the film enjoyed a record run of 320 performances at Marcus Loew's Palace cinema, to be replaced by Rex's *The Prisoner of Zenda,* which in turn was replaced by his *Trifling Women.*[53] Dublin audiences had to wait until January of 1923 for the film's opening at the La Scala Theatre. But when it came, *Four Horsemen* was as lavishly presented in the city of Rex's birth as it was anywhere else, with months of preparation going into the opening.

Metro need not have worried that audiences were weary of war films. The success of Rex's film ushered in a new era of epic productions, many of them with antiwar plots, such as *The Big Parade* (King Vidor, 1925) and William Wellman's *Wings* (1927). Other films on the scale of *Four Horsemen* followed, including Cecil B. DeMille's *The Ten Commandments* (1923) and the vexatious *Ben Hur.* For now Rex was indeed king at Metro. Visitors to the studio's New York office found themselves greeted by three statues. To the left stood a bust of Rex by Lee Lawrie. Just opposite stood one of Ibáñez by E. T. Quinn. On the desk, in pride of place, was Lawrie's figure of the Four Horsemen.

5

Conquering Metro

If there was one lingering cloud on the horizon of *The Four Horsemen of the Apocalypse,* it was the relationship between the film's star and its director. "He didn't let me do what I wanted," Valentino complained to Robert Florey. "He seemed to think more about his compositions and his lighting effects than about my performance, and that sometimes annoyed me."[1] Florey, who knew Valentino well, guessed that he would have hated being corrected by Rex on set in front of other people and tended to sulk when this happened.

Relations between the two men further deteriorated as they launched into their second production together. Metro was keen to capitalize on the unexpected reception of *Four Horsemen* and the success of the Mathis-Ingram-Valentino-Terry combination. June Mathis wrote an adaptation of Balzac's *Eugénie Grandet,* and she and Rex worked on getting it swiftly to the screen. Rex had another reason for ensuring that the film be completed promptly. Yale had contacted him with the news that it was going to award him a bachelor's degree in fine arts in recognition of his direction of *Four Horsemen.* The ceremony was to be held on 22 June 1921; thus the new picture, titled *The Conquering Power,* had to be finished by then. "My failure to get a degree had been a great disappointment to my father, so I determined that nothing would stop my getting to New Haven on time. Night work resulted, which frayed everyone's nerves, including my own."[2] In all, the film took five weeks to shoot.

Familiarity with Balzac's source story is not much guidance for the viewer of Rex's new film. Mathis played fast and loose with the original, which sees its focus gradually shift from the miser, Père Grandet, to his daughter Eugénie. In the novel Eugénie's happiness is awoken when her father's nephew, Charles, comes from Paris to visit their provincial home. It is soon revealed that Charles's father has committed suicide as a consequence of his indebtedness. No sooner have Charles and Eugénie fallen in love than Père Grandet dispatches his unwanted nephew to the West Indies to recoup the family fortune. Eugénie gifts him all her life's savings and waits devotedly for his return. But Charles turns out badly after all and comes back not to Eugénie but to a society bride, leaving the innocent provincial cousin to spend the rest of her days nursing her loss. In the novel, the conquering power is greed; in the film it is love. In Mathis's version, Charles is faithful to Eugénie, and the two lovers are eventually reunited.

The opening intertitles explain why another alteration, this time in the novel's period, had to be made: "Commercialism tells us that you, Great Public, do not like the costume play. Life is life, so we make our story of today, that you may recognize each character as it comes your way." The scenes that immediately follow this doggerel do, as promised, bring the viewer to Paris of today rather than Balzac's 1819. The location is a nightclub where Charles Grandet (Valentino with a monocle) cavorts with flapper girls and exotic dancers against one of John Seitz's hazy, smoke-filled backgrounds. The film then shifts to the French countryside and the home of the miser Père Grandet (Ralph Lewis) and his beautiful daughter, Eugénie (Alice Terry), a setting that bears a much closer resemblance to period drama than the opening titles had suggested. Alighting onto this rustic scene, Valentino, in an immaculate pale-colored suit and tossing elegant gloves from hand to hand, flinches at the sight of such an unsophisticated milieu before introducing himself to his uncle. His arrival at the Grandet home is rendered even more exotic by the addition of an elaborately clipped poodle on a lead. The camera completes a rare movement, following in close-up the young man's examination of his uncle's rustic garb from toe to head. Valentino is exquisitely decadent, and the camera revels in his perfection. It is only once he arrives in Martinique, in accordance with his uncle's plan to remove him as far from Eugénie and his rightful inheritance as possible, that he rolls up his sleeves and takes on a more conventionally manly demeanor, just as he did in *Four Horsemen*.

The most striking sequence in the film, however, does not feature the young star. Instead it takes place in Père Grandet's hideaway. Crazed by his own greed, the old man can only watch in horror as the cradle holding his gold begins to rock of its own accord. Ghostly emanations of those he has wronged start to materialize around him. In the garden, Eugénie reads the love letters from Charles she has discovered concealed in Grandet's cabinet, still unaware of the fact that he is not her true birth father. Grandet hurls himself against the walls, tearing his hair as the cradle keeps up its demented rocking. Two skeletal hands emerge from the cradle, then through the bars of the window. The walls of the room begin to close in on the miser, and the ghostly figure reveals itself to him announcing, "I am gold! All your life you have sought me—now you are mine!" Grandet collapses to the floor, pulling the coins down on top of him as he breathes his last.

The sequence has its origins in Mathis's scenario. In her version Grandet inadvertently locks himself into his storeroom, and as he tries to escape he becomes gripped by a kind of claustrophobic panic. The ghosts appear and dissolve out, the doors of the cabinets of gold open, and the walls seem to grow in on him. He grasps at the cabinet, and the gold pours out on top of him; the walls move back, leaving him lying crushed to death by his precious coins. Embellished and expanded, the scene now becomes the dream that Rex had been carrying in his head since his teens, and his nightmare vision of the end of the Lambert household in Galway. It was as close as he ever came to including Irish material in his films, even if no one viewing *The Conquering Power* would likely have made that connection. Yet it was always there, that lurking Gothic sensibility, that sense of horror erupting into everyday life.

Insulting Valentino

The dynamic of *The Conquering Power* is driven by the relationship between Eugénie and her father, with Charles remaining absent for much of the story (as he was in Mathis's script). If Valentino's character is sidelined on screen, the actor also felt sidelined during the making of *The Conquering Power*. His director greeted with stony indifference his strong (and correct) belief that he was now a star. Valentino had further gained in confidence through his new relationship with former ballerina, now costume designer, Natacha Rambova, another startling figure on the Metro lot. Clad in turbans and exotic jewelry—quite a reinvention for a woman born Winifred Kimball Shaughnessy in Utah—she added a new, mystic presence to the group around Mathis and Valentino. Like Mathis, she believed in reincarnation and, like Rex, was to become fascinated by Egyptology, becoming a notable collector. One imagines they had little else in common.

Now Valentino decided to assert his own opinions as to how the film should look. For a start, since he loved to dress well, he made it known that his own design ideas would dictate what his character should wear. Rex had no intention of letting this happen. Rambova and Seitz both recalled a flare-up over clothing leading to extraordinary tensions on set. One day Valentino came in, and Rex said to him, "Valentino, that's an American suit you got on in the picture." Valentino had prepared his clothing for the midnight entertainment scene at the film's opening with his customary care, so he flashed back that Rex knew nothing about clothing—otherwise why would he always wear the same old trench coat around the studio? Englishman Frank Elliott was called in to adjudicate on the basis that he would be familiar with the correct code of attire for such an occasion. Elliot came down on Valentino's side. Rex was furious and proceeded to taunt his leading man by cleaning his fingernails with his penknife during Valentino's most important close-up. A few weeks later Rex was invited to an official dinner at Metro. Finding that he had no suitable clothing, he asked Valentino for the loan of evening dress. Valentino without hesitation complied.[3]

Rex meanwhile was drawing in people from his wider artistic circle to work with him, a practice he would continue throughout his career. He had already turned to Lee Lawrie to create the sculpture for *Four Horsemen*. As he was preparing to shoot *The Conquering Power,* he contacted another old friend, inviting Ralph Barton to the West Coast. Barton was appointed set director on the film but quickly found moviemaking uncongenial: "The pace was too frantic and the process too fragmented for his orderly, deliberate methods of working: too many people seemed to be doing the same thing, or nothing, and he felt no control over his own vision," his biographer notes.[4] Something of an insomniac, the caricaturist was used to all-night entertainment in New York. In Los Angeles in the middle of the night, there was nothing to do. Still he stayed on in Hollywood for a while, picking up work for *Photoplay* and reporting back on the glamorous circles in which he was moving for *Vanity Fair*. One of his illustrations, from September 1921, for *Vanity Fair,* titled "When the Five o' Clock Whistle Blows in Hollywood," shows a cluster of stars and directors in front of the Hollywood Hotel as the movie studios were closing. The figures include Cecil B. DeMille, Harold Lloyd, Will Rogers, Elinor Glyn, Buster Keaton, Charlie Chaplin, Mary Pickford, Gloria Swanson, and Rex Ingram standing beside Alice Terry. Rex is dressed in his regulation trench coat, with a pipe and what looks like a polka-dot tam-o'-shanter. The monocle, if it ever existed, has been abandoned.

Valentino does not feature in Barton's sketch, and if he had he certainly would not have been standing beside Rex. Now certain of his star status, Valentino asked for a pay raise. Metro told him they couldn't afford it and didn't feel he was worth it: "Rex and I had a talk and I asked for a hundred dollar raise. We argued and argued, and finally he gave me a raise of fifty, making my salary $400 [per week]."[5] By the end of the shoot, they were at constant loggerheads. Rex was becoming increasingly dogmatic and intolerant of dissent; Valentino was becoming increasingly aware of his own worth. "I never saw as conscientious an actor, especially on this picture," Seitz later remembered. "He was a hard and conscientious worker, the most conscientious actor I ever met."[6] The final split, according to Seitz, came at the end of the production. Rex wanted to finish off a sequence, and Valentino wanted to take a break since it was his birthday and a party was being held for him. Rex was insistent: "No, he's no better than the rest of us. He has to go to the restaurant with the rest of us." Valentino went to the restaurant, and when Seitz joined him, he said, "Johnny, I think I'll kill this Irishman." The next day, according to Seitz, he went over to Jesse Lasky and signed to do *The Sheik*.[7] In fact Valentino's birthday was on 6 May, and he signed the contract with Famous Players–Lasky in July of 1921. Still, Rex's account of the split confirms Seitz's to the last detail, except their parting words. "You'll have a tough time finding someone to take my place in your next picture," Valentino said, according to Rex. "It's taken already," Rex responded.[8]

If Valentino's move from Metro to Famous Players–Lasky was not quite as abrupt as Seitz remembered, it was at least in part Rex's doing. Rex himself explains concisely in his memoirs why he had no sympathy with the actor's aspirations: "I said I was not interested in directing stars. I preferred a cast of comparatively unknown players who would be accepted as the characters they portrayed, and if a picture of mine happened to boost one of them to stardom I would rather find someone else for the next. I was only interested in the production as a production."[9] This was a little disingenuous, as Alice starred in nearly all his films, and Ramón Novarro would star in five. In Rex's mind, the model for a sculptural figure was seldom recognizable so why should the identity of an actor be? The answer to this was, and remains, because the Hollywood star system was crucial to the financial success of the industry. For Rex, this was anathema. Or as DeWitt Bodeen writes, "He was a starmaker, but he was not a star's director. *He* was the star, and everyone who worked for him respected him and his masterly talent."[10] If they did not, they encountered Rex's deep intolerance of dissent. Sometimes this emerged in thoroughly obnoxious behavior. Although occasionally the victim of his intolerance and he made up, others were cast as enemies, snubbed in public, sneered at privately, and treated forever with contempt.

Jesse Lasky remembered in his memoirs going to see *Four Horsemen* at the Lyric Theatre. "That picture thrilled me as *The Birth of a Nation* had," he writes. "Everything about it was magnificent. Rex Ingram's direction of his first important picture was outstanding, June Mathis's script was superb, the camera work incomparable, and, to top it all, an unknown young Italian actor discovered by June Mathis gave one of the best silent-screen performances I have ever seen."[11] Several days later—about a month after the release of *Four Horsemen*—his secretary announced that Rudolph Valentino was in the office and would like to see him. When Valentino asked Lasky if he might have a part for him, the latter couldn't believe he was serious. How could Metro not realize what an asset they had on their hands? He guessed that the knowledge that Rex and Valentino had quarreled on set had given Valentino a bad reputation around the studio; in addition, Rowland was distracted by the pending deal (actually 1920) to sell Metro to Marcus Loew. He did indeed hire Valentino on the spot and took the precaution of hiring Mathis too. In fact, correspondence suggests that Lasky and Rex entered discussions with a view to Rex joining him as well.[12] Lasky had been searching for a lead for his upcoming film, *The Sheik;* now he had one.[13]

Just where June Mathis stood on the split between Rex and Valentino isn't clear. It must have been evident to her that her professional future, at least, lay with Valentino and with molding his stardom through creating scripts that would show him off at his best. She may also have worked out that Rex would chafe against her control—she was still his senior in position as well as years—ever more as he developed his own very particular working methods. She may have quite simply resented both Metro and Rex for their treatment of her protégé, Valentino. Later, as we will see in the next chapter, an opportunity came her way to show Rex just who was in control. And she took it.

The Conquering Power opened on 8 July 1921. The critics were enchanted by what they saw on the screen, with the National Board of Review declaring that with this film Rex had outdone *Four Horsemen*.[14] Most of all, it was the painterly, artistic quality of the images that reviewer after reviewer praised:

> If true art be determined by its symbols of beauty, its rhythm, its formal perfection and its reality, then "The Conquering Power" . . . is the artistic picture of the year. I might even go further than this and say that because of its failure at any point to offend the esthetic sense—pictorially speaking—it is the one really artistic picture. It represents photography, and with it the art of photographic composition, as adapted to the screen, in its highest form to date.
>
> With the screening of this picture, Rex Ingram, the director becomes a master of the beautiful in visual expression.[15]

The *New York Times* too agreed that this was the film that realized the promise of *Four Horsemen*.[16] That paper's critic singled out Rex's frequent facial close-ups as a signature of his style, both artistically in the way they were captured and as a method of shedding light on the characters' thoughts and emotions. Opinions differed on the performances. The *Los Angeles Times* critic found Alice Terry unduly melodramatic with a limited range of expression, while *Variety* thought her "sweetly beautiful and beautifully sweet." More gallingly for the screen's number-one Latin lover, Valentino was deemed by the *Los Angeles Times* to have given merely an "acceptable performance," though again *Variety* was more encouraging, pronouncing that "his performance . . . proves his right to stardom in motion pictures."[17] The star of this show was without doubt its director.

Jessie Lasky now tried to tempt Alice Terry with an offer to star opposite Valentino in *The Sheik*. Rex, however, firmly announced that she was to be in his next picture, *Turn to the Right*.

Turn to the Right (1922)

Metro paid a hefty $500,000 for the screen rights to Winchell Smith and John E. Hazzard's play *Turn to the Right*. John Golden, the New York theater impresario, had already sold a half interest in the stage production to Marcus Loew, who was confident that the play's spectacular success would be replicated on screen.[18] Mathis had written a draft of the script before leaving Metro, and the task of completing it went to Mary O'Hara, a name that later would resound with generations of children as the author of *My*

Friend Flicka. "He looked too young to be famous. There was not a mark of experience on him," she later wrote of meeting Rex. "He was very quiet, as if always slightly abstracted. He could have been twenty-five or forty-five. He was mysterious, like every true artist."[19]

The story of *Turn to the Right* followed Joe Bascom (Jack Mulhall) as he left his farm, his widowed mother, and orphaned sister to make a fortune in the city and marry Elsie Tillinger (Alice Terry). In the city Joe turns to the left, falls into criminal ways, and is falsely imprisoned. On his release, he resolves to turn to the right and go straight. He returns to the farm, but two of his old friends from the criminal fraternity follow him there. After a series of comic encounters with country life, Elsie now comes into her own and, with the assistance of her mother's peach jam, reforms the criminals. As the description suggests, this was moralistic, populist fare, without any of the class of *Four Horsemen*. Still John Seitz took his task seriously, reflecting the picture's sentimentality with soft, warm lighting. His director proceeded to encourage Harry Myers and George Cooper as the two criminals to ratchet up the humor, so much so that at least one critic suspected that he was undermining his own material.[20] The *Variety* critic was one among several, however, in finding the picture "satisfying despite its old fashioned situations."[21]

Certainly this kind of Americana, familiar with it as he was from *Shore Acres,* was not to Rex's taste. Yet the film is identifiably an Ingram film. The sequences in New York recall his prewar works—the interior of the bar where Joe turns to the left could just as easily be that of *The Flower of Doom.* In darkened, subterranean rooms, men smoke, drink whisky, and fight; they gamble and play pool, their faces marked by life's harshness. John George puts in an appearance as background color in the pool hall sequence. In prison, as Joe sits thinking of Elsie, shafts of light fall through the bars of the window, while by contrast the country characters, particularly the good Mrs. Bascom (Lydia Knott) are brightly lit, as are their surroundings. Alice Terry, with her characteristic sweetness, was well-suited to this kind of fare. Rex dressed her in pale costumes and flower-bedecked hats, emphasizing the pastoralism of the village setting. The countryside is bathed in sunlight, its vistas framed by peach trees and its innocent charms enhanced by the inclusion of a family of gamboling kittens. It is also a place associated with womanly virtues and values, of church and kitchen, a nod perhaps to the rectory at Kinnitty.

The humor, on the other hand, is deeply unsubtle and in this instance tinged with anti-Semitism. The sequences of exchanges between the two Jewish characters, some of them in untranslated Yiddish, seem to be there primarily to provide cheap laughs. So unproblematic was this that it went unremarked by the commentators of the 1920s, many of whom would have shared with Rex easily provoked prejudices around Jewishness. Indeed, the suspicion of a nudge and wink to a knowing audience is obvious throughout, though nowhere more than in the final sequence. Mrs. Bascom watches the beams of Joe's car as he drives up to the house he has built for his life with Elsie. The lights go on downstairs, then off, then on in the upstairs window. A shade is drawn down, as if the final curtain were lowering, and the film closes.

The combined departures of Mathis and Valentino would have been devastating for many directors but not for Rex. He was still carefully constructing a group of people with whom he could work comfortably. "Ingram was a very independent Irishman," Metro's publicist, Howard Strickling, who was to enjoy a long working career with Rex, commented. "He was not hostile to people—but he was selective as to his friends and associates."[22] Director Norman Taurong later told Paul Kozak: "I was told by people who were fond of Rex that he never got into terrific arguments or fought you right away. He would absolutely clam up. Just clam up. Then the other person would say, 'Rex, what's the matter? What happened?' *Then* he would tell you. But when you were off guard, not when you were at your full strength. And he'd tell you in no uncertain terms."[23] To friends and family, Rex remained always generous, always loyal, someone who veered between intense intellectual thought and a love of pranks and practical jokes. He was stubborn and, despite the best efforts of his father, also largely self-taught. With that came the obstinacy of the autodidact, a reluctance to heed contradictory opinions, but also a real hunger to learn. He was charming to some, offensive to others, unforgiving, contradictory.

Once the split with Valentino was final in terms of working together, the former antagonists settled into a somewhat improved personal relationship, propelled most likely by Alice Terry's old friendship with the actor. They all dined together several times in New York in 1922, and later Valentino looked them up when he was visiting the South of France. As she explained to Liam O'Leary, the two men were never great friends, but there was no bitterness between them at the end.[24] Ironically it was Valentino who would later make public claims for Hollywood's potential as Art rather than Industry, citing Charlie Chaplin, Douglas Fairbanks, D. W. Griffith, and Mary Pickford in his defense, a position that would surely have appealed and applied equally to Rex.[25]

Having lashed out so much money, Marcus Loew made the decision to release *Turn to the Right* at top price ($1.65) in an upmarket venue, the Lyric Theater. Full orchestral accompaniment was laid on, though the *Variety* critic felt that the "claquers" (who were paid to warm up the audience by clapping on cue) were overdoing their work and that the bass drummer needed to be suppressed.[26] In what now seemed inevitable, the film was greeted with admiration. "After this sweep from Ibañez to Winchell Smith, we would back Rex Ingram to do anything," the *Picture-Play* critic declared.[27] Metro too would back Rex to do anything. It seemed that whatever he touched was a success, with or without Valentino, no matter what the source material. Following the vast historical pageant of *The Four Horsemen* and the two more modest melodramas, they now assigned him to a different genre again, the swashbuckler. And he rewarded them with another masterwork.

6

Swashbucklers and Other Romances

Metro's next project for Rex was *The Prisoner of Zenda,* a rip-roaring swashbuckler based on Anthony Hope's best-selling 1894 novel of the same name. It was Hope who invented the mythical kingdom of Ruritania, and so popular did his series of novels set there become that they and their successors and imitators became known as "Ruritanian Romances." *The Prisoner of Zenda* was the first in the series and already contained all the ingredients that were to set Victorian hearts aflutter.

A glitch in the legitimacy of the family tree sees the idle aristocrat Rudolf Rassendyll take a trip to the Kingdom of Ruritania, where his cousin, Rudolf of Ruritania, is to be crowned king. Tempted to take a look at the family estate in Zenda, which is occupied by Rupert's conniving sibling, Black Michael, Rassendyll stumbles upon a plot by Michael to abduct his brother and seize the throne. At the same time, it is revealed that Rassendyll is a dead ringer for his carefree namesake. The only way to save the day is for Rassendyll to assume Rudolf's identity and ascend to the throne. This will give the king's loyal servant, Colonel Zapt, time to rescue the real king and thus foil the plot. Once crowned, Rassendyll must resist the tempting charms of the fair Princess Flavia and determine just what part the darkly beautiful Antoinette de Mauban is playing in the dastardly plotting of her lover, Black Michael. With his ready wit, flashing steel, and love of adventure, Rassendyll is a hero in the best tradition of the genre, and it is no surprise that Metro lined up Hope's best seller as sure-fire box office. Indeed, *The Prisoner of Zenda* would be remade over and again, with a version appearing nearly every decade of the twentieth century. Mary O'Hara once again wrote the screenplay, retaining much of the original story in her adaptation.

Increasingly a Rex Ingram film was a personal project, with Rex demanding, and receiving, sole authority over the production. Now, for the first time, he was guaranteed 50 percent of the profits. Ever generous with those he loved and admired, he signed over 10 percent of that 50 percent immediately to John Seitz, who later said that he made more on this than on "a lot of films put together."[1]

When Rex started on *The Prisoner of Zenda,* he was taking on a story whose plot and look were already well established in the public eye. His youthful hero, Charles Dana Gibson, had provided the sketches for Hope's novel. However, the style of the film is so identifiably his that it is hard to argue that Rex was greatly influenced by Gibson's illustrations. Nor are the sudden pratfalls and Ingramesque horseplay in the original novel or screenplay. From the casting onward, he stamped his mark firmly on the production. It was an easy decision to choose Alice Terry as the virginal Princess Flavia; for the leading roles of the identical cousins he picked Lewis Stone. This was to be Stone's first time working with Rex, and he soon became an Ingram regular, appearing in a succession of his films. Rex quickly took to the former stage actor, saying that Stone was "a great delight to any director, because it is not necessary to instruct him, and the time saved can be used to good advantage by the busy producer."[2]

More challenging was the secondary part of Rupert of Hentzau, a charismatic villain, described in the novel as "reckless and wary, graceful and graceless, handsome, debonair, vile, and unconquered."[3] A young unknown named Samaniego now pushed himself into the limelight. His first attempt to contact Rex was abortive, and all he met was an official Metro brick wall. Still, he persisted, now forwarding Rex a personal letter of introduction from Ferdinand Pinney Earle, a mutual friend of both Rex's and Mary O'Hara's. Earle was a well-known figure around Hollywood and an even better-known name in the gossip columns (it was they who christened him "Affinity Earle" after he abandoned his French wife, Emillie Marie Fischbacher, and took up with Julia Kuttner, whom he called his "affinity wife"). The letter made it through to Rex.

Born José Ramón Gil Samaniego on 6 February 1899 in Durango, Mexico, the unknown actor who arrived in Rex's office was one of a large, once comfortably-off family whose fortunes had been shattered by the Mexican Revolution in 1910 and by Samaniego Sr.'s inability to work following illness. Ramón and his brother Mariano fled the revolution, escaping to El Paso and from there to Los Angeles. Arriving in a city on the cusp of emerging as the capital of the movie world, Ramón immediately set his heart on becoming a film star. However, reality dictated that he start out as a floor washer, a grocery clerk, and a busboy before finding work as a singer and dancer in cafés. Eventually he began to accumulate minor roles in Hollywood, and in 1922 Ramón was hired, along with his sister, Carmen, as extras on *The Four Horsemen of the Apocalypse*. According to Rex's memoirs, Ramón worked on this film and on *The Conquering Power*, although there is no further evidence of the latter. He also writes:

> I never gave him anything particular to do, but I could not help noticing the way he did whatever he had to do. He was one of those people a director never dared place too close to the principals in the foreground action. His personality drew the eye at once. In one scene in *The Four Horsemen* I had put him standing behind Rudolf [Valentino]. It was in the French café where they were singing the *Marseillaise* the night of the declaration of war. Everyone was on their feet to join Rose Dion, arrayed in her Alsace-Lorraine bonnet, as she sung:
>
> "*Allons enfants de la patrie-e*
> *Le jour de gloire est arrivé*"
>
> After two rehearsals I had to switch Ramón over to the other side of the set. He was killing Rudolf's scene. I decided to make a screen test of this Mexican.[4]

There is no reason to privilege Rex's version of their encounter over Ramón's, particularly since it reads most of all as the settling of old scores with Valentino. This lingering hostility, mixed with admiration over his professionalism, toward his former star is remarkable. It seems to have really irked him that Valentino eluded his control and asserted his own star value over Rex's value as a creative artist. Rex did not care to have people challenge him, particularly those who were successful as a consequence of their looks rather than what he identified as talent. In the specific case of casting for *The Prisoner of Zenda*, he had been intending to use Valentino in this film and in a sequel, *Rupert of Hentzau,* so he cannot have anticipated at that point that Valentino would strike out without him.

Rex now invited Ramón Samaniego to come and see him. The young dancer and bit-part player sensed that his appointment with Rex was to be the "turning point of my career."[5] Clutching the letter, Ramón introduced himself. Rex told him that he was "just the opposite of what I want," which was an actor "six foot two, blonde, Teutonic."[6] This was a departure from Gibson's sketches, which showed a dark, quite slight, and bearded villain. The character was also to be around a dozen years older than Ramón. Rex turned over Earle's letter and began sketching out his vision of the actor he wanted for Rupert of Hentzau. The younger man's heart sank: "But I was good at make-up and fashioned a false moustache and beard. Mr. Ingram studied me a long time, and finally took me out on a set and made a camera test of me. In the next few days he made four tests of me as Rupert. After the third test he said, 'No, you're still too young.' But he then changed his mind. 'Let's try a test with a monocle, too,' he said."[7] At last Rex was satisfied, and Ramón landed the part on the understanding he grow a moustache. Rex started him on a contract of $125 a week. "He said I would be his new leading man and that he would groom me for stardom. I was deliriously happy, and didn't dare believe him. But that's exactly what he did."[8]

Alice and Rex both warmed instantly to their new lead. "I think of all the actors I have ever been with," Alice told Liam O'Leary:

Ramón was really the best actor of all. I think there was no picture that you could put him in that he couldn't have reached every scene and I think the others couldn't have. I think that Valentino was such a type that he couldn't have played certain scenes. . . . Ramón I could have seen in almost any part outside of an American Boy. . . . Ramón would attempt anything, comedy, drama, crazy scenes, anything, and he could do it and I always thought he was capable of doing better than almost anyone, possibly besides [John] Barrymore, who I think had the same thing.[9]

One can only speculate as to what kind of star Rex might have made of Valentino had they worked together for longer. With Ramón, he had that opportunity. The latter was to prove more amenable to taking directions and remained, to the tragic ending of his life, devoted to the director who gave him his first real chance in Hollywood.

Before *The Prisoner of Zenda* was released, Sam Goldwyn spotted Ramón in the rushes playing a scene in which Hentzau toasts Antoinette de Mauban in the cellar and was impressed. He instantly offered to sign the actor for $2,500 a week without option. His agent was delighted, but Ramón sensed that it was Rex on whom he could best rely if he were to enjoy further success on the screen. "I said 'Mr. Ingram is the one that believed in me. He gave me a chance. If anyone is going to cash in on me, it's Rex Ingram.'" The infuriated agent went to the Samaniego parents and attempted to persuade them to intervene. Ramón was further angered by this. Rex heard what was going on and took his young discovery to one side: "Say, kid I hear that Sam Goldwyn has made you a very good offer." Ramón explained how grateful he was to him. "You have no business being grateful in this business," Rex responded sharply. "Get your money when you can and that's that." Ramón insisted that he'd rather be with him. "I can't afford to pay you that salary anyway," Rex warned him, "but if you want to, I mean I can sign you up and then just keep you in my pictures." That suited Ramón, who signed with Rex personally for two years and happily dropped the arrangement with Goldwyn.[10]

Ramón Samaniego was only one of the unknown actors Rex discovered in the casting of *Prisoner,* although he was to become the most famous. Another new face to the screen was Malcolm McGregor, who played Count Fritz von Tarlenheim. He had been a classmate of Rex's at Yale and shared his love of boxing; he was another handsome young man with looks that subsequently landed him numerous silent-era romantic roles. Rex cast another unknown, Lois Lee, as the Countess Helga. The fan magazines anticipated a triumph for this "quiet little thing with a kind of sparkle hidden away down inside, if you know what I mean—the sort who doesn't effervesce but has to be drawn out, the kind of personality that intrigues you into wanting to know more of it."[11] Regrettably for Lee, after one more appearance that year, in George D. Baker's *Don't Write Letters,* she vanished from Hollywood screens. A more turbulent career awaited another rising name in Hollywood who appeared as Antoinette de Mauban in *The Prisoner of Zenda.* Barbara La Marr had already gained some notoriety after reportedly being kidnapped by her half-sister in California. She followed this by becoming a screenwriter for Fox and United Artists. Screen roles as a seductive vamp quickly materialized, and she earned herself the sobriquet of "The Girl Who Is Too Beautiful." *The Prisoner of Zenda* was not her first film, but it was her most significant screen role to date. She took on the part with relish, her dark looks counterpointed to Alice's fair complexion, her movements smooth and lithe and bewitching.

It was highly unorthodox to cast so many unfamiliar actors in a film that was widely anticipated to be a mainstream success, but it also guaranteed Rex total control. No one in the cast would challenge his authority, and the Metro executives were learning to stay well away. With John Seitz and Grant Whytock on his crew, Rex had two collaborators who knew exactly how he wanted the film to look, and he was confident that he could ease the new actors into their roles and mold their performances. He proceeded with his customary attention to detail. His male leads were to learn to fence properly and to adopt a military bearing on screen. He insisted on the costume department making handsome new uniforms for the legion of military extras, an incidental detail that cost $80,000.[12] Particularly challenging were the sequences where Lewis Stone had to appear as both Rassendylls, including one in which he had to shake hands with himself. Whytock remembered later that they accomplished this by shooting one side, then the other, and that they took and retook until they got a perfect match.[13] Under pressure from Metro to try out color stock, he agreed to have Technicolor film for an exterior sequence, but "we thought the people looked like dark colored oranges, so we took it out of the picture and threw it away," Whytock told Richard Koszarski.[14]

The film is another visual triumph, with Rex and Seitz working closely together to create an effect of three-dimensionality. This was achieved in part through the layout of the sets. In an early scene, for example, as Rassendyll is traveling to Strelzau, the story moves to an inn. In the foreground three men are sitting, playing cards and smoking. Midway into the room, to the right, a coat of arms dominates a wall, and then at the back of the room and to the left, a man—Rupert von Hentzau, Ramón's first appearance in the film—is seated playing piano. He looks so much smaller than the characters in the foreground that one suspects the use of a double exposure. To take in the scene, the eye is drawn from the foreground, to the left and farther back to the right, giving an extraordinary depth to the image. At the very end of the room, a window frames the town, adding even further depth. When von Hentzau moves forward and into the main frame, his face is picked out over and again with Seitz's lighting, at once pale and shadowed, the perfect romantic villain.

In subsequent sequences, characters move simultaneously into the foreground and the background, creating diagonals of movement that enhance the impression of depth. Light runs down staircases into darkened dungeons, tracing villainy. Often, these scenes are themselves framed by arches and doorways, adding a further dimension to their architecture.

Lighting picks out characters, so that in a wide shot Alice's Flavia is well lit and central, with dimly lit secondary characters surrounding her. For close-ups, the light sculpts her face, throwing one side or the other into relief. The cathedral where the coronation is held has enormous vaulted ceilings; Seitz placed his camera so that in one shot it is down low looking up and in the next high up looking down, again creating a sense of limitless depth. Incidental details—the presence of pet dogs who glance offscreen or run across the set—animate indoor scenes, while outdoors the waving leaves of trees create the same effect. Many of the sequences, such as one of horses' hooves throwing up dust into beams of light, are repeated from *Four Horsemen*, yet *Zenda* is also a more intimate film and more recognizably generic. This was consummate filmmaking, edited at a pace and filled with eye-catching performances. The actors were required to work as an ensemble, and while Ramón made for a gleefully wicked villain and Alice an equally romantic innocent heroine, Stone anchors the film in the dual roles of Prince and Pretender, with Barbara La Marr and the other cast members all adding color to the drama. Once again, the audience was denied a happy ending; *Zenda* concludes on a bittersweet note of departure. Princess Flavia and Rassendyll have fallen in love but now, having saved the king, he must leave the country, and she must stay and honor her royal duties.[15]

During the production of *Prisoner*, Rex added another new name to his burgeoning company. A young journalist had turned up on set on the hunt for an interview. As he approached the cameras, Alice was shooting the sequence where she has to cry out, "Rudolph, if love were all I would follow you to the ends of the earth, but if love were all you'd have left the king to die" and burst into tears. Willis Goldbeck later told Kevin Brownlow: "And she couldn't cry and she was cursing Rex because she had no music so he came to me and said 'Do you play the piano'? There was an old prop piano there, and I said well I know one or two things and I played and she promptly burst into tears which made Ingram hire me apparently for the publicity."[16] Goldbeck became Rex's press agent, only to be fired and replaced by Herbert Howe and then hired again to work on the screenplay of *Scaramouche*.

Having a Rather Good Time Together

Rex and Alice's relationship continued on the somewhat haphazard course it had always followed. He was certainly good-looking—Alice thought he looked better than the Prince of Wales—yet their encounters lacked passion. Asked by Liam O'Leary if she was in love with Rex, Alice replied: "No, not particularly. We were very good friends and he used to come down and we went out to dinner to a tea room and he would tell me about what he was doing and ask me about what I was doing (well I wasn't doing anything, except trying to study) and we'd go out and then he would take me home and then everyone on the set would tell me where he had been the night before, all the other girls, you know, and I thought 'good for him,' and I kind of liked him but I thought 'that's not for me.'"[17]

Was Rex really seeing "other girls"? This was a man who, if his memoirs are to be trusted, found women attractive but who had sex with prostitutes by choice. Intimacy seemed to threaten him, except with a few of his most trusted male collaborators—Seitz, Whytock, Edward Connelly, Louis Stone—and, by distance, his brother Frank. He had married Doris Pawn on impulse and found himself ill-suited to such a relationship. He writes:

I was quite convinced that my feeling for her [Alice] was platonic. I had no intention of getting married again. In the evenings I often drove her home; and if the day's work had not been too strenuous we drove around for an hour or two before I dropped her at her house. Her tranquillity was a sedative for studio nerves. Even if I was in an irritable mood when I joined her my bad mood soon passed. She listened to all I had to say about my troubles and those who caused them, but without committing herself on any issue. She just heard my complaints in silence and with a smile. At times I would ask her what she thought was so comic, and if she took no interest in my work. Her laugh was so infectious that in the end she would have me laughing at myself. With her, I got glimpses of myself as others saw me, and came to realize that, after all, I really had very little to kick about.[18]

Rex further recalls what Alice does not, that she had a suitor—he may even have been a fiancé—with "an objectionably highpowered roadster" who sat with Harry in Harry's Greasy Spoon, drinking Coca-Colas and smoking "endless cigarettes tranquilly, patiently, good-humoredly" as he waited for Alice to finish at the studios.[19]

Enraged by the competition, Rex claims he decided he must marry

Alice. Alice's own recollection of Rex's proposal was equally prosaic: "We were walking along the street one night with Elizabeth Waggoner and Ralph Barton and Rex said, 'Do you think we have enough in common to get along?' And I said, 'I think we get along pretty well.' And he said, 'Well I mean to get married.'" She was unenthusiastic, nor was she sure that Rex really wanted to marry her. Then again, did she want to marry him? Yet, she said to herself, if it doesn't work, then we could always get a divorce. If they were married, Rex promised her craftily, she wouldn't have to work again. That was more tempting. Alice accepted.[20]

Most of what is known about Rex Ingram and Alice Terry's long marriage comes to us courtesy of a series of interviews she gave film historians after Rex's death. During their working career, it was he who gave the interviews, with Alice often appearing in the background to smile cheerfully at the interviewer and agree with her husband. The later interviews were invariably prompted by interest in Rex, and Alice slipped easily into the role of guardian of his memory. As she reconstructed their life together, she cast herself as an actor of very modest talents, whose success, if that was how it could be termed, was the consequence of her husband's strong will and artistry. What she seldom mentioned was how involved she was in the making of the films. Yet, as we shall see, it was Alice who took over the direction of *Where the Pavement Ends* when Rex went AWOL, and she shared the direction of her husband's final film, *Baroud*. She almost certainly managed their affairs later when they worked in France at the Victorine studios if not before. Their relationship piqued the interest of the press during their marriage, and long intervals of separation gave rise to numerous rumors that the union was going the way of so many Hollywood marriages. Their habit of occupying separate accommodations for lengthy stretches added to the mystery of their marital circumstances.

But neither time nor Rex's memoirs shed further light on what exactly passed between them during their decades as husband and wife. It is hard to be convinced that she was the "beard" for his gay activities, just as it is hard to be convinced that Rex was a gay man or even bisexual. Certainly both had lovers, and home movie footage from their later years suggests that their lovers were also each other's friends. Both also were comfortable in the company of gay men and, off set, Rex enjoyed an easy physicality with other men and with women.[21] Sex, particularly unusual sex, fascinated him, and he subscribed selectively to the conventions of morality. That he was an exasperating companion is easier to imagine, or to sense, in interviews Alice gave. It is more convincing to see her as the calm center around which Rex and his assortment of gifted, often anarchic friends, actors, writers, and fellow filmmakers revolved. He certainly consulted with her on his productions, though the final decision was most likely understood to rest with him, this most controlling and single-minded of directors. It seems equally evident from her letters that Alice loved Rex deeply, if not with the sexual passion of more conventional marriages. Rex in turn, despite his restless, searching nature, seems to have found in Alice the emotional stability he needed to keep his life from going off the rails. And she was fun, with a sense of humor that punctuated Rex's own self-absorption, particularly on set.

The marriage between Hollywood's handsome director and his leading lady could have been the story of the decade, with limitless publicity potential. Instead Rex and Alice refused then, as they refused for the rest of their lives together, to perform for journalists. Of course it is part of the language of celebrity coverage for the journalist to claim a "just happened by" intimacy with their subject and for those subjects to cooperate by acting up their casualness, yet in this case the couple's refusal to play to the camera rings true. "They have a rather good time, these two. And they don't 'put on a show' for interviewers," one journalist confided shortly after their marriage.[22] Having a rather good time together (with some notable lapses) describes the marriage well.

Although Rex announced his marriage to Alice during the making of *The Prisoner of Zenda,* the press subsequently reported that the two would not wed until they had completed one more picture. Surprisingly they added that Rex did not wish his bride to work after marriage, while Alice wanted the opposite. In the same article, Rex is quoted as saying that he hoped to marry in Ireland.[23] That was not to happen. Instead he and Alice married on 5 November 1921, during the filming of *The Prisoner of Zenda,* in a quiet and almost unannounced ceremony. As a favor to Rex, Lou Strohm, Metro's location manager, scouted a suitable location. His son Walter told Paul Kozak: "I remember when he wanted to get married, he wanted a romantic place. And Rex loved Mediterranean and Spanish things. My father found a place for him. El Molino. It was out in Pasadena near the Huntington Hotel. It had been an old Spanish or Mexican mill. That's where he was married, in this romantic spot."[24] Dr. W. W. Edmondson, a chaplain of the American Legion, officiated, and only a few intimate friends were invited to attend. Echoing the previous tone of press coverage of their relationship, it was reported that the bride would retire from motion pictures.[25] They reappeared on set the next day and only took off on a honeymoon in early March 1922 after the film had wrapped. Then they went to San Francisco, where they spent much of their honeymoon touring Chinatown and the city's jails in the company of the city's mayor. "I thought the world would change immediately after the ceremony," Alice commented in *Photoplay*. "But when we drove away from the church and I saw people walking around just as though nothing important had happened I realized that it was utterly useless to impress humanity. Nothing you do matters in the least to the world."[26]

Their home was one of several in the grounds of Canary Cottage, a property built by Jack Donovan, the charismatic actor turned producer and occasional architect, at 6633 West Sunset Boulevard. He designed the buildings to be a blend of English cottage and French country house, with thatched roofs, dovecotes, and a goldfish pond. Rex had moved in there prior to shooting *Four Horsemen*, and Alice was happy to stay. Their house was modest by Hollywood standards, timber-clad with vines growing over the porch, its interiors draped in ruby damask with blood-red velvet carpets. Donovan planned to create an artists' colony there, and so Alice and Rex had as neighbors such people as the director Frank Griffin and the popular, if scandalous, author Lorna Moon.[27]

The Prisoner of Zenda opened at Loew's State Theater in Los Angeles as the cinema's first "A movie." Increasingly the studios were labeling their films as A or B listers, with the glory going to the big budget spectacles that Rex, DeMille, Josef von Sternberg, and the other star directors created. To emphasize the high-class nature of the evening's entertainment, the picture was preceded by an elaborate musical introduction, with an orchestra playing "Ode to Ruritania," "If Love Were All," and the *Zenda* waltzes. In New York's Capitol Theatre, the evening closed with an organ solo by the distinguished organist and composer Melchiorre Mauro-Cottone. In Dublin the film opened in the La Scala Theatre, with a prologue presented by the celebrated Abbey actor Frank Fay, alongside fellow actors Joseph O'Neill and Gertrude Mortimer.

The press headlined the new Ingram release, lavishing his production with the now customary praise for its pictorial beauty, even if, as always, there were caveats. The *Los Angeles Times* reviewer found the picture more dramatic than previous works, with the final duel scene as "tense an affair as any that we have had lately in pictures." He was less impressed with the performances: Alice Terry was, as usual, lovely but not in any way aristocratic, while Ramón was accused, not unfairly given his habit of squinting through his monocle and raising the eyebrow of his other eye, of "clownish mugging." More praiseworthy were Barbara La Marr and Malcolm McGregor, with Lewis Stone taking the lion's share of the acting laurels.[28] The *New York Times* sounded what was becoming a familiar warning about Rex's tendency to veer into slapstick, finding the film's comedy crude: "Sometimes it takes itself quite seriously and at other times it seems to be jazzed up for the sake of an allegedly democratic country."[29] In an insightful comment on Rex's developing practice, *Variety* noticed that the director had cast the better-looking actors in the least sympathetic roles, adding, "Nobody loves a handsome man except himself and his sweetheart. It's a wonder nobody ever thought of it before. Ingram is a pathfinder."[30] Despite these caveats, *Zenda* further reinforced Rex's reputation as the foremost artist of the Hollywood screen. Comparing it with another recent release, Robert Z. Leonard's *Fascination,* the *Picture-Play* reviewer sighed, "Why can't everybody be Rex Ingram?"[31]

Ben Hur

At this stage Rex was already planning his production of *Ben Hur,* to star Alice Terry, Edward Connelly as Simonedes, and Ramón Samaniego in the title role. When he had settled on terms with Metro, he believed that they included an arrangement that they would purchase the *Ben Hur* rights and he would direct. However, Goldwyn Pictures bought the screen rights to Lew Wallace's hugely popular biblical epic, and by now June Mathis was working with Goldwyn as chief scenarist, a position that effectively placed her in charge of all her productions. For *Ben Hur,* on which she began working in July 1922, this meant that every detail of the film—not just the script but also the casting, the location, the costumes, the makeup—would be her responsibility. It seemed like an obvious move for Rex after *Four Horsemen,* and with its massive scale, antiwar message, and spiritual element, he was confident that he would soon be occupying the director's chair. Mathis of all people would know how suited he was to the project. Goldwyn Pictures ratcheted up the suspense by announcing a nationwide hunt for the lead role. Intense industry speculation focused on this and the choice of director.

Around the same time, Rex began to talk of working abroad: "Just two more pictures, and then I shall be on my way to Europe," he announced to a journalist. She blamed his departure on increasing censorship, citing his difficulties with the making of *Turn to the Right,* since censors had announced that theft couldn't be shown on the screen. Apparently at this stage he had already lined up Nice as a possible new home.[32] In October 1921 Marcus Loew announced that he would be sending Rex overseas to film his next picture. Loew made it clear that it was not his policy normally to relocate his productions to Europe and that he would be focusing his activities on Los Angeles.[33] Throughout 1922 the papers continued to report on Rex and Alice's desire to settle in the South of France. Metro, meanwhile, told the press that Rex would be following *Zenda* with an adaptation of Victor Hugo's *Toilers of the Sea,* to be shot in Maine. Rex, however, said that he planned a remake of his earlier *Black Orchids.*[34]

On 18 April 1922, Rex signed a new contract with Metro, the terms of which stipulated that he make three more film spectaculars to follow *Four Horsemen* and *Zenda* and one "superfeature" that was to outshine all previous productions. He also announced that he would continue to work with his stock company, Alice Terry, Ramón Samaniego, and Edward Connelly.[35] Into this contract he inserted a clause permitting him to take time out, if necessary, to direct *Ben Hur.* Asked about the future of cinema, he was also firm: "I think the real hope of the motion picture is the establishment of separate theatres for adults and children. We cannot go on limiting our entertainment to the intellectual level of a twelve-year-old child. This is the only hope I can see to save the movies from going to the dogs."[36]

Trifling Women (1922)

Rex's new film confirmed his commitment to making pictures for adults. With a plot replete with lust and treachery, it was certainly quite unsuitable for children, even more so once the vampish Barbara La Marr was confirmed in the lead opposite Ramón Samaniego. *Black Orchids* soon became *Trifling Women,* though much of the original film, with its story-within-a-story, remained. At the same time, Ramón Samaniego became Ramón Novarro. Alice was now holding Rex to his promise, and this was to be the only film since *The Day She Paid* in which she didn't play any part. Novarro and La Marr in turn had become overnight stars after *Zenda.* The former, the *Film Daily* declared, "brought a new charm to the screen," while La

Marr stood out as a "very interesting type."[37] Novarro, another critic suggested, "resembles the sort of chap every married woman hopes her next husband will be like."[38]

Apart from the omission of Alice, the cast list looked familiar. Edward Connelly and Lewis Stone had prominent roles, John George reprised his part, retitled Achmet, from *Black Orchids,* and now Hughie Mack joined them. He and Rex had known each other since the Vitagraph days in New York, and Mack's rotund figure had already ensured him a long career as a comedian. His was just the kind of personality that Rex loved. Erich von Stroheim shared this fondness for the fat man, and between these two directors they kept Mack in work long after others had tired of his modest abilities. Rex also took on three dwarfs, who were to act as servants to La Marr's character, Jacqueline de Sévérac.

One further performer from *Black Orchids* also reappeared, namely the ape Joe Martin. According to numerous sources, the animal developed a fixation on Barbara La Marr. "He adored Barbara La Marr, and he was very jealous of the men," John Seitz explained, recalling a scene where Ed Connelly had to place a necklace around Barbara La Marr's neck, which she would then take off and put around the monkey's neck. "We did several takes of this scene and on the third take Ed pushed the monkey away and he attacked him and squeezed him so hard that the blood came out of his fingernails. Then the rather sadistic trainer, he was fired for his cruelty to animals, anyway he got him off."[39]

Although this is a lost film, surviving production stills suggest that it was visually complex and striking. Seitz had been developing his process of using matte shots to add depth to the image, and it was with *Trifling Women* that he finally felt he had perfected his technique. This involved photographing a large painting and then adding it in to the scene to give greater emphasis to the background. Other still images suggest dramatic lighting effects, Rex's inevitable framing device of arches curving over the performers, and sinister, cluttered Gothic interiors. It was to become one of his favorites and catapulted La Marr and Novarro into superstardom.

The plot was widely dismissed by the critics as trifling, and many objected to the film's sugary morality. A common complaint was that the framing story—of a novelist trying to warn his daughter against flirting—was unnecessary and that it would have been better to open with the main story. Those who could ignore the plot structure found much to praise in Rex's Gothic images: "pictures of a Circean woman, of men made foolish and mad by her, of queer medieval towers and castles, of dark dungeons and cellars, of duels and murders, and of characters, definitely stamped and oddly real characters, passing through it all to give it the passing semblance of reality."[40] But it was his execution of the film's climactic action sequences that, most agreed, showed the stamp of the master: "It closes with a smashing climax, depicting the vengeance of a deceived man, which, in its visual suggestion of horror and absolute doom, is one of the best things Rex Ingram has yet done."[41] Metro again launched the film in the top price category ($1.50 per seat).

By now Rex Ingram was a name to reckon with. "When I go into the theatre and listen to the lulling music of the orchestra, a magic flash comes to the screen bearing the words 'Rex Ingram Productions.' Instantly the atmosphere of the theatre changes, I am ready to enjoy the mystery, romance, and beauty that this cinema master gives so freely in his pictures," one fan wrote to *Photoplay* after seeing *Trifling Women*.[42] With this kind of fame, Hollywood society beckoned. Rex hated formal events, and journalist/publicist Herbert Howe took some relish in watching the famous director suffer in public. In one of his columns for *Photoplay,* Howe reported back from a farewell party thrown by the screen actor Bert Lytell to mark his departure from Hollywood to the East Coast. Rex and Alice showed up late, he noted, with Edith Allen, whom Rex would shortly cast in *Scaramouche.* Marshall Neilan had already taken to the floor with Blanche Sweet, and other Hollywood celebrities were scattered around the tables and on the dance floor. Rex, Alice, and Edith Allen were taking their table when Rex spotted Willis Goldbeck seated across the room. Proudly holding aloft his newly acquired copy of Desmond Humphrey's *Why God Loves the Irish,* he charged over to him. Then he rushed out onto the dance floor and stole Mae Murray from her husband, Bob Leonard, who cut his losses and joined Alice at her table. "Dinner with Rex Ingram and Alice Terry," Howe recorded, "after which Rex spent the evening rapturously killing flies."[43] Alice, however, loved dancing and dragged her husband to the Hollywood hotspot of the moment, the Montmartre Café. He went, Howe observed, with the sacrificial air becoming to a martyr.[44] When forced to abandon his habitual khaki and change into a dinner jacket, Rex was miserable.

Throughout 1922 he continued to plan *Toilers of the Sea.* Part of the excitement of the Victor Hugo project was the prospect of shooting underwater sequences on location. In this case, that was to be Jamaica and to include the scene in the novel where the central character, Gilliat, wrestles an octopus. While he was working out these details, Rex took off for a couple of weeks with Alice to New York to escape Hollywood and reacquaint themselves with their artistic circle. The director was evidently in high spirits, with a slate of challenging projects ahead of him, not least *Ben Hur*. Better still, these projects entailed foreign travel—with the West Indies now emerging as the most likely location for shooting exteriors on what would become his next picture, *Where the Pavement Ends*.

Where the Pavement Ends (1923)

As it turned out, Rex and Alice made their base in Florida, with some filming in Cuba for *Where the Pavement Ends,* returning to Hollywood in the fall of 1923. The film was based on John Russell's short story "The Passion Vine," which had been published in his collection of short stories, *Where the Pavement Ends,* in 1919. It tells the tragic tale of Motauri (Ramón Novarro) and Matilda (Alice Terry). She is the beautiful daughter of a missionary; he is the young islander who falls in love with her. Harry T. Morey plays the foul Capt. Hull Gregson, who ingratiates himself so thoroughly with Matilda's father, Pastor Spener (Edward Connelly), that the latter agrees to their marriage. Knowing that he can never marry Matilda because of the race barrier, Motauri gives her his cache of pearls and hurls himself to his death from the top of a waterfall. John Russell joined the film shoot in Florida and helped supervise the building of a Samoan village to replicate the one in his novel.

Rex was drawn to the film's exotic setting and particularly to the idea of having a "native" as the film's hero. In the film Motauri is treated with sympathy; one intertitle refers to "the eternal slur cast on his race by the white invader." This is an addition to the original short story, which, while not unsympathetic to Motauri, is much more interested in the titillating potential of forbidden racial attraction. Its opening provides a taste of what is to come:

> It is difficult to find an excuse for Miss Matilda. She was a missionary's daughter, committed to the sacred cause of respectability in a far land. Motauri was a gentleman of sorts and a scholar after his own fashion, a high chief and a descendant of kings; but he was also a native and a pagan. Strictly, it should have been nothing to Miss Matilda that Motauri looked most distractingly like a young

woodland god, with a skin the exact shade of new heather honey, the curly ringlets of a faun, the features of a Roman cameo and the build of a Greek athlete.[45]

Even Rex had to admit that the public would not tolerate a story with a love affair between a man of color and a white woman. Hollywood shared with its audiences a fascination with exotic (native) female types, as the career of Theda Bara demonstrated, but a relationship between a member of the "fairer sex" and a native man would have been out of the question. Rex's exoticism was of a different order from the popular obsession with "sexually potent natives," and he despised this constraint. One solution (not in the original novel) was to have Captain Gregson articulate the toxic ideology of white supremacy when he says to Matilda, on finding out that she is seeing Motauri: "God, when I think how I dreamed of you—wanted you—you sweet, cold white saint you, and a devil after all. A missionary's daughter—too respectable to touch . . . what are you now, that's been out in the night—with a *yellow dog!*"[46] Another departure from expectations was to have Motauri sacrifice himself—more conventionally it was the woman who sacrificed herself for love.

Metro were concerned that the ending was too bleak and prevailed upon Rex to write a prologue that made the hero really white but brought up as a native of the islands. Rex shot this ending, and they tested it on audiences. Although this is the ending indicated in the list of intertitles, judging by the reviews the final version retained the original ending, with Motauri committing suicide. Once again Rex seems to have correctly gauged the tastes of the "adult" filmgoer and found them much more tolerant of unhappy endings and nonstandard moral messages than was widely believed to be the case by the industry.

The shoot seems to have been a happy one for the Ingram unit, with a sense of vacation settling on them once they were away from Hollywood. Rex fooled around cheerfully, inserting himself into scenes, a practice he enjoyed. Whytock equally predictably edited out his director's appearances:

He always played little bits himself and afterwards he'd say, "You took me out of the picture." I'd say, "Yeah. It wasn't very good." He enjoyed doing them. He just had little scenes here and there. Little comedy gags. Sometimes they might have stayed in. But generally they had nothing to do with the picture.

I remember in *Where the Pavement Ends* we had a brothel built into what was supposed to be a beached ship. He played a character bit inside there. He'd learned a cigarette trick. He could make it disappear up his nose and come out his mouth and all. Well, I took it out. It came at a place where it disturbed the story.[47]

While they were there, Rex gave Whytock a copy of Bram Stoker's Gothic novel *Dracula,* telling him he was considering filming it. Regrettably nothing came of the idea.[48]

Although the crew remembered clearly that Rex and Alice did not travel with them to Cuba, Rex devotes several pages of his memoirs to the description of a highly exoticized encounter there with the young Rosita Garcia, whom he hired on the spot only to discover that she came with an extended family (three automobiles full of Garcias). Later she would rejoin the Ingram crew and remain a lifelong friend and, reputedly, Rex's lover. For now, she just made a brief screen appearance. Rex recalled:

Before we sailed, I asked Alice how she would like to live there on a hacienda with a river and a house with a big patio and a tropical garden.

"I wouldn't," she said. "Hollywood is more my style. If you want to live here, you'll just have to look around for another little wife."[49]

The tone of her words rings true, but whether any of the remainder of the recollection is accurate or not is lost to history.

At last news came through about the final decision as to who should direct *Ben Hur.* In September 1923 June Mathis announced that George Walsh, brother of Raoul Walsh, would be the star and Charles Brabin the director.

No one, least of all Rex, was prepared for this, and the response from the industry was one of deep surprise. Years previously Brabin had directed Rex in *The Necklace of Rameses,* but his career since had been far less distinguished than that of his bit-part actor. Indeed, he was as well known for being the husband of Theda Bara as for any of his screen credits. Adela Rogers St. Johns, who shared the view that Mathis was in love with Rex and felt jilted when he favored Alice Terry, even hinted that this was Mathis's best revenge.[50]

Whatever the reason for Mathis's decision, nothing about it was to turn out well. The fiasco that accompanied the filming of *Ben Hur* has been well documented.[51] Charles Brabin made Rex look easygoing and once in place refused to let Mathis have anything do with the production. George Walsh turned out as insignificant as everyone assumed he would be. Even after the newly merged Metro-Goldwyn rid themselves of the troublesome Brabin, they did not contact Rex but hired Fred Niblo to retrieve the project. By then thousands of feet of footage, and with it a more than equal amount of dollars, had been wasted, with anything that Brabin shot being discarded. At the same time, Mathis was relieved of her duties on the film, and, of all ironies, Ramón Novarro found himself cast in the lead role.

When Rex heard the news about Mathis's decision, Seitz recollected, "this made for a sudden change in his personality. Everything had been going so well and he had been having his way in almost everything. This came as a great shock."[52] His immediate reaction, according to Novarro, was to hit the bottle; the second was to refuse to work further on *Where the Pavement Ends.*[53] Alice took over direction in his absence.

Once again, Rex (with Alice's help) had made a hit. Crowds lined the block around Loew's State Theater for the Los Angeles opening night. Once again, the critics were enthralled. For some, such as Edwin Schallert in the *Los Angeles Times,* this was the film that finally fulfilled the promise of *Four Horsemen:* "Poignant poetry pervades the love scenes of the picture," Schallert wrote before moving on to praise its leads: "Both Alice Terry and Ramón Novarro in the leading romantic roles accomplish a remarkable variety in expressiveness. Navarro seems to have found a part that suits him perfectly and plays it with the rarest feeling. Miss Terry brings loveliness and a remarkable sincerity to the portrayal of the heroine."[54] As he so often did, Rex had taken a familiar genre—the South Sea island romance—and breathed fresh life into it: "It makes every other South Sea island film look as if it had been sunk under an earthquake in the Pacific," the critic for the *Sun* noted. "This is a picture without hokum, without the lovers embracing in the last scene, a picture that clings closely to the author's story, and one in which there is rare characterization," the *Tribune* agreed.[55] Only *Variety* was less impressed, labeling Alice's beauty "flawless but frigid" before continuing to praise the film's pictorial achievements. In particular the critic was struck by the underwater photography, notably one sequence where the hero dives for pearls and finds himself almost within touching distance of a shark the size of himself.[56] Years later

DeWitt Bodeen would remember *Where the Pavement Ends* as "one of the most hauntingly beautiful movies ever made."[57]

Alice and Rex returned to Los Angeles, where they lived in a house off Vine Street belonging to actor-director couple James Cruze and Margaret Snow, who had recently divorced. On the surface of it, Rex's career was now unmatched. He enjoyed exceptional creative freedom and used that to combine commerce and art in a manner that was not supposed to be possible in the movies. The critics were in awe of his talent, audiences queued to see his latest opening, and money from his films was pouring into the Metro coffers and, as a result of his contract, his own. He was working with a cast and crew who understood his ambitions and would put up with temper tantrums and obsessive behavior to realize them. Yet, at the heart of his career, he found nothing he liked.

There was only one solution and that was to leave Hollywood. He would make one last film, he concluded, and then he would go.

Scaramouche (1923)

Scaramouche started filming with a flourish, Rex having purchased the rights to Rafael Sabatini's novel in September 1922. After seven months of preparation, shooting was due to commence on 19 March. The press suddenly announced that he would instead begin shooting on St. Patrick's Day, 17 March. Rumor had it that he was too drunk to start for several days after that, but this seems more like lazy Irish stereotyping, or thoughtless publicity, than the truth. In reality Rex despised people who let alcohol come in the way of their work, and there is no evidence that he excepted himself.

Sabatini's historical romance told of one André-Louis Moreau, a law student who vows to fight against the aristocracy to avenge the death of his friend, Philippe, in a duel with the Marquis de la Tour d'Azyr. Deserting his sweetheart, Aline, André joins a troupe of traveling musicians, winding up in Paris at the outbreak of the revolution. There he becomes embroiled in politics and makes a fortune as a fencing instructor. At the film's climax, he discovers the truth of his parentage and rescues Aline and his newly discovered mother from the rioting hordes. To construct a scenario, Rex gave Willis Goldbeck the book and told him to go to New York and write a script. When Goldbeck handed him the finished script six weeks later, "he was very generous in his praise of it. He should have been for the $65 a week he was paying me. And he fired me two weeks later—I came back here [Los Angeles] and found an office with my name on it and he fired me because I happened to get into a fight with his assistant and he said, 'I'm afraid I need him more than I need you. And he won't stay if you stay.'"[58]

Again Rex planned his film using the principle that if a film looked right, its audiences would find it credible. To this end, he hired a historical advisor to investigate details of costume, architecture, and period design. Houses were to be thatched just as they had been in France in the eighteenth century, and a map of Paris revealed the layout of the city's streets from the period, while key buildings such as the Palais de Justice and the Tuileries were reconstructed from old engravings. For six months a special research department gathered information: "Hundreds of reproductions of the Paris of that day had been sent to us from the Musée Carnavalet," Rex remembered, "together with innumerable costume plates of the epoch. Photographs and casts of death masks and portraits cast from life by Houdon had also been obtained, these latter of inestimable value in recreating historical characters. The fact that the contour and structure of a man's face and mind reflects his personality is often ignored in producing period pictures."[59]

No expense was spared on *Scaramouche*.[60] Rex built two complete villages, one on the Metro lot and another in the San Fernando Valley. Alice Terry was to take the lead as Aline de Kercadiou, Ramón Novarro would play André-Louis, Lewis Stone was to be the marquis, and Edward Connelly a minister to the king. In a nod to the director of *A Tale of Two Cities,* who was his early if reluctant mentor, Ingram cast William Humphrey as the Chevalier de Chabrillone. The usual army of extras, this time some fifteen hundred people, was hired, of whom one was Novarro's brother Mariano.

Surveying his kingdom one day, Rex fixed his attention on the orchestra, which was running through "La Marseillaise," and abruptly bawled down the loud hailer "For the love of God, will you play an Irish piece?" The Tuileries Palace toppled to the tune of "Back to Erin." Only Alice was spared the worst of his temper, as she was still prone to bursting into tears when shouted at. Inevitably as shooting progressed, Rex became more and more fatigued and tense, with his mood deteriorating rapidly. On set, the usual dwarfs and sundry crazies were lined up for his distraction, often to be subjected to bizarre physical pranks, and to bring him luck. Crazy Mary was one such character who had a job on every one of Rex's pictures. She brought him holy medals and blessed him and prayed for his conversion. He responded by having her dance an Irish jig. Just before shooting started, Rex received a letter from a Vincent J. Danton, a writer from Boston, who claimed to be the great-grandson of the revolutionary Georges Danton. He attached with the letter a tricolor rosette that he said Danton gave his wife before ascending the scaffold to his death. Rex solemnly read this out before shooting commenced on the scene in which Danton (George Siegmann) makes his striking cameo.

As the production progressed and finally exploded onto the screen in all its glory, it accumulated so many tall tales along the way that it is hard now to tell which were pure fiction and which had some basis in fact. A vigorous debate arose over gloves—to wear them or not? Research revealed that the noblemen of the revolutionary period did not wear gloves. More work landed on the makeup team when Daumery discovered that Danton was pockmarked. This led to further discussion. Did that render him somehow morally suspect? Rex swiftly intervened to remind his crew that about one-third of the entire population of France at that time would have been pockmarked (in Sabatini's original, pockmarks feature prominently). In the end, Siegmann's face was made up to look pitted, an extraordinary visual effect that Rex made the most of with some startling close-ups.

John Seitz continued to develop his practice of matte photography to lend depth to the shot, and many of the film's most striking images were created using miniatures. He shot these sequences with no backlighting so that the miniatures would blend easily with the set. Thus many of the set pieces appear to be shot against vast locations or in ornate, detailed interiors, where in fact these are tricks of the eye. Into these sets, Rex placed a moving gallery of physical types. The king's lieutenant at the Palais de Justice, where André-Louis begins his quest for retribution, is shot in extreme close-up, his face grotesque, thickly powdered, with a bulbous nose, a monocle, and a slightly weepy eye. In contrast, the camera cuts back to a close-up of Novarro's young, handsome face, framed equally tightly. The crowd scenes are a tour de force. Early in the story, the French mob moves with choreographed beauty, rows within rows swaying one way or another, causing ripples within the greater mass. In the closing sequences, keeping faith with Sabatini's original, they erupt in a howling, crazed riot, now wearing ripped, dirty clothing, grotesque expressions, and accompanied by half-naked women executing barbarous dances.

If the film's visuals illustrate how Rex was refining his artistry, the other notable development was in Novarro's performance. He now not only looked handsome, but he had abandoned the insecure acting tics of *Zenda*—the twitching monocle and raised eyebrow—for an ambiguity of expression that gave this particular role its meaning. He should be the hero of the tale, but his actions are, as the novel also suggests, more often those of a villain. His proposal to the young woman, Climène Binet (Edith Allen), whose father is the traveling players' founder, is an unfair piece of deception. Knowing this, he holds her to him roughly, rather than tenderly, then fiercely chastises Aline for selling herself to the Count de la Tour d'Azyr (Lewis Stone). Expressions flicker across his face, and he indicates disdain with a slight movement of his mouth. Physically, just as Rex had predicted, he dominates the screen.

Making period dramas was now a Rex Ingram signature. In part this was simply a response to audience taste. Swashbucklers were perennial favorites, and as recently as 1921 D. W. Griffith had made his own French Revolution drama, *The Orphans of the Storm*. Yet one may guess that Rex was happier in another era as well as in another place. Over and again, he returned to Europe for his settings; if not to Europe, then to some exotic Caribbean island. Contemporary American life, and the corrupt, teeming New York slums, no longer found any place in his work. And the Europe that he constructed with such care and richness of detail was inevitably a place far off in time, where moral codes were unclouded by the ambivalences of twentieth-century thinking. As Jazz Age America celebrated the liberations of modernity, so Rex insisted that the real energy lay elsewhere: "The American woman," he declared in a *Picture-Play Magazine* interview, "is tired of the bright young business man and his weary elders. To arouse her interest a man must have an exotic, instant appeal, awakening feminine curiosity, stirring feminine imagination, giving her some quality of the unknown to ponder on. The Latin type of man offers that as no other type can. The American businessman is too easily read, too frank, too obvious. To the American woman he is like a book, a rather naïve book which she has read and yawned over many times."[61] Others were of a like mind, though the solution to the dullness of the American businessman was not always to take a Latin lover but, as in *Foolish Wives*, directed by Rex's friend Erich von Stroheim (1922), to dally with a charming European cad (played of course by von Stroheim).

There were also mundane reasons for Rex's love of exotic period settings. One was simply the collector in him, that same impulse he had confided to his Aunt Cissie on arriving in New York City and that would accompany him to the end of his days. Herbert Howe has left us with a colorful description of walking down Hollywood Boulevard in Rex's company: "He'll drag you down alleys, up firescapes [*sic*], into stores, and probably into trouble. He's utterly Irish in whim and daring. He reminds you of the Irishman who, seeing a couple of fellows fighting in a saloon, rushed in to ask if it were a private fight. Where another person will look into a shop window and see his own reflection, Ingram sees everything in the store and is liable to burst through either the door or the plate glass to find out how it is made."[62] Design fascinated him, and at least according to Jesse Lasky, it was Rex who "designed" his white Packard Special after Ralph DePalma's racing car. It had speed, Lasky said, at the expense of power in the forward gears. "It could climb hills only by backing up them, a rather inconvenient and humiliating procedure, but then sports cars aren't supposed to be practical."[63]

In an article titled "Pictures Secondary in Cinema Success," fellow studio great Cecil B. DeMille warned against films becoming too pictorial. Was he perhaps taking a potshot at his celebrated peer, whose *Chalice of Sorrow* borrowed from his own *Carmen*? Although DeMille doesn't mention Rex, the article is illustrated with images from *Scaramouche*. A coincidence, maybe, but it reminds one of just how influential Rex's intensely visual filmmaking was on the cinema of the day. Still, a murmur of criticism was beginning to become louder, and DeMille was picking up on it when he wrote, "It is a pity that so many of our promising younger directors become so engrossed in creating individual charming pictures on the screen that they forget to create that clash of characters, which is the sole and only thing that can hold the attention of an audience through a feature photoplay."[64]

In the case of *Scaramouche,* no such criticism could be made. Following the success of the *Four Horsemen* roadshow, Metro again gave *Scaramouche* the gilt-edged treatment, setting up twenty-three roadshows to tour the country.[65] As with *Four Horsemen,* the strategy paid off, and Rex's film was another box office winner. Most important, it drew the middle classes into the cinema. As one reporter commented, it was an unusually undemonstrative audience that attended the opening night at Los Angeles' Criterion Theater (where *Scaramouche* ran for an impressive two months). Instead of breaking into loud applause at every stage, they watched the film with a "charmed and generally attentive interest that betokened the arrival of the luxurious and elegant entertainment that appeals especially to those who possess the taste for finer things." The same critic recommended the film's drama and especially Novarro's performance but reserved his strongest praise for the production's pictorial qualities, likening the visuals to the works of the great European painters and sculptors and proclaiming Rex the master etcher of the screen: "You might even say that the plot is simply a canvas in the background, and though individual situations have a telling fervor, and there is a steady ongoing allure to what happens before your eyes, the great attraction of 'Scaramouche' is not that of drama, but of beautiful and glorious pictures."[66] "Not since *The Four Horsemen* has the young Irish director made such a picture," the *Morning Telegraph* declared.[67] "He [Rex] may not have previously been placed on the same plane as the greatest directors," *Variety* responded, forgetting their earlier review of *Four Horsemen,* "but he certainly stands with the best that there is in the industry after this, and there are only two or three that can be mentioned in the same breath."[68] Novarro too came in for fulsome praise: "He is better looking than Valentino, more versatile, more plastic, more animated and a more accomplished actor," the *Herald* declared.[69]

"I know when I saw the roadshow of *Scaramouche* at the White Theatre in Fresno, California," DeWitt Bodeen writes, "an awesome suspense gripped the audience when those deceptively sweet Mozartian notes sounded, while the sheer ecstasy of *La Marseillaise,* as played by a full symphony orchestra, when the liberty-crazed mob, led by Rose Dione, swept through the streets of Paris in a murderous carmagnole, made the walls and ceilings of the auditorium quiver with sound."[70] These were not silent movies, but true moving images that needed no words.

The film reached even greater critical heights when it won the $10,000 cash prize offered by Adolph Zukor to the author of the best story or play produced between 1 September 1923 and 31 August 1924. The terms of the prize meant that the award went to Sabatini, but the surrounding publicity seldom failed to mention Rex's name or omit his status as one of the greatest directors of the artistic film.

The financial success of *Scaramouche* (as well as performing strongly in the United States, it broke all records in London and was a hit in Paris) ensured that Rex was now comfortably off. However, he was ill—he was suffering from stomach ulcers—and tired. He also was more restless than ever and disenchanted with life in Hollywood. At last Marcus Loew made good on his promise of overseas filming, and Rex now readied himself for his first voyage to North Africa. It was an experience that was to change his life.

7

Escape to the Desert

In his later career, Rex would be accused of losing touch with Hollywood; no such charge could be leveled against *The Arab* (1924). The film is a little-disguised riposte to Valentino's 1921 triumph *The Sheik,* directed by George Melford. In the place of Valentino, Rex cast Ramón Novarro in the title role. The Valentino film is partially set in Biskra, Algeria; *The Arab* was shot in Biskra and in Tunisia; both films have at their heart a romance between a handsome Arab man and a European woman; and both revel in the visual opportunities presented by Arab costuming, interiors, and dance. Publicity materials spared no cliché: "A story of a son of the desert at war with his own people—a clash of civilizations, a tale of modern crusaders, of howling mobs of frenzied fanatics crying for blood, with one heroic Bedouin standing between the girl he loves and death for her and the children within her gates. Don't miss *The Arab.* It has all the magic wizardry of the world's greatest screen director revealed in scenes and action that reflect the glory and glamor of the East."[1]

The extraordinary and unanticipated success of *The Sheik* was largely ascribed to its popularity with female audiences, notably because of the casting of Valentino. The film's décor and setting further reinvigorated the public love affair with exoticism, one that was now given increased currency with the discovery of King Tutankhamun's tomb in 1922. As the archaeological explorations revealed, and as travelers' tales had always rumored, Egypt was home to a history of androgynous kings and bewitching women, of life preserved in death, of harems, sheikhs, magical invocations, and Arabian nights. In the same year, Sid Grauman responded by building the Egyptian Theatre, a magnificent monument to Hollywood's interpretation of North African settings, complete with massive columns decorated with hieroglyphics, tiled interiors, exotic plants, palm trees, terracotta pots, and a fountain. Soon Egyptian Theatres were springing up across the United States. Fashion and home decoration turned Egyptian, and dancers stepped out in time to the "Tutankhamun Rag." Egyptomania was all the rage.

It is no wonder that Marcus Loew was happy to greenlight Rex's newest project. The production was announced in September 1923. Long drawn to the idea of travel in North Africa, Rex must have been happy to go. However, what started off as just another "sheik picture" was to become increasingly complicated by its director's own experiences of this ancient culture and his encounters with actual Arab sheiks and Arab life. The "frenzied fanatics" promised by Metro publicists were to become close friends.

On 30 September 1923, he and Alice departed on the *Leviathan* from New York on a visit, it was reported, to Ireland.[2] In October 1923 the *Irish Times* informed its readers that Rex had traveled to London and was planning to visit Ireland.[3] Again, on 15 November, he was said to be going to Ireland on a visit from New York.[4] On none of these occasions did he in fact return home. Alice Terry later told Liam O'Leary that "Rex wanted to go to Ireland many times—but as he finished one picture along came . . . another studio—to do another picture—so he finally gave up."[5]

Had Rex returned to Ireland, he would have found a country much changed. Years of agricultural depression, combined with the enactment of legislation aimed at forcing the sale of land at favorable prices to tenants, had eroded the value of the Irish estates. This had coincided with increasing political hostility toward the estates' owners, many of whom were Protestants. During the War of Independence, the Irish Republican Army (IRA) carried out a campaign of burning the big houses. In 1920 alone, thirty were burned down, and more in the following year.[6] Kinnitty and its surroundings were at the heart of the IRA's battleground, and many of the homes that Rex remembered with fondness from his childhood went up in flames. Often those shot were, or the IRA suspected were, Crown informers. One of the most notorious of these incidents took place in June 1921, when the IRA executed two brothers, members of the staunchly loyalist Pearson family, at Coolacrease, and burned the house. Coolacrease was about five miles from Kinnitty, and Reverend Hitchcock was a friend of the Pearsons. He was deeply shocked by the deaths, yet a year later he reacted with equal horror to news that Protestant militias in the North of Ireland were carrying out pogroms against

Catholics. Like others, he spoke out publicly about the good relations enjoyed by members of the Protestant faith in his diocese and their Catholic neighbors: "I have always found my Roman Catholic brethren, laity and clergy, most genial and lovable, as all true Irishmen are, and ready to co-operate in everything that is for the public good; and I have, in my wide and varied experience of all sorts and conditions of people, never known one case of religious intolerance. We can not only live and let live down here; we have learned the secret of living and helping to live—a far sounder proof of our common Christianity."[7]

The sense of abandonment felt by many Protestants was epitomized by the decay and ruins of their homes. As Elizabeth, Countess Fingall, wrote of her own home: "The front of the house seems to have had a blank look, the windows staring across the country like blind eyes. It has a look that the windows of Irish country houses often have, as though indeed that was the spirit inside them, the spirit of the colonist and conqueror, looking out across the country which they possessed but never owned."[8]

The following year, sickened by all he had seen, Reverend Hitchcock left Tipperary forever, settling in the parish of Tolleshunt Knights in Essex. Frank too settled in England, and so Rex's ties to home were gradually loosened. He may not have been particularly sympathetic to the old Protestant order but, with his love of antique and precious items, he must have been shocked at the wholesale burning of these houses and their historic collections.

Instead of Ireland, Rex traveled to Paris, where on 14 October he announced that he had quit America forever. "I will never make another picture there if I can help it," he told the press, adding, "I suppose I might have to go back to America but I intend to do all my work abroad and remain here permanently."[9] Returning to London, Rex addressed a formal luncheon, where he shared his opinions on the evolving American system of production: "They [American producers] live on formulae. They believe that the box-office is the only test of success. They will not allow you to do anything new, but if you do it and it succeeds, everyone follows you like sheep. It is the film producer's duty to withstand the financier's demand for a maximum number of films and to make just what films he likes, and only those to which he can give sincerity and an individual touch."[10]

After a short reunion with his father in London, Rex traveled on alone to Africa. It seems possible that at this point he visited Egypt to view the tomb of King Tutankhamun. Certainly he had been following daily reports of the excavations in the newspapers.

In November 1923 Alice and Ramón Novarro met with Herbert Howe in Paris. From there, after a few days sampling the delights of the Moulin Rouge, they embarked on the *General Grévy* for Tunisia. When they sailed into the Bay of Tunis, Rex met them, greeting them in the traditional Arab manner, shaking Howe's hand and then kissing his own.

Rex had hired Howe as his publicist, which at that time meant placing favorable articles in fan magazines and daily newspapers. Aside from his writing skills, Howe came from an Irish American background, and that must have recommended him too. Howe spent the next three months in North Africa with Rex, Alice, and Novarro, much of it in Tunisia, where *The Arab* was mainly shot. According to both Anthony Slide and André Soares, Howe subsequently became Novarro's lover.[11] One way or another this little band of expatriates made for colorful company: Rex, with his extraordinary looks, his moods, the intensity that left him exhausted to the point of illness; Alice, calming him and helping behind the scenes as she prepared for her performance; Novarro, now a full-fledged Hollywood star; and witty, cynical Howe, chronicling and embellishing their activities for the entertainment of readers back home.

Rex was starting to feel reinvigorated. "Already in Algiers," he writes, "I had begun to feel the change. I had landed there the nervous wreck that Hollywood's film makers become after three or four years of taking their careers and selves too seriously, but from the moment I stepped off the gangplank of the Lamoricière, the incessant torture of gas pressure on the stomach—due to my Hollywood, or ulcerated duodenum—began to ease up. To my new surroundings, to the Berbers and Arabs, with their poise, unconcern and unquestioning acceptance of destiny I reacted as to a Scotch highball after a hard day's work." Perhaps, he speculated, there was something in him that was half-Arab.[12] Already he was casting North African culture as a sanctuary from Western materialism, a not uncommon projection among his intellectual set. Howe, on the other hand, recognized that his job was to attenuate Rex's seriousness and to reconstruct their journey as an exotic adventure among a half-savage people.

Rex and Alice drove from Tunis to Algeria, stopping in Bou Saâda, an Algerian town on the plateau of the Ouled Naïl Mountains and home to the French painter Étienne Dinet. Rex was an ardent admirer of Dinet's work, and he was to become a major collector of Dinet's paintings. These included *Amparo, Fandango Dancer* (Amparo, danseuse de fandango, 1900), *Naked Boy in the Oasis* (Gamin nu dans l'oasis, undated), *Dancers in the Palm Trees, Moonlight* (Danseuses dans la palmeraie, clair de lune, 1920s); and *The Women Cut Off Their Own Hands* (Elles se coupèrent les mains, 1902). It was not just Dinet's art that Rex admired, however, but his way of life. Dinet had converted to Islam and in 1913 announced that he was taking the Muslim name Nasr-Eddine. He was determined not to reproduce the traditional Western fantasies of the mysterious harem or to depict life in Algeria as backward and impoverished. Instead his paintings are warm, richly colored depictions of the people of his adopted home. They feature washerwomen at work, turbaned Arabs riding donkeys, children playing, and gazelle hunters armed with rifles. Women tend a dying man; men pray. They also depict naked and seminaked dancing women, sometimes clad only in turbans, bracelets, and necklaces, set against a background of lush Arab scenery. Despite their creator's best intentions, they were inescapably exotic, if more palatable ideologically, and found a ready market among Parisian and other collectors.

Dinet wrote novels about Algerian life as well, including one, *Khadra, Ouled Naïl Dancer* (Khadra, danseuse Ouled Naïl, 1910) about a nomad child whose mother wants her to settle down against her will. Although it would be simplistic to suggest that Rex modeled his own dreams of the future on Dinet's life, there are remarkable similarities in their trajectories. Rex's paintings too were clearly influenced by Dinet's. Although there is no record of the two men meeting on this occasion, it seems most likely that they did since Dinet held open house on Sundays and was often visited. Rex certainly came to consider Dinet a friend.

Bou Saâda had become a popular tourist location for Westerners who wanted to experience the "real" Sahara. It was a three-hour bus ride from Algiers and, after World War I, a destination for over thirty thousand visitors a year, twice the local population.[13] The Ouled Naïl dancers were one of the main draws, with their vivid clothing, lavishly worked jewelry, and their hands and feet decorated with henna. It was this too, according to ethnographer François Pouillon, that attracted the Orientalist painters, notably Dinet, who realized that here, uniquely, Arab women would willingly pose nude. During the day, the dancers performed in costume for families traveling with children, while at night they danced naked. Later again, they secured their dowries through prostitution.[14] Rex too became fascinated with the Ouled Naïl dancers, sketching and painting them naked from the waist up, with vast rounded breasts and swaying skirts.

Casting locals was therefore not just a matter of creating background color but of being as faithful to the locale as he could be. An inadvertent consequence of involving people from the region in his films was to encourage the dream of an indigenous cinema. When Rex was preparing to film in Algeria, he met the young actor Tahar Hanache (also known as Benelhanache Tahar). Hanache may already have played a small role in Jacques Feyder's 1921 French hit *Queen of Atlantis* (L'Atlantide), much of which was shot in the Sahara, and which became a massive worldwide success, most of all because of its extraordinary photography and full-on exoticism. It is very likely that Rex saw Feyder's film; certainly its success made Rex's own proposal to shoot in the desert seem less outlandish. He was delighted to meet Hanache, whom he hired not just as an actor but on the understanding that he direct certain of the scenes as he could liaise with the other local actors. Hanache stayed on with Rex and Alice, playing in *The Garden of Allah* (1927) and *Baroud* (1932), Rex's later desert films. He subsequently made what is considered the first Algerian feature film, *At the Gates of the Sahara* (Aux Portes du Sahara, 1938), and enjoyed a long career in film and later television.[15] Although no record remains of exactly which sequences Hanache directed in *The Arab,* even the fact of his participation in this manner reflects Rex's own commitment to a more truthful representation of North Africa than that of the earlier "sheik films" or *Queen of Atlantis,* as well as his willingness to treat the local people as equals.

Another young Arab, Haydée Chikly, played a minor role in the film but a major role in Tunisian filmmaking. Her father was the pioneering Arab filmmaker Albert Samama Chikly, who, along with a photographer named Soler, had organized the first film screenings in 1897 in a Tunis shop. Chikly also introduced his fellow Tunisians to the bicycle, the radio, and X-rays. In 1908 he filmed over Tunisia in a balloon and, after war service in France, returned to Tunisia, where he devoted his life to documenting all aspects of local life. Haydée worked closely with her father, writing the scripts, starring in the films, and editing them while still in her teens. After she appeared in *The Arab,* Rex was so taken with her that he invited her to Hollywood; her father, however, insisted she stay in Tunis to complete her baccalaureate.[16]

These local actors were joining a cast that was already international;

only Alice and Ramón Novarro were Hollywood stars. The rest of the nonlocal performers were assembled in Europe and included the French theater actor Max Maxudian; the rising French director Jean de Limur, who had also worked in Hollywood; Florica Alexandresco of the Theatre Royal in Bucharest; Giuseppe di Campo; and the English stage actor Jerrold Robertshaw. The latter drove Herbert Howe crazy, loudly declaiming lines from *Macbeth* in the hotel room next door to his.[17] The crew remained Rex's choice of Hollywood regulars, notably John Seitz, his assistant Gordon Avil, and Curt Rehfeld. Grant and Ota Whytock had stayed behind in the United States.

The party moved on from Bou Saâda to shoot in Biskra and then returned to Tunis, stopping off in Sidi Bouzid in the interior of Tunisia. Rex would head off to scout locations while Alice stayed behind in the small hotels where they lodged. He threw himself deeper and deeper into Arab life, but Alice, who had never left America before, found it strange. "There were always funerals going by, and the crowd sort of chanting," she later remembered.[18]

Back in Tunis, the main party stayed in the Majestic Hotel, where Rex presided over a caravan of extras passing before his demanding eye in a last costume check before shooting started. Beside him sat Alice, and it was to her he turned for a final decision. When the traveling costume department was unable to come up with a garment for Novarro that satisfied Rex's requirements, Alice plunged herself into the labyrinthine souk, the Arab shopping district, to come forth with a stunning array of burnooses and turbans. As Howe tells it, she even inveigled El Beji, the merchant prince of Tunis, to come along and personally drape Novarro in the costumes.[19]

Rex, Alice, Novarro, and Howe celebrated Christmas 1923 with others of the cast and crew. They found a small tree and retired to Howe's room for appropriate festivities. Alice strummed the ukulele, while Novarro gave impressions of any film star the group called out. On another occasion, Rex came across Novarro dancing on the roof of the Majestic Hotel. Fearful that his star would fall, Rex banned dancing, and Novarro was restricted to singing practice at his piano. Rex suggested sparring as an alternative to rooftop dancing, but Novarro was uninterested.

One day Rex left Alice at the hotel and went off with Howe and some of the crew to scout additional locations. Their car broke down, and they had to wait for help, which arrived in the shape of a Bedouin caravan led by a young woman. After some small persuasion, she danced for Rex and his entourage. Herb Howe was fascinated: "Never have I beheld such savage beauty and natural magnetism as possessed by this Rheba of the Nomad tents. With that sublime composure that is the traditional heritage of the Arab she never for one moment was self-conscious. . . . When she danced the dance of the Ouled-Nail women she could have fascinated a flock of cobras."[20]

Rex Engaged the Dancer Right There, the Tribe Also

Soon the party was off again. They drove along the coast to Gabès, and as their automobile pulled into the town, Howe gasped at what he saw: "A thrilling spectacle whirled before our eyes. Five hundred Bedouins on horseback, their white burnouses flying from them like banners, rode madly, skimmingly over the sands, firing rifles into the air, leaping from their horses and back again, standing loftily in their saddles as with their hands they touched their breasts and turbans in proud Arabic salutes. Around and around our car they circled in their *fantasia* of welcome."[21] Rex was entranced and threw himself into horse races with the Bedouin. At Gabès, Howe accompanied Rex and Alice to a banquet with eight local sheiks. One of the sheiks bathed Rex with attar of roses, and Rex responded by getting up and declaring that they sprang from the same stock as the Irish. "The Arabs," Howe remarked, "continued to look pleasant; evidently they had never heard of the Irish."[22]

Further shooting took place in Gammarth, also on the coast. Even though it was now January, the American cast and crew found themselves working in searing daytime temperatures that then plummeted at night. They learned to hate Rex's camels—eight hundred of them–employed strictly for background color. John Seitz remembered that their contact there was the chief of the secret police, a man who was part Italian, part Arab. Apparently he was responsible for much of the local casting.[23] He was, according to Rex, the stepson of a Mr. Hanech, private executioner to the bey of Tunis.[24] The bey, Muhammad VI al-Habib, and Rex had become friendly, and the bey gave Rex his personal jester, a dwarf named Abu Ben Harish, or "Shorty," as he became known among Rex's retinue.

Howe reports that Rex and Alice acquired several Arab children as protégés, including a young Bedouin girl of ten named Zina, a Sudanese "negress" of twelve named Mazourka, and a young Arab whom Alice dubbed the Malcolm McGregor of Africa because of his smile.[25] Just before they left, Rex stopped in the street in Tunis where he had seen a young Arab boy being terribly treated by a Parisian couple. He and Alice rescued the child and apparently adopted the boy, Kada-Abd-el-Kader, on the spot. An uncredited Arab boy who closely resembles Kada-Abd-el-Kader appears in the schoolroom scenes in *The Arab*, where he is foregrounded by the camera, and it seems likely that Rex gave him a small role in the film.

Now he and Alice "owned" an Arab dwarf, an Arab child, and an Ouled Naïl dancer. "In Barnum style we disembarked at Marseille," Rex writes, "that is to say with two camels, an assortment of bedouins, including Mlle. Reb'ha-bint-Yussef-ben-Amor [Rheba], Shorty Mahmoud, P-E. Hanech and Reb'ha's father, her widowed sister and some cousins—all needed for interior scenes in the old Pathé studio."[26] In February 1924 Rex and his entourage moved to Paris for interior shooting at the Joinville studios. He stayed in the Hôtel Chambord on the Champs-Élysées, the Bedouins at a less salubrious address.

The Futility of Everything

On 3 March 1924, Rex announced that he had bought a house in Tunis and that he had decided to quit the cinema forever in order to devote the rest of his life to sculpture. Filmmaking, he suggested, had only been an interim occupation, but sculpting was his true vocation.[27] On 11 March Rex and Alice disembarked in New York from the *Aquitania*, Novarro having preceded them a few days earlier. Rex stayed on in New York to edit *The Arab* while Novarro and Alice, with her sister Edna, who had joined them in North Africa, continued on to Los Angeles. There Novarro confirmed to reporters that Rex had decided to give up filmmaking and settle in Tunis to concentrate on sculpting. He might still, he added, make the occasional film, and Alice had received generous offers to appear in other films, which she would probably do for the moment.[28] Howe wrote in a column for the *Los Angeles Times* that the director had purchased a magnificent old Moorish house on the site of ancient Carthage and was planning the construction of an artist's studio there where he would pursue his sculpture. The house overlooked the Bay of Tunis, twelve pillars from the ruins of Carthage adorned its courtyard, and its walls were hand-carved to resemble ivory lace. But what won Rex over most of all was the fact that an old Greek galley filled with bronzes and marbles was rumored to lie in the waters below the house.[29] "It is not easy to explain, this urge of mine to go and battle in a country thousands of miles away from all the places that have become identified with life for me during the last years," Rex told the press. "But I know—or rather, feel—that there will be satisfaction out there in Tunis."[30]

As for Alice, she told Herbert Howe that she always did believe in the futility of everything except just sitting, and "sitting is the chief attitude of the Mohammedan."[31]

This pronouncement was hardly a bolt from the blue. Rex had been signaling his desire to move abroad for some time. In North Africa he found a way of living that was much more agreeable than anything in America, and he felt an affinity with the local people. He also had an artistic and spiritual model in Étienne Dinet, and his health had improved. (He fell ill almost as soon as he returned to America, and the editing of *The Arab* was put on hold.) Subsequent announcements, however, subtly toned down the initial decision, suggesting that Rex might in fact make one or two more films.

The other influential factor in determining Rex's future as a filmmaker was his relationship with Metro. On returning to Hollywood, Rex and Alice found the industry much changed. On 16 May 1924, Marcus Loew had merged Metro Pictures with the Samuel Goldwyn Company and Louis B. Mayer Productions, and out of this Metro-Goldwyn-Mayer was born. With Louis B. Mayer came his newly appointed production head, Irving Thalberg, Rex's old bête noire. Metro brought to the merger a raft of prestigious, if notoriously difficult, directors and a reputation based on one massive hit, *Four Horsemen*. At the old Metro, Rex had worked directly with Nicholas Schenck; now suddenly he was faced with a new regime and one that he did not like. Most people agree that it was over for the untouchable directors of the silent system when in October 1922 Irving Thalberg fired Rex's friend Erich von Stroheim from the set of *Merry-Go-Round*, replacing him with Rupert Julian. Rex had lasted longer, buffered by the personal support of Marcus Loew and the phenomenal success of his films. Now, however, the kind of autonomy that he enjoyed was unacceptable. Polled on his opinions by *Photoplay*, he firmly pronounced: "My sympathies are with those directors who stand or fall on their own merits. I have too often seen a good picture, and the career of a promising director, ruined through so-called *supervision*."[32]

Erich von Stroheim and the *Greed* Debacle

Mayer and Thalberg might have had more to say at that moment if it weren't for the financial risk of losing Rex. Another distraction was looming in the shape of Erich von Stroheim's production of *Greed*. Von Stroheim had arrived back in the fold as an employee of the Goldwyn Company and now found himself facing off against Thalberg again. By March of 1924 he was losing his battle over his ten-hour version of the film. At first he cut it down from forty reels to twenty-six, but Thalberg balked at the idea of having the film screened over two evenings. Trusting few people to touch his masterwork, von Stroheim turned *Greed* over to Rex. Rex and John Seitz sat down and watched the film together. They liked what they saw, so Rex passed it on to his editor, Grant Whytock, who had worked with von Stroheim before leaving him to join Rex's unit. Whytock spent the summer on the twenty-six to twenty-eight reels that arrived in his office, with a view to dividing the film in two and eliminating any unnecessary shots. Rex was pleased with Whytock's efforts, as were the executives from Metro who attended a screening in New York. However, the reprieve was short-lived, and rumblings over the production soon reemerged. Rex flew to his old friend's defense and telegrammed Mayer, threatening that "if you cut one more foot I'll never speak to you again." An unimpressed Mayer simply told von Stroheim that he didn't care about Rex or him and removed him from the picture. Joseph Farnham, an editor whom von Stroheim despised, finished it off.[33] Next up was *The Merry Widow*, which again the studio cut radically before releasing in 1925.

The Arab opened in America in July 1924. Reviewers were torn between the obvious flimsiness of the story and the visual splendors of the location shooting. The story was indeed minimal. Novarro plays Jamil, son of a Bedouin lord. After carrying out a raid during the feast of Ramadan, he is disowned by his father and leaves for Turkey, where he falls in love with Mary (Alice Terry), the daughter of a Christian missionary. As the Bedouins threaten the mission, Jamil learns that his father has died. He risks his life to save the mission's schoolchildren and win the hand of Mary.

The *Los Angeles Times* critic, who one feels liked the film despite himself, noted that "an Ingram picture is always much above the average" and reserved particular praise for Novarro's performance, specifically for his satirical humor. The other actor he singled out for admiration was the

Gypsy girl, Rheba (now Justa Uribe).[34] Other reviews were less flattering, particularly when it came to Alice, whom the *Film Daily* dismissed as "plump and not as pretty as she was in previous pictures."[35] In New York the *Bulletin* echoed many opinions when its reviewer remarked that "what is lacking in *The Arab,* and what has also been absent from several of this director's most recent pictures, is drama. There doesn't seem to be any fire, pep or punch in it." The *Daily News* may have been closest to the mark when its writer guessed that "Rex Ingram has made better pictures than *The Arab,* but I should like to bet he never enjoyed making a picture so much. It's brimful of sly satire and open horseplay."[36] Surprisingly the most celebratory review came from the normally cynical *Variety,* whose critic proclaimed *The Arab* to be "the finest Sheikh film of them all." The settings and characters were so authentic that the critic, who had been to North Africa, felt it to be more real than anything else he had seen and more beautiful, for "he [Ingram] has an artist's rare faculty for making a single tree throw into perspective on a screen a vastness and grandeur supplied by the imagination and memory."[37]

The film is indeed punctuated by sly humor and open slapstick. The sequences in the missionary school show a mischievous Jamil taking the opportunity to squeeze the hand of his fellow female student, while Shorty, on listening to the devout believer Iphraim (Paul Vermoyal) proclaiming in prayer the greatness of Allah, remarks, "You're right! . . . but there is no better tobacco than in the mission."

What stands out most, however, are the snapshots of local life. Many of the sequences depict everyday scenes: men praying, traders haggling, herders driving their goats, women dancing. The settings of courtyards and alleyways are framed by the camera like a travelogue, with the bustling of background characters catching the eye as much as the foreground activities.

Novarro's Jamil is a more robust sheik than Valentino's Sheik Ahmed, while Alice's Mary Hilbert has a role to play as the missionary's daughter that gives her a moral authority denied Agnes Ayres's Lady Diana. It allows her, for instance, to chastise Jamil for having purchased a wife, although he counters that it was her father who bought him for his daughter. As they fight over the young woman, Myrza (Justa Uribe), Mary snatches Jamil's whip and strikes him with it. However, the relationship has none of the air of dangerous sexuality that made *The Sheik* such a hit, not least because of Alice's demure bearing (in this film, she appears as a brunette). Jamil's character is not unlike that of Julio Desnoyers in *Four Horsemen*. Initially, he is something of a buffoon; disowned by his father, he has no position in life and refuses to live up to his heritage. In his relationship with Mary, he behaves more like an importuning child than a full-blooded sheik, sitting at her feet while she reads him lessons in English and looking up at her in adoration until he distracts her. Later, like Julio, he will redeem himself by saving the missionaries and leading an Arab charge across the desert and, in doing so, restore his masculinity.

Unlike Julio, however, Jamil doesn't dance. And it is the dancer who carries much of the film. She first appears in a street scene where Jamil introduces her as an Ouled Naïl from the desert. Rex shot this sequence much as he had shot Valentino's tango sequence in *Four Horsemen*, except that the young woman is in an open street surrounded by onlookers and other entertainers. As in the earlier film, the sequence opens with a long shot and then moves in to a close-up of the dancer's ankles, alternating between distance and intimacy. Despite having hired a real Arab dancer, Rex cast Florica Alexandresco as the Ouled Naïl woman, dressing her in imposing headgear and flowing garments. Alexandresco has a startling screen presence, at once statuesque and mysterious, and reappears throughout the story, spying on the governor as he plots the downfall of the missionaries. By virtue of her identity as a native woman, the film suggests that she can move around the town incognito, no better cover for a spy. It is she who reveals to Jamil the crucial information of the governor's treachery, prompting the prince to assume his rightful role of Bedouin lord and leading the final attack that will save the mission and the children.

The author of the original play was Edgar Selwyn, who also starred in the 1915 version of *The Arab* and shared adaptation duties with its director, Cecil B. DeMille. In the DeMille version, Jamil has to give up Mary so that he can become the new sheik, thus conveniently sidestepping any question of an interracial marriage. Rex left the matter unresolved, concluding on an ambiguous note that requires the audience to decide whether the couple has a future. It is hard to comment in detail on the film's aesthetic as, at the time of writing, the only viewing copy is missing the finale in the desert and is in poor condition.[38] However, as the reviews indicate, Rex was moving away from conventional Hollywood narrative structures and toward travelogue films that would combine documentary imagery with minimal plotlines, the kind of films his near-contemporary, Robert

Flaherty, was also producing. But where Flaherty made his name with these quasi-documentaries (*Nanook of the North* came out in 1922), audiences for a Rex Ingram release expected fiction films with strong story lines and compelling heroes. They were tolerant of his habitual refusal to cast well-known stars, of his often-jarring horseplay, and even of his discomfort with the "happy ending," but he was to face a challenge of much greater magnitude in attempting to convert them to films in which the scenery was the star.

Farewell to Hollywood

Just as *The Arab* was due to be released, Rex discovered that the titles were to read "A Metro-Goldwyn-Mayer" picture. Furious, he demanded that they be changed to "A Metro Picture" and sent the photographer Gordon Avil round to the lobby of the Capitol Theatre in New York to take pictures of the offending publicity materials. These he sent on to his attorney. From then on, despite the reality of the new studio, Rex refused to allow Mayer's name to appear on his films. His only true allies at Metro now were Marcus Loew and Nicholas Schenck, and even Loew was warning him that he had to start making films with happy endings. Rex was sick too, exhausted by the demands he set for himself when working on one of his vast pictures and always prone to stomach complaints. On advice from his lawyer, Nathan Burkan, he traveled to Cuba, and in his absence Burkan met with Schenck. These two men then met with Louis B. Mayer and smoothed the passage for an extraordinary arrangement. Mayer summoned Rex, and the principal antagonists agreed on two more productions, both to be shot overseas, in Spain, Paris, and Italy. Both too were to be adaptations, one of Jakob Wasserman's *The World's Illusion* and the other of Vicente Blasco Ibáñez's *Mare Nostrum* (Our Sea).[39] What was remarkable about the agreement was that Mayer also agreed that Rex should now work out of the South of France.

It was a coup that only a director of Rex's stature could have pulled off. Difficult as the Irishman was, he made pictures that spelled prestige and income in equal measures. In that year, he appeared in the top three of Hollywood directors in the *Film Daily* and *Photoplay* polls (alongside James Cruze and Cecil B. DeMille in the former, and Cecil B. DeMille and D. W. Griffith in the latter). If this was the way to keep him at Metro and out from under the new management's feet, then it would be done.

Mayer's only stipulation was that Nicholas Schenck supervise Rex's activities in France.

Rex started to ready himself for the move. The plan was that Alice would return to Los Angeles and sell the house and furnishings; she would also continue to make herself available to take roles in other people's productions. Novarro too would be returning to Hollywood.[40] Rex would stay in New York. Inevitably rumors as to the ending of the celebrity couple's marriage swiftly circulated around Hollywood.

The first of Alice's films was *The Great Divide* (1925) for Irving Thalberg at MGM. Because she had been working with Rex for so long, she had no "Hollywood salary" other than the $750 a week that Rex paid her as part of his unit. With advice from Rex ringing in her ears, she demanded $2,500 a week. Thalberg packed her off to Louis B. Mayer. She explained to the mogul that she needed this amount of money because they had to send their adopted Arab son to school. He would look after that, Mayer assured her. She needed a car, she continued. MGM would pay for that too. Finally, she was living with her mother and wished to move out. Mayer announced that he would take care of that, and Alice left the meeting pleased with herself. Thalberg was impressed too. Once it came to shooting the film, however, Alice's confidence fell away. She had become used to working with her perfectionist husband and suddenly felt unsure about appearing before the cameras without him. To make matters worse, the film's director was Reginald Barker, who had fired her from his production at Inceville so many years before. This time, however, it was his turn to be fired, and John Stahl replaced him.[41] Alice next appeared in the leading role in Victor Sjöström's *Confessions of a Queen* (1925) for MGM and in *Sackcloth and Scarlet* (1925) and *Any Woman* (1925), directed by Henry King. After completing *The Great Divide,* she joined Rex in New York, putting to rest stories of their estrangement.

Alice may have played up the cost of educating their adopted child, but in reality the hastily made plan was not working out. In August 1924 a columnist on the *Los Angeles Times* noted wryly that "Alice has wearied of being fond mama to a half-portion sheiklet from the Sahara Desert" and that she had deposited him with Rex in New York. He in turn had decided to send the boy back to North Africa to finish his education in the language of his fathers; then he would set him up in the Oriental carpet business.[42] For the moment, this did not happen, and Kada-Abd-el-Kader traveled with his adoptive parents to France.

Old friends and new were lined up for the voyage. One of the new faces was a fellow Irishman, albeit Irish American, the mercurial Dudley Murphy. He was on the rebound from a recent experiment in filmmaking, the fantastical *Ballet mécanique* (1925), when he met Rex. The Metro-Goldwyn attorney, J. Robert Rubin, introduced the two men. "He was one of the handsomest and most glamorous men I have ever seen," Murphy wrote in his memoirs. "When I showed him some of my films, he engaged me to work with him on his forthcoming picture. But instead of Hollywood, he said we sail for Paris Wednesday morning."[43]

Work on *Mare Nostrum* was about to begin.

8

Escape to Nice

On 1 October 1924, Rex set sail for Europe. Increasingly his heart was in North Africa, and so he determined to find a workplace that was as close to there as was practicable. He had agreed on Nice with Louis B. Mayer, but his stop was Paris, where he briefly considered a studio but dropped the idea. Instead he spent some time looking up old friends, catching up on the latest exhibitions, and casting *Mare Nostrum.* One of the exhibitions was by a young American artist, Harry Lachman, at the Galerie Hernheim. Rex dropped by and purchased one of Lachman's paintings. Meeting the artist, he invited him to dinner and over the meal spelled out his desire to settle in France, probably in Nice. Would Lachman consider accompanying him? None of Rex's staff spoke French. Rex then invited Lachman to take over the running of the studios, which he did, in doing so displacing Dudley Murphy as Rex's liaison man with the French authorities. Soon Lachman took over production duties, though he also took over the role of chief interviewee, relishing press interviews whereas Rex hated them. This neatly afforded him the opportunity to recast Rex's life in his own words, regularly briefing journalists, for instance, on Rex's studies at Oxford University and his brilliant career in the Royal Flying Corps. His own part in the development of the Rex Ingram Studios was also never understated, nor was his centrality to shooting the films. Later Rex signed a photo of himself for Lachman with the inscription "Jack of all Trades, Master of Some."[1]

Once in Nice, Rex took up residence in the Hôtel Ruhl, a majestic Victorian building on the Promenade des Anglais, much beloved of the wealthy 1920s sojourners. Initially he shuttled back and forth between Los Angeles and Nice, as he interspersed his search for suitable studios with arrangements for filming *Mare Nostrum.* Later, when they were shooting *The Magician,* he and Alice moved to another famous hotel of the day, the

Hôtel Negresco, which remains one of the landmarks of the Promenade des Anglais. And later again, they purchased their own home, the Villa Binh-Hoa, in Saint-Maurice.

It did not take long to decide on the best location for Rex Ingram Productions. In 1913 the great French film pioneer Léon Gaumont founded the original Victorine studios in Nice in an old white villa that stood in around ten acres of grounds. Gaumont was drawn to Nice by its abundant natural light, but he never followed up his initial purchase with any serious development of the site. In 1919 entrepreneur Serge Sandberg set up the Ciné Studio there with his partner Louis Nalpas. Their aim was not just to create a studio on the Victorine site but to establish a film center on the Riviera that would return French filmmaking to its prewar glory. The French industry now boasted multiple small production companies that needed a supply of studio space. Nice promised not only year-long sunlight, but also spectacular mountain ranges rising above the pretty cobbled town, palm trees, and Mediterranean waters—in other words, a location to please every type of filmmaker. The fact that films were already being made in the area also meant that they could easily hire experienced personnel, both for production purposes and as actors and extras. Sandberg and Nalpas invested heavily in the enterprise, borrowing sufficient capital to erect four studios, an open-air theater, workshops, and other buildings.

However, by 1921 the relationship between the two men was coming under increasing strain, not least due to the burden of the financial debt they had taken on, and in 1920 René Navarre took over from Nalpas as head of the studio.[2] Sandberg left the business at this point.

Rex and Lachman quickly agreed that this was the site for them. Nicholas Schenck refused to buy the Victorine for Rex, though MGM did foot the bill for renovations, charging the cost back to the production. In addition a French ruling decreed that a foreign purchaser of French property had to pay an additional 25 percent on top of the asking price. Rex returned to Los Angeles to discuss the proposed move with MGM. By January 1925 he was back in Nice, staying at the Hôtel Ruhl and now sporting a beard.

An undated, unsigned document in the Sandberg papers proposes that Rex Ingram Productions would lease the Victorine with a purchase option in six months, based on a valuation of seventy-seven francs per square meter and to include no less than twenty-five thousand square

Terry and Novarro in *Scaramouche. Courtesy of Bill Grantham*

Ingram and Erich von Stroheim. *Courtesy of the National Library of Ireland*

Alice Terry publicity shot. *Courtesy of Trinity College Dublin Archives*

On the set of *The Arab* (1924). *Courtesy of the National Library of Ireland*

Novarro and Terry in *The Arab*. *Courtesy of the National Library of Ireland*

The laboratory staff at the Victorine studios, mid-1920s. *Photograph by Garry Alderson courtesy of Valerie Pearce*

Ingram in Nice, mid-1920s. *Photograph by Garry Alderson courtesy of Valerie Pearce*

Entry to the Victorine. *Photograph by Garry Alderson courtesy of Valerie Pearce*

Shooting at the Victorine, mid-1920s. *Photograph by Garry Alderson courtesy of Valerie Pearce*

Shooting at the Victorine, mid-1920s. *Photograph by Garry Alderson courtesy of Valerie Pearce*

Victorine studios, mid-1920s. *Photograph by Garry Alderson courtesy of Valerie Pearce*

Victorine studios, mid-1920s. *Photograph by Garry Alderson courtesy of Valerie Pearce*

The Victorine's café, mid-1920s. *Photograph by Garry Alderson courtesy of Valerie Pearce*

L-R: Antonio (Tony) Moreno, Rex Ingram, and Vicente Blasco Ibáñez, 1926. *Author's private collection*

Alice Terry rehearses a scene with Michael Powell. *Courtesy of the National Library of Ireland*

Poster for *Mare Nostrum* (1926). *Courtesy of the National Library of Ireland*

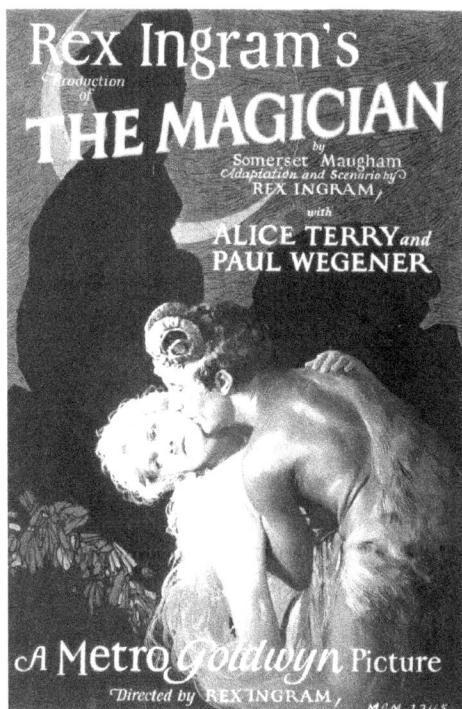

Poster for *The Magician* (1926).
*Courtesy of the National Library
of Ireland*

The Reverend Francis Hitchcock, Rex Ingram, and Alice Terry in Nice, 1927. *Courtesy of Trinity College Dublin Archives*

Pierre Linevitch (double for Iván Petrovich in *The Garden of Allah*) and Ingram sparring on the beach at Nice, 1927. *Courtesy of the National Library of Ireland*

Iván Petrovich and Alice Terry in *The Three Passions* (1929). *Courtesy of Bill Grantham*

L-R: Capt. F. C. Hitchcock, Madame Milivoyevich, HRH Prince Pierre of Montenegro, Alice Terry, Iván Petrovitch, HRH Princess Violet, and "Hadji," the prince's equerry. *Courtesy of the National Library of Ireland*

Alice Terry (undated). *Courtesy of Trinity College Dublin Archives*

Ingram in the High Atlas, Morocco, with unidentified companions, 1932. *Courtesy of Trinity College Dublin Archives*

(Above) Ingram with "Shorty" (Abu Ben Harish) plus unidentified other. *Courtesy of Trinity College Dublin Archives (Below)* With unidentified companion while making *Baroud* (1932). *Courtesy of Trinity College Dublin Archives*

Ingram as André Duval in *Baroud. Courtesy of Trinity College Dublin Archives*

Production still, *Baroud. Courtesy of the National Library of Ireland*

Image from Ingram's personal files, possibly used to accompany press article. *Courtesy of Trinity College Dublin Archives*

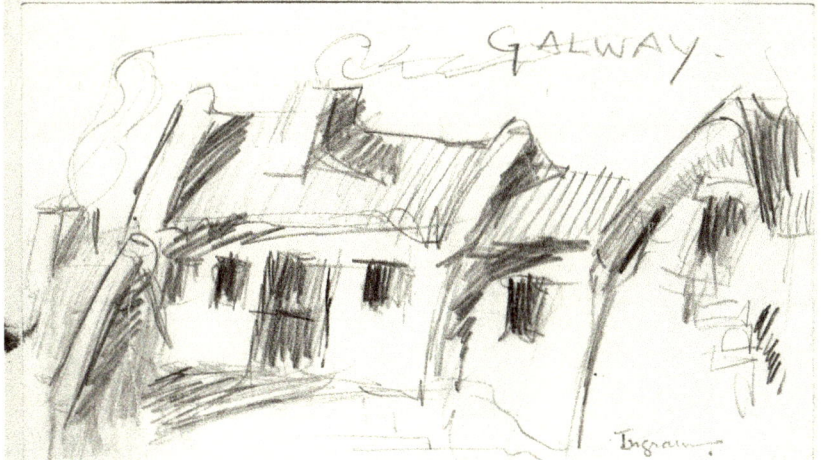

Undated sketches of a young woman and a Galway cottage by Ingram. *Courtesy of Trinity College Dublin Archives*

Rex Ingram in his 1935 Auburn 851 Supercharged Speedster. *Courtesy of Trinity College Dublin Archives (with thanks to Michael Boland for identifying the model)*

Ingram in the 1940s. *Courtesy of Trinity College Dublin Archives*

Undated Ingram sketch of *Ahaggar* Tuareg man. *Courtesy of Trinity College Dublin Archives*

Head of a Jester, sculpture by Rex Ingram. *Courtesy of the National Library of Ireland*

Mother Earth, sculpture by Rex Ingram. *Courtesy of the National Library of Ireland*

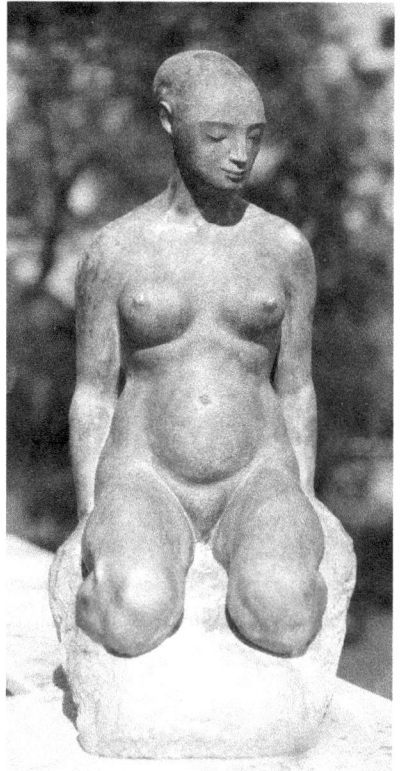

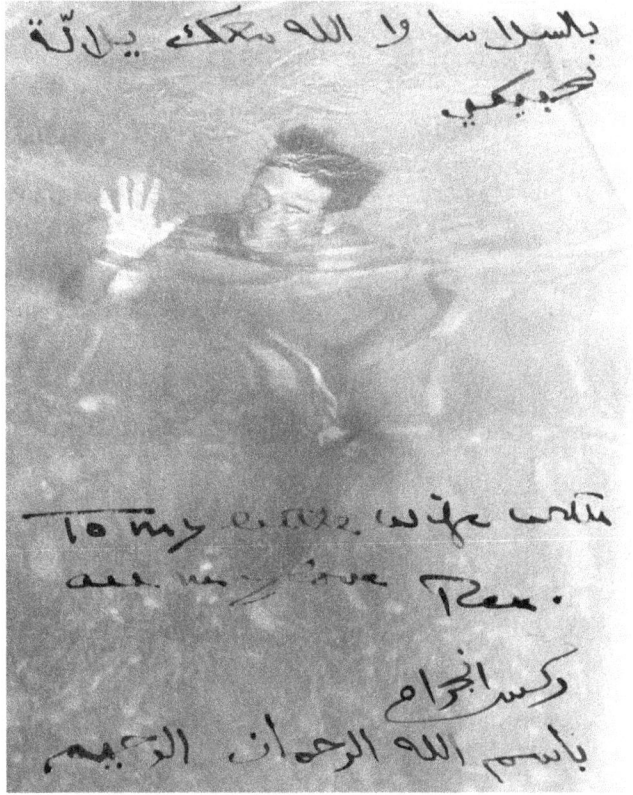

Inscribed item
from Ingram
to Terry.
Courtesy of
Trinity College
Dublin Archives

Ingram in his office at 11554 Kelsey Street in Studio City. *Courtesy of the National Library of Ireland*

Painting of Rex Ingram by Alice Terry. *Courtesy of Rick Spector*

meters, with the purchase to be conducted by the Menton-based solicitor Edouard Corniglion-Molinier.[3] In March 1925 Sandberg and George Noffka signed a lease with Rex Ingram Productions that allowed Rex and his company to set themselves up in the Victorine for two years on a straightforward rental basis, commencing on 1 April (for the time being, the proposed purchase was shelved).[4] Corniglion-Molinier, who was the son of an eminent politician in the Midi, was retained as the company solicitor. In April 1925, with some fanfare, Rex and his cortege moved in.

With the arrival of Rex Ingram Productions came an injection of Hollywood celebrity that was soon the talk of Nice. Many of the old crew moved with Rex to the South of France—Howard Strickling continued to organize unit publicity, John Seitz stayed on as cameraman with Davie Howell as his assistant, and Grant Whytock, still working with Ota, remained Rex's editor of choice. Joseph Boyle and Donald Murphy traveled as assistant directors, Benjamin Carré was art director, Willis Goldbeck scenarist, and George Noffka, who had worked on *The Arab,* was appointed by Metro to keep an eye on their interests at the studios. Also on the Ingram ticket was his mascot, John George. New faces joined the group, including Max de Vaucorbeil, whom Rex had met on *The Arab,* and Jean de Limur. Many of these, particularly Vaucorbeil, were now staunch friends with whom Rex liked to spend evenings in conversation after the work of the day had ended. Rex himself cut a dashing figure around the streets and environs of Nice, where he was to be seen driving his custom-built Rolls Royce, another eccentric experiment with car design, this time with no body—just two basket chairs.

The French press was fascinated by the comings and goings. Although Rex had moved to escape the clutches of the studio system, he was greeted on arrival as a famous Hollywood director. From *The Four Horsemen of the Apocalypse,* the French cineastes had followed his career closely, lavishing him with the same praise that he had received from American critics and audiences. He in turn now assured them of his love of France and reminded them of the many French stories he had already filmed. Most of his actors, he told the press, would be French or drawn from the international community; he would be hiring few Americans. He was also careful to reassure them that he was himself Irish, not American.

Alice did not appear in Nice until after production on *Mare Nostrum* had started, as she had been working on her other films. As soon as she arrived, the cameras flashed again—catching her as she strolled around

Nice in the sunshine, posing with Rex, her blonde wig abandoned, twirling dark glasses, and smiling. She was delighted with the move to France and later told Anthony Slide that whenever she felt the need for some relaxation, she would scour publicity until she found an inadvertent reference to one of her husband's films being a "Metro-Goldwyn-Mayer" production and show it to Rex.[5] He would fly into a temper tantrum, production would be closed down for the day, and Alice would go off to the beach. Sometimes the famous couple was accompanied by Antonio Moreno, the star of *Mare Nostrum,* on other occasions by the book's author, Vicente Blasco Ibáñez, and his wife, Elena, who were living in Menton, just up the coast. Rex and Alice in turn were frequent guests at the Ibáñezes' villa. Now a very wealthy man, Ibáñez dreamt of creating a writers' paradise. The gardens of his mansion, the Fontana Rosa, were filled with Spanish flowers and citrus trees, and he furnished a library with a collection of more than fifty thousand books. Fellow writers were encouraged to dip into his collection and wander out to the gardens to read in peace under the shade of the tall trees.

The studios were in the suburb of Saint-Augustin, about six kilometers from the center of Nice and reached by a rattling tram. They were not as well equipped as Rex had become used to at Metro. Like most French studios of the time, the Victorine boasted two massive glass barns to make the best of the natural light.[6] Because the general electricity in Nice was cut off at four o'clock to allow enough power to light the streetlamps, two electricity generators took over for evening work. Rex swiftly replaced the generators. He then persuaded the council in Nice to supply him with round-the-clock electricity and covered the entire studios with a blackout curtain so that he could shoot under lights.

One of their first additions was a twenty-by-twenty-five-meter pool that Rex planned to use for the underwater scenes in *Mare Nostrum* (the pool remains in place to this day, as does much of the original studio). In pride of place, raised on a slight incline, stood the villa that Rex made his base, often sleeping there when he was working, while Alice kept an apartment of her own about twenty minutes away. Rising three stories to a hexagonal turret, with tall windows looking out toward the Mediterranean in one direction and the mountains on the other, the villa was dim and shaded by day when the shutters were closed and filled with sunshine when they were opened. The grounds were brilliant with jacaranda trees and mimosa, the shade coming from the waving fronds of palm trees and tall cypresses. Balconies ran around the outside of the villa, and wide steps led up to the front doors. Inside the walls were hung with paintings, including an original Il Sodoma and various works by Arab artists. The hallway housed a number of busts and was dominated by a huge fireplace flanked by giant candlesticks. One room was devoted to Rex's sculptures. In his library he had a complete set of the works of Arthur Machen, the popular author of supernatural tales, another complete set of the works of the Irish writer George Moore (untouched), and shelves of books in Arabic. He was an intermittent reader and later told F. Scott Fitzgerald, "I read about one Novel and this Koran a year."[7]

The production company set up its main office in a second, smaller villa in the grounds, and the crew—carpenters, plasterers, prop men, and others—was housed in a barn-like building of about two hundred feet in length. This was also to double as an indoor set. A further building housed the laboratory where the stills photographer Tomatis worked developing the negatives. Here too the film was tinted.

Rex's Hollywood friends soon took to stopping by, as did the swelling numbers of the Riviera expatriate community. Some were from Ireland, including one of the Saunders boys from Killavala, by now Maj. F. Grant Saunders, who enjoyed watching Rex make his films. Frank turned up with his young son, Rex's nephew, also called Rex, who remembered his uncle giving him a model ship from the filming.[8] Others hoped that they might find work with the famous Irish director at the Victorine. One such was a young man who left behind a vivid account of the early years at the studios. In 1921 the Welsh army officer Capt. Thomas Powell bought a lease on the Hôtel du Parc (which he subsequently renamed the Hôtellerie de la Voile d'Or) in Saint-Jean-Cap-Ferrat. The Riviera of those days, as his son Michael later wrote, was a place for wintering only: "Nobody who was anybody would have been seen dead there in the summer months. It was too hot. All the grand villas, all the terraces and colonnades, all the fountains and ornamental pools, all the gardens full of oranges and lemons, loquats and figs, bougainvilleas and geraniums, were silent and deserted. The idea of lying in the sun to make your body as much like an African native as possible would have been greeted with shrieks of horror."[9]

In January the season began in earnest. Every train discharged a new contingent of elegant travelers loaded with suitcases. At night the casino hummed, and the opera seats filled with women in white furs. In the early evening, the Hôtel Negresco hosted a *thé dansant,* while later, Maxim's, on the Place Masséna, with its American Bar and all-night dancing, was packed with revelers. The Theatre Victor Hugo catered to English and American visitors with performances of English-language plays. Alongside the social set, a more sober collection of guests was to be seen strolling along the Promenade des Anglais. These were the ill and the overworked, many of them politicians or businessmen, for whom the clear air and the tang of the sea were considered a bracing tonic.

All this was to change in 1923 when Cole Porter and his wife, Linda, introduced the idea of a summer vacation in the South of France to their friends Gerald and Sara Murphy. The Murphys were at the heart of Jazz Age America, and their story has been recounted over and again.[10] Gerald's family was Irish Catholic from Boston, and his father was the owner of the luxury-goods business Mark Cross. Sara's father was a self-made millionaire of Norwegian parentage, her mother a wealthy socialite in her own right. Gerald was an aesthete who shunned commerce; Sara, who was several years his senior, was smart, beautiful, and independent-minded. Frustrated by the opposition of their families to their marriage, they decamped to Europe and the avant-garde art scene. The relative strength of the dollar enabled the twosome to settle first in Paris, where Gerald took up painting and where they swiftly became friendly with the leading lights of the artistic circle of the 1920s. Their decision to purchase a villa, soon renamed the Villa America, in Cap d'Antibes was the turning point in Riviera life, introducing a whole generation of bohemian and other vacationers to the pleasures of treasure hunts, yachting, picnics, and sunbathing.

By 1923 the Americans were in full flight to France. In that year, of the over 135,000 Americans who visited the country, only 10 percent were on business. The rest were there for pleasure.[11] In an often-quoted letter of 1925, F. Scott Fitzgerald wrote: "There was no one at Antibes this summer except me, Zelda, the Valentinos, the Murphy's, Mistinguet [*sic*], Rex Ingram, Dos Passos, Alice Terry, the MacLeishes, Charles Bracket, Maude Kahn, Esther Murphy, Marguerite Namara, E. Phillips Openheim, Mannes the violinist, Floyd Dell, Max and Chrystal Eastman, ex-Premier Orlando, Etienne de Beaumont—just a real place to rough it and escape from all the world."[12] He might have added Pablo Picasso, who was a regular at the Villa America, or Ernest Hemingway, who stayed nearby. Far from roughing it, the Murphys' guests were treated with immense kindness and warmth by their ever-solicitous hosts. Fitzgerald continued his curiously ungrateful response to the hospitality of the Murphys and others by lampooning them in *Tender Is the Night*, where the central character, Dick Diver (a little-disguised Gerald Murphy), already sees the charm of the Riviera fading: "The pastoral quality down on the summer Riviera is all changing anyway—next year they'll have a Season."[13] Howard Dietz, MGM's head of exploitation and publicity in New York, was one of the guests at the Murphys' place, and one may assume that Rex and Alice came to know them, though no record of their acquaintance exists.

Not long after Rex had set himself up, Michael Powell took a break from his dull job at the National Provincial Bank in London to visit his father, whose business was blossoming with the influx of tourists. Captain Powell had recently come across an American film crew working in Nice and invited them to dinner at Maxim's so that they could meet his son, whom he knew had a yearning to work in film. Unbeknownst to him, the crew was Rex Ingram's. Michael was overjoyed and not a little nervous, since Rex was one of his greatest heroes. Dinner must have gone well because the next day Harry Lachman offered the young man a job as his assistant working in the stills department. So began a career in cinema that was indebted to Rex, not just for the underpaid position at the Victorine, but for a lifelong commitment to film as art and to a fascination with the supernatural. In all, the future British director and partner of Emeric Pressburger in such extraordinary films as *Black Narcissus* (1947) and *The Red Shoes* (1948) was to spend three years working with Rex and Alice at the Victorine. Unsurprisingly, Michael Powell's first impression of Rex was of his looks. Rex was, he later wrote, one of the best-looking men he had ever seen.[14]

Mare Nostrum (1926)

Mare Nostrum was to test the will of those who had made the move to France with Rex. Rex chose to bring his own influence to the script, adding supernatural elements that were not in the original. Willis Goldbeck adapted the story for the screen. Alice had long been insisting that she wanted her husband to cast her against type. Now came the opportunity, with the lead role of Freya Talberg, the Austrian spy who seduces the sea captain (Antonio Moreno) to win his loyalty to the enemy side. The Spanish

Moreno was a familiar face to filmgoers, having appeared in films since the early 1910s, often in Latin lover roles. He first met Ingram at Vitagraph, where both acted in *Goodbye Summer*. In 1923 Moreno married the wealthy socialite divorcée Daisy Canfield Danziger, and for a few years their soirées were second only to those of Mary Pickford and Douglas Fairbanks at Pickfair, leading him to be dubbed "The It Man" by Elinor Glyn. Their marriage was, however, rumored to be one of convenience, a cover for Moreno's homosexuality. As Michael Powell observed during the filming, no spark of sexual fire flew between Alice and Tony Moreno on set.[15] Another drawback was that Moreno was noticeably too old for the role.

The rest of the cast were an international mix—as well as Moreno, they featured the famous French strongman and wrestler, Uni Apollon (as Titon), and Mademoiselle Kithnou, a dancer and actor of part-Indian heritage. Rosita Garcia played a minor part, while Kada-Abd-el-Kader took a small role as the young Ulysses Ferragut. The expatriates who dropped by the Victorine willingly allowed themselves to be roped into Rex's eccentric circle of occasional performers. One of these was the larger-than-life American artist Waldo Peirce. A massive man with a long beard, he found himself unexpectedly cast in *Mare Nostrum* as Triton Number 3. As he told his friend, the art critic and collector Harry Salpeter, "I swam under water off Juan Les Pins with a live octopus in one hand and a live lobster or crawfish in the other, in about four feet [of] water and could barely keep my derrière submerged. The octopus was dam [*sic*] tired having already done a six hour day."[16] Not only did the octopus suffer, but shooting was so delayed that the lobsters in the Victorine's pool baked in the heat.

Peirce was joined by a legion of White Russians whom Rex recruited as extras for the sequence in which the *Californian* is sunk. As the day grew longer and the water colder, they were kept supplied with shots of vodka—after every take, another shot of vodka. The Russians were delighted, according to Seitz, and kept demanding more takes. In the end, they were so drunk they had to be dragged out of the water.[17]

Another new recruit, who would go on to act in *The Three Passions* and *Baroud* for Rex, was the Russian-born German actor Andrews Engelmann. He had appeared in just two films (and had abandoned an education in medicine) when Rex strode into the Paris office of his manager, Louis P. Vérande, had a quick look at him, and said, "OK" to Vérande before turning and striding out again. His role was to play the square-jawed German U-boat commander.

Later Alice said that Freya Talberg was her best part: "I feel that *Mare Nostrum* was the only picture I ever did really, as far as I was concerned, and I was ready to stop right then. I thought 'I will never get another part like that, I will never like a part better, and I will never have the luck I had on that.'"[18] She looked magnificent: the audience's first sight of her is as she walks into the frame in the ruins of Pompeii, clad in a tight, elegant black dress, cape, hat, and pearls, looking nothing like the rather homely Mary of *The Arab*. Right to the film's ending, she remains a woman of elegance who insists that her uniform is her fine clothing and jewels. Not long after, Josef von Sternberg would play homage to Rex's film, and Alice's role, by casting Marlene Dietrich in a very similar part in *Dishonored* (1931). George Fitzmaurice's classic *Mata Hari,* also of 1931 and starring Greta Garbo, is equally in thrall to *Mare Nostrum*.

Filming lasted for over a year. The French government loaned Rex two submarines that they had captured from the Germans. In addition he chartered an elderly schooner in Marseille. One day he set out to sea with actors, crew, and sailors divided between the schooner and the tugboat he was using for filming. As the schooner tacked toward the shore, one of the crewmen let out a wild call and pointed to a dark object skimming past them on the water. At first glance it seemed to be some sort of fish, but when Rex and the crew rushed to the rail and saw the object go spinning past, less than ten feet from the bow, they realized that it was a torpedo. Seconds later a second torpedo flashed past them. They had sailed into the practice field of two French submarines. To make matters worse, the schooner was "in costume"—in other words, it was flying a German flag.

With occurrences such as this, and the motley crew of performers that the film attracted, *Mare Nostrum* took fifteen months to shoot. In addition the scale was so lavish that Rex had to appoint Seitz to the second unit to direct the Spanish sequences with Tony Moreno in Barcelona. Because of Ibáñez's reputation with the Spanish government, filming had to be carried out clandestinely. When Seitz returned to Nice, he found that Rex had fallen out with Benjamin Carré and fired him, so he continued on without an art director. Rex would make a sketch of the scenes, and Seitz would try to interpret them. Luckily, soon afterward, Henri Ménessier, the Gaumont art director, whose assistant Carré had been, dropped into the studio. Rex hired him immediately.

Alongside the filming, the studios were being renovated, which contributed to the lengthy shooting time of *Mare Nostrum*. At first the plan had been for Rex to shoot the outdoor sequences in Nice and return to the Metro lot in Hollywood for the interiors. However, soon after they had settled in and commenced shooting, Rex decided to shoot the entire film in Nice. The renovations were stepped up, with Harry Lachman fuming at the slow progress of the local entrepreneurs who had taken on the job. They did not understand the phrase, he told one journalist, "time is money." He gave them two weeks to complete the laboratory, which, he said, would have been quite enough in America; they demanded twenty-two days. As long as they delayed, the costs of the production mounted, with the masons and the carpenters, who were on the MGM payroll, unable to work.[19]

Undeterred by a lack of appropriate equipment for the indoor sequences, Rex dispatched the production team to Rome to raid the equipment left behind by the troubled *Ben Hur* shoot. Louis B. Mayer had just recalled Charles Brabin and his crew to America and was determined to keep a closer eye on his runaway and chaotic production. Since the equipment in Rome was Mayer's, Rex had no qualms about helping himself to its most useful stock, including generators and lights for indoor work. He also hired a legion of Italian electricians, whom he put to work alongside the French construction men and the Hollywood crew. Now he was set to make his entire film far away from his nemesis. Of course, this all added to the length of time it took to complete *Mare Nostrum,* but its director didn't mind.

It sounded like chaos, and to many of the new recruits to an Ingram film that was their first impression of a shoot under the command of the famous fugitive from Hollywood. Yet, as Michael Powell and others visiting the set discovered, Rex remained as much a perfectionist in France as he had been in Hollywood, working on each shot until he had achieved exactly what he wanted.

The final version of *Mare Nostrum* came in at over one million feet. When Mayer saw the completed film, he cabled Rex: "It's a travelogue, take out a thousand feet, and you have a swell picture."[20] According to Grant Whytock, the only way they could reduce it was to take out whole reels, which they did, including one entire story line that was three and a half reels long.[21] It seems likely that MGM cut it further before opening it. Indeed, it is impossible now to trace which print was screened in any one territory and to guess which version any one national audience saw. One key sequence, in which the two lovers embrace in front of an octopus in a Naples aquarium, seems familiar because of its ubiquity as a publicity still. It is, however, nowhere to be seen in the television print.[22] Rex continued to insist that Mayer's name should not appear in the credits of any of his films. Running into the mogul in a Paris restaurant, he introduced him to Dudley Murphy as "Louis B. Merde."[23] *Mare Nostrum* was credited as a "Metro-Goldwyn" production.

Mayer was right to point out that Rex had made a film that looked like a documentary. That was what he had intended to do. After *The Arab* he remained convinced that this was how best to overcome the tired formulas of Hollywood plots: "Documentary films, that is to say, the news-reels and travel pictures, had always interested me more than films of studio fabrication. It was a Mediterranean newsreel which finally convinced me that if I filmed the exteriors of the picture *sur place,* making use of local characters, the result would give that same feeling of actuality the book possessed."[24] The problem with this, of course, was that newsreels and travel pictures advertised themselves as such, and audiences attended them knowing what to expect; audiences for Rex Ingram films rightly assumed that they were paying to see fictional dramas and were now becoming increasingly disconcerted to find Rex's eccentric hybrids appearing in their darkened cinemas. The American press blamed what they concluded was a Continental influence, but, despite Rex's casting of European actors in European stories, his films were not quite European art films either. In an increasingly commodifed industry, to be without a defining marketing niche was a dangerous position to occupy.

Certainly *Mare Nostrum*'s location shooting is eye-catching, even if much of it is now lost. When the story moves to Naples, the opening sequence has the camera placed on a height looking down over the bay with a gaunt tree in the left foreground. Next is a low-angled shot of one of the ships in the harbor. A third shot is a bird's-eye view of cargo being unloaded with a crane. These sequences are followed by a view of Vesuvius framed by two columns and the ruins of Pompeii. Ferragut (Moreno) has come to explore the site, and the camera explores it with him. This too is where he first encounters Freya, who reminds him uncannily of a painting he owns of the goddess Amphitrite. He moves on to Paestum with Freya, who is accompanied by of one of Rex's inevitable figures of fun—the stout, overdressed, monocle-wearing, Austrian female archaeologist and spy Doctor Fedelmann (Mme. Paquerette, aka Pâquerette). The casting is full of such visual jokes, with one of the most grotesque being Hughie Mack as the captain's servant. Mack was now so appallingly overweight (and would die the following year still only in his early forties) that there is something immensely discomforting about his presence and his relentless slapstick, just as there is with the double act of John George and Shorty as two other servants. The French actor Fernand Mailly, who plays Count Kaledine, is equally one-dimensional and, with his military bearing, monocle, and starched collars, seems to have been cast more as a jokey nod to Rex's friend Erich von Stroheim than as a serious contributor to the dramatic action.

Even with the lengthy "travelogue" sequences deleted, there is something decidedly odd about *Mare Nostrum,* with strange lapses in plot and pacing and tone. Yet it still bears many of the hallmarks of the best of the earlier films. Interiors are either cluttered, often with religious statues and paintings, or bare and arched. The sequence where the troops march through Naples is structured along the same flowing lines that distinguished similar scenes in *Four Horsemen,* with the viewer's attention being drawn from foreground to background and corner to corner of the frame in order to follow the movement of the marching men. Another poignant and understated sequence is the moment where Ferragut realizes his betrayal, turns to look at the men on the ship who loll among the cargo both physically and mentally distanced from him, and turns back to gaze across at the sea and the disappearing submarine, alone. And, although the sinking of the *Californian* is too obviously created using miniatures, the hunt for survivors is strikingly shot in the darkness, with just one beam of light picking out the small, life-size craft on the sea, followed by a second beam streaming down on a dead woman floating face-up on a lifebuoy.

Another defiantly unhappy ending sees Freya step bravely up to her execution, requesting only that she wear her "uniform" of furs before facing the firing squad. Shortly thereafter Captain Ferragut sets sail for war in the *Mare Nostrum* to be torpedoed by the very submarine that he helped man. His final act is to sink the submarine before his own ship disappears into the nighttime waters. In the closing sequence, Freya/Amphitrite rises from the ocean bed to embrace the sinking body of her lover and welcome him to her ocean kingdom.

The audience at the film's American premiere was, the *Los Angeles Times* reported, "enthusiastic, though bewildered." The *New York Times* agreed, observing that the "audience . . . appeared to be left slightly dazed by the weird delivery of the film." Others snickered at the film's old-fashioned intertitles, with their overemphasized foreign accents. The *Los Angeles Times* was more receptive to Ingram's latest work, praising the artistic merits of *Mare Nostrum* but doubting that audiences would flock to it; if anything, the paper opined, it might be a slow-burn, word-of-mouth release. The images of the Marseille waterfront particularly delighted the reviewer, who also found space to lavish praise on the performances of Antonio Moreno and Alice Terry.[25] The *New York Times* reviewer, on the other hand, found that "Alice Terry is fair, but unconvincing in the rôle of the German spy." She was, the writer considered, "too phlegmatic for the part."[26] Other critics agreed, most of them praising the film's photography while lamenting its pace and plot development. Once again, Metro elevated Rex's film to its "specials" category, opening it in its upmarket theaters.

The French press, however, was won over by *Mare Nostrum*. *Cinéa* praised Rex for his decision to relocate to Nice, vowing that this gave the film an authenticity that one could not have expected of a stranger to the country. *Mare Nostrum* was a film that glorified "our old Greco-Latin civilization, our countryside, our monuments and our traditions of honor."[27] *Les Spectacles* called *Mare Nostrum* "vital and perfect," adding that Alice Terry had performed at the height of her talent.[28] Shortly after the film's opening in France, in September 1926, the French government bestowed on Rex the Légion d'Honneur. The Irish press too was enthusiastic, praising both story line and acting.[29]

Not surprisingly, the Germans were outraged by this second attack on their national character, following the previous assault on them in Rex and Ibáñez's *Four Horsemen*. The German ambassador to Paris asked the French ministry of foreign affairs to ban this "tendentious and hateful [representation] of our country," a representation, he added, that might actually prevent France and Germany from reestablishing positive diplomatic relations.[30] Andrews Engelmann became a hated figure in his home country. MGM withdrew the print from circulation and cut certain sequences but to little political effect.

Expatriates and Other Friends

The Irish were well represented on the Riviera, and Rex knew most of them. They often met in the Riviera Tea Rooms at 15 rue de France, run by the sister of the editor of the expatriate magazine *Continental Life,* the Irishman John J. Dempsey. With ham imported directly from Ireland and hot scones served dripping with butter, its clientele could savor the pleasures of home. The McDermotts from Bray, County Wicklow, owned the three main cinemas in Nice—the Picture House, the Arcadia Gardens, and the Gardens. The well-known Irish journalist and politician T. P. O'Connor (widely known as "Tay-Pay") was a regular visitor. Another was Frank Scully, who was later to achieve notoriety for his reports on flying saucers and his 1950 book *Behind the Flying Saucers.* He had come to the South of France for his health and, he claimed, to ghost a life of George Bernard Shaw by Frank Harris. He stayed on to write publicity stories for MGM about the Victorine. Frank Harris, the Galway-born publisher turned American citizen, now living near Nice in Cimiez, was already in the midst of his scandalous and fanciful four-volume autobiography *My Life and Loves* when he and Rex met each other. But the Riviera Tea Rooms did not just serve Irish guests. On one occasion, the president of the Executive Council of the Irish Free State, W. T. Cosgrove, and his wife enjoyed Ceylon tea in the inner room, while members of the English royal family sipped China tea in the outer room.[31]

The most famous of the Irish Americans to visit the Riviera in those years was also a friend of Rex and Alice's. Rex had read and relished *The Great Gatsby,* writing to F. Scott Fitzgerald that "Gatsby is very fine: it is full of sentiment without being sentimental—Gatsby was a sentimentalist but on so heroic a scale that he was magnificent. Everyone of your characters prove that the U.S.A. is uninhabitable."[32] According to Alice, the two men exchanged other letters, of which all she would say was that they were obscene.[33] Fitzgerald responded to their friendship by modeling one of his characters on Rex. It was, as the Murphys were to discover, a hazardous fate to find oneself recreated in one of Fitzgerald's fictions, yet Rex escaped relatively lightly from the process, which suggests that the two men shared a genuine affinity. The fictionalized Irish film director underwent multiple reworkings in the mid-1920s as Fitzgerald struggled with a new novel, to become *Tender Is the Night.* In the 1929 version, Lew (Llewellen) Kelly is a Yale man on his first trip to Europe, where he plans to live on the French Riviera. He is accompanied by his wife, Nicole, who buries the pain of her life in alcohol. On board the ship with the Kellys, traveling with her mother, is the ingénue, Rosemary: "She was seventeen and nearly complete but the dew was still on her."[34] Rosemary is determined to meet Lew Kelly and eventually contrives to do so. Her first impression of him:

He was about twenty seven; he was tall and his body was over spare save for the bunched force gathered in the shoulders and upper arms. His bright blue eyes were like glittering worlds and for a moment she lived in them eagerly and confidently. She noticed his strong scornful mouth and his nervous young fore-head, already lined with fretful and unprofitable pain. At the moment he was, save for Griffith, the most successful picture director in the United States. To Rosemary he was more than that—he was the gate keeper of the promised land, he [was] the portal itself to all that was desirable. Look at me, her heart cried, See me now when I'm beautiful. How can you let a second of this be wasted? Here is a violin for your bow, clay for your clever hands. Take me and use me, wear me out and throw me away.[35]

Kelly's companion, the writer Bowman, tells him that he ought to make a test of Rosemary, but the director is scornful: "I'm sick of all that. Pick them out of the gutter one day and they want gold plates tomorrow."[36] At a party on board that he hadn't wished to attend, Kelly falls into conver-sation with the consul general of Bucharest's wife, Mrs. Woodle. Hearing that he is traveling to Nice in summer, she is horrified: "It'll be roasting. It's impossible. There'll be no one there at all."[37] He tells her that he is tired and all that he wants to do is to test the light to see if he can make a picture later: "All the French film seems blurred and dark to us but I think maybe its [sic] the technical equipment and the methods."[38] He is leaving America for Europe because, seen from Hollywood, Europe seemed "warm, unified and clear, a movement from the diverse and thin toward the definite and concrete. . . . He expected, in any case, a completed world, a world he would not have to make or mould."[39] And, finally, it was "a copy of Leger's Ballet Mechanique which had found its way to the coast that had given him the idea of going abroad. And they were secure—he had saved half a million dollars."[40]

The depiction of Lew Kelly in this version, which Fitzgerald later largely discarded, is convincingly close to Rex and suggests conversations between the two men in which the director explained certain of his deci-sions to the writer. In the same year, Fitzgerald published the short story

"Jacob's Ladder" in the *Saturday Evening Post*. In it the narrator introduces the young and beautiful Jenny Delehanty to the Irish film director Billy Farrelly. He is described as full of bitter Irish humor, "in contempt for himself and his profession."[41] Farrelly makes a star of Jenny, who in turn falls for a Valentino lookalike, Raffino. Again this seems a very close, if exaggerated, fictionalization of Rex's personality, with little of Alice's identity traveling into the writing. We may guess that Rex's own ambivalence, veering into contempt, about Hollywood found a ready echo in Fitzgerald's attitude toward the industry to which he willingly sold his writings but that he despised as a medium "capable of reflecting only the tritest thought, the most obvious emotion."[42]

Eventually all that Fitzgerald left of the Irish director and his European studio was a small section of the published novel (the 1934 version) where Rosemary visits the film director Brady in an old Gaumont studio in Monte Carlo; despite the Irish-sounding name, he has a "faintly defiant cockney accent."[43] Rex was to return once more as a ghostly presence in *Tender Is the Night* when the poet and novelist Malcolm Lowry wrote his unproduced (and unproducible) five-hundred-page screen version of Fitzgerald's novel. In it a disconsolate Dick Diver walks down Broadway while a collage of effects illustrates his state of mind. He enters a cinema playing *Mare Nostrum:* "Immediately on the screen in this cinema a man is seen drowning beneath the sea: the scene of drowning now fills the screen so that we feel ourselves almost drowning in the sea through which now appear other electric apron fronts of other theatres which we feel Dick still walking into."[44] It is a delirious projection, perhaps, yet one that the much saner Rex Ingram would have certainly appreciated.

Michael Powell observed Ingram's court at the Victorine with pleasure and fascination. Rex loved to rub shoulders with people of all kinds but most of all, "like many autocrats, Rex surrounded himself with a court of odd-balls, among them dwarfs, hunchbacks, apes and clowns."[45] Shorty, the dwarf gifted to Rex by the bey of Tunis, functioned as Rex's court jester, there to "be teased and provoked and kicked around like a football. He knew his place and invited the treatment. He was made of rubber. He had a huge head and torso, no legs to speak of and was smart. He wore Arab dress. If Rex wanted a butt for a joke, or just a punching ball, Shorty was always on hand. He made actors uneasy."[46] Nor was Alice pleased about "Rex's damn dwarfs," though she was resigned to her husband's whims.[47]

Rex liked to have dwarfs, John Seitz said, because being Irish he was super-stitious.[48] Willis Goldbeck, however, thought otherwise:

> He was the most romantic looking man, or the handsomest man I've ever seen in my life. Women used to practically swoon for him but he didn't seem to have much of an eye for them. I mean, he liked them, but his eye was more or less for the grotesque in things. . . . He saw beauty in ugliness, if you know what I mean. When we went abroad and had our studio in Nice, he was always looking for not a beautiful woman but a woman of some extraordinary facial characteristic or turn of neck or something. These were the people that fascinated him.[49]

This comment has the ring of truth to it, given that Rex so relied on Alice and his latest Latin lover type to embody beauty and showed little interest in experimenting with new looks or types. Ugliness—whether Danton's pockmarked face or a leering drunk—endowed his works with a visual complexity that beauty never could.

In the end Rex grew fed up with John George because he was using his overtime money for gambling and handed him a second-class ticket and some money and told him to leave. The actor raised a fuss, but Tony Moreno took him to one side and said, "Beggar boys like you and me shouldn't be particular. You've got money and you'll have money when you get to New York."[50] So George left and returned to Hollywood and a long career in film and later television, working up until the 1960s.

Later, in January 1927, Rex found himself at the center of a Riviera scandal. When Isadora Duncan wrapped herself in a purple cloak and walked out to sea only to be rescued, as the water rose to her chin, by an English officer, the Riviera gossip columns were full to overflowing. To add spice to the story, one of the English papers reported that she had done so after leaving a party in her studio where Rex and she had had a bet to see how long she could stand in cold water. The party swiftly was amplified into an orgy, and as rumors grew, and the events of the Fatty Arbuckle scandal were remembered, so it seemed that now Hollywood had indeed taken over Nice. Duncan, however, assured Sewell Stokes, her first biographer, that Rex had not even been at the party, although Jean Negulesco (in his less than reliable autobiography) swore he was, as were, among others, Jean Cocteau and Picasso, and that later they piled into Rex's big sedan and drove to Chez Basso in Marseille for a midnight bouillabaisse while Cocteau ogled the handsome sailors.[51] In any case, the event that triggered this grand gesture had nothing to do with Rex and everything to do with the dancer's jealousy over the solicitous behavior of her lover, Victor Seroff, toward a dinner guest whose glass Isadora had apparently topped off until she became ill.[52]

Had anyone stopped to consider the story, it would have been most uncharacteristic of Rex to participate in orgies on the Riviera with Isadora Duncan. He still loathed public appearances that required attention to dress and the making of small talk. Only Alice liked to dance. In her column for *The Riviera Season,* the same Isadora Duncan wrote of catching a glimpse of the star at a *thé dansant,* "flitting past you like a draft of rare Arabian perfume, looking like a veritable ray of moonlight, wrapped in her silvery furs, her little feet shod in Damask and disappearing before you have had time to feast your hungry soul upon the fairy dream."[53] Rex meanwhile was hurrying through the lobby, pushing his way politely but determinedly through the bevy of young female fans eager to secure his autograph. With many and profuse apologies, he made his escape, leaving a long string of "oohs" and "aahs" trailing in his wake.

9

The Magician of the Riviera

If to the French press Rex and his entourage breathed the life of Hollywood into the Victorine studios, in fact his working methods were eccentric and autocratic in a manner that would never have been tolerated in the newly organized industry back in Los Angeles. In the mornings, he liked to toss a ball around on the beach, "La Grande Bleue," or swim, putting in a couple of hours of good exercise. By now Rex was so well known that eyes would turn in his direction as he strolled down to the sea, and aspirant stars made it their business to be seen to their best advantage when he came into sight. He was a strong swimmer and, the press reported, on one occasion dashed into the water fully clad to rescue a bather who was in trouble.[1] He also liked to strip down to his bathing suit and lie out enjoying the feel of the sun on his body. No filming was to take place until after lunch, when the light was softer.

At lunchtime, everyone—actors and crew—ate together at long tables set in the gardens and shaded by palm leaves. To his staff Rex was generous. On his instructions, a canteen was set up to feed the laborers at the studios sandwiches and fruit and serve beer and tea; alcohol was permitted as long as it wasn't abused. Every Christmas he purchased a huge tree and decorated it, buying gifts for the workers and their children of toys, clothes, pipes, and other items, many of them valuable. Friends and strangers continued to drop by, some by appointment, others on the off chance of gaining an interview with the famous Hollywood director.

It is thanks to Rex's many illustrious guests that one can piece together some sense of the working atmosphere at the Victorine. One of these was the Jamaican poet, writer, and intellectual Claude McKay, a key figure in the Harlem Renaissance. McKay's wanderings around America and

Europe form the backdrop to his autobiography, *A Long Way from Home*. Often penniless but open to the unpredictable encounters a life on the road threw up, McKay was introduced to Rex in the spring of 1926 by another leading name in the Harlem Renaissance, the literary critic Max Eastman. All shared a common friendship with Frank Harris, who had been instrumental in launching McKay in America. All were friends too with another acquaintance of Rex's, the actor Paul Robeson. In *A Long Way from Home*, McKay recalls being welcomed by Rex, whom he described as having a "sympathetic mind and an insatiable curiosity about all kinds of people and their culture."[2] The director was especially interested in North Africa, he recalled, and had learned to speak Arabic. They swapped poetry, and McKay was impressed with his host's talents. Rex in turn gave his visitor a job reading through a selection of novels and summarizing their plots with a view to potential film adaptations. More shockingly for the day and age in which both men lived, he invited McKay to eat dinner with them, a crossing of the racial divide that particularly enraged some of the American technical staff working in the studio. When the studio manager got wind of the information that McKay had visited the newly formed Soviet Union, he was doubly incensed. Unconcerned about the furor he was creating, Rex spent the evenings deep in conversation with his guest. "Rex Ingram," McKay found, "held some very advanced ideas on world politics. He was interested in the life and thought and achievements of minority groups, and whenever he ran into me had something interesting to say."[3] An incident on the street in Nice saw McKay draw a knife on one of the studio's Italian employees who was taunting him about his skin color. The poet instantly regretted his reaction and was ashamed for Rex, whose friendship he valued. For the rest of his stay at the Victorine he kept away from his patron; Rex for his part understood what had happened and turned a blind eye to the incident. When the time came for McKay to leave, he sought out the Irishman to thank him and bid him farewell. Rex "encouraged me to go on with my writing, told his bookkeeper to give me a free ticket to Marseilles and gave me a gift of six hundred francs."[4]

If no account is without the gloss of time, it is remarkable how consistently their authors remark on Rex's hospitality, his open-mindedness, and his pleasure in exchanging ideas. Off set, he was charming; on set he remained a tyrant. Being his own master allowed him to organize his time as he saw fit and to hire people who caught his eye or with whom he felt like working. Nor was he under the same pressure as he would have been in Hollywood to attend functions and formal events just to keep his name in the gossip columns; instead he could dress as he pleased. "One of Rex's peculiarities was his liking to dress like a bum," Harry Lachman remembered. "Old sloppy clothes, no sox and open sandles [sic]. On the trip we took to New York on a luxury liner with the great lawyer Nathan Burkan Rex appeared for supper in the sloppy clothes and no sox. I overheard a couple of husky Americans say we aught [sic] to beat that fellow up. I told Rex and the next night he appeared in a Tuxedo, impeccable and of course handsome."[5] Another object of fascination for visiting journalists was the ring Rex wore on the little finger of his left hand. Garnished with an ancient Egyptian gem, it was only matched by the inevitable gold bracelet on his wrist. "My brother never talked cinema except to cinema people," Frank told Liam O'Leary. "His conversation was boxing, sport, Arabs, books, Ireland, history, swimming, shark-fishing, cartoons of natives etc. Everything but cinema!"[6] If pushed Rex would name the films of D. W. Griffith and von Stroheim, Robert Wiene's *The Cabinet of Dr. Caligari* (1920), and Merien C. Cooper's *Chang* (1927) as works he admired.

Increasingly guests and journalists were treated to Rex's views on the loss of values in Western society. Money had become the cause of much unhappiness, in his view; fame was transient, his own included; and only one's health and the pleasures of the outdoors were important. For all his open-mindedness, he had his blind spots: communism was a scourge, and he remained irrevocably anti Semitic. In some ways, he was growing closer temperamentally to his father, the opinionated and dogmatic Church of Ireland rector; in other matters, they were set on a collision course. Meanwhile "North Africa was becoming a habit," he wrote in his memoirs. "Taking the boat in Marseilles before noon, I would be in the port of Algiers the next day in time to have a cous-cous lunch in an Arab eating-joint near the *marché*."[7] Nor did he stop in Algiers, but traveled onward, leaving behind him the last Western travelers and keeping the company of Bedouin hunters and camel traders as he camped under the stars, halted in oases, and sat drinking mint tea with the villagers. The people he met and the situations that he found himself in were later to form the basis of his unpublished short stories. But for now he was still officially a Hollywood filmmaker, if an expatriate one.

In early October 1925 Alice returned to Los Angeles after nearly a year in France with Rex. On 15 October Antonio Moreno followed her. Rex too was forced to return to America intermittently, both for business and to consult his doctor. By the mid-1920s, despite his vigorous outdoor life, rumors of illness were appearing in news reports about him, only to disappear again without further elaboration. In December 1925 Rudolph Valentino went to Monte Carlo to spend New Year's Eve with the actor Mae Murray and Manuel Reachi, the husband of actor Agnes Ayres, and the press reported that Alice and Rex would join them.[8] Whether it was then or when he was staying at the Hôtel Negresco (in early January 1926), Alice remembered that they did indeed meet up.[9]

The Magician (1926)

For his next film, Rex had planned to adapt the Somerset Maugham novel *The Moon and Sixpence,* whose rights MGM already owned. However, the lukewarm reaction to *Mare Nostrum* put him off the idea of another war story, and he turned instead to *The Magician.* He chose the novel, he said, to provide a starring role for Paul Wegener. His source material he otherwise dismissed as "cheap melodrama" with an ending that had to be changed if it were to see the light of day as a film.[10] This baffled and displeased Maugham in equal measures: he couldn't understand why anyone would purchase his story and then alter the ending. He made his displeasure widely felt, and despite being neighbors on the Riviera (Maugham's villa was at Cap Ferrat), the two men never hit it off.

The Magician was first published in 1908 and, as Somerset Maugham later acknowledged, drew liberally for its central character, Oliver Haddo, on the notorious figure of Aleister Crowley:

> At the time I knew he was dabbling in Satanism, magic and the occult. There was just then something of a vogue in Paris for that sort of thing, occasioned, I surmise, by the interest that was still taken in a book of Huysman's, *Là Bas.* Crowley told fantastic stories of his experiences, but it was hard to say whether he was telling the truth or merely pulling your leg. During that winter I saw him several times, but never after I left Paris to return to London. Once, long afterwards, I received a telegram from him which ran as follows: "Please send twenty-five pounds at once. Mother of God and I starving. Aleister Crowley." I did not do so, and he lived on for many disgraceful years.[11]

Unhappy with his fictional reincarnation, Crowley had already reviewed Maugham's novel in *Vanity Fair* (under the name of Oliver Haddo), dismissing it as plagiarism and including extracts from the sources he had detected Maugham using. He topped this off by speculating, "After studying the make-up of *The Magician,* we are constrained to wonder whether any of Mr Maugham's numerous plays have been composed in the same way."[12]

Crowley had every reason to be displeased with his fictional alter ego. Haddo is a huge man, standing well over six feet tall, obese, and arrogant, with "the look of a very wicked, sensual priest."[13] His peculiar powers have been learned in the East, and in revenge for a slight he proceeds to seduce the young Doctor Burdon's fiancée, Margaret. Despite his physique and demeanor of evil, she experiences a sexual ecstasy with Haddo that the dull Burdon can never match. Haddo steals Margaret away from the doctor and Parisian society and works his evil desires on her. Unable to rescue his former, now defiled fiancée, whom Haddo finally murders as part of his scheme to create human life, Burdon does manage in the end to kill Haddo and burn his gruesome laboratories to the ground. It isn't vintage Maugham—more of a potboiler than anything else. But it offered Rex the chance to play with the kind of visual trickery and magic that he had used so effectively in the fantasy sequences in *The Four Horsemen of the Apocalypse* and *The Conquering Power.* It also allowed him to draw in friends from the art world as he so liked to do—the faun, for instance, that makes its appearance in one sequence, he commissioned from the sculptor Paul Dardé.

Filming began on 10 February 1926 in Paris and finished in Nice in May 1926. The opening sequences in the capital are a visual tour de force, looking down at the bridges over the Seine and across to the Eiffel Tower from a height, with a cluster of gargoyles on the right of the frame apparently sharing the view. From a shot of the Latin Quarter with its artists and bustle, we enter the studio of sculptor Margaret Dauncey (Alice Terry as a blonde again), who is working on a massive sculpture while her friend Susie Boyd puts the finishing touches on a sketch, *Sunrise on the Seine.* Susie (played by Gladys Hamer) sits back, chews her pencil and then makes an alteration. The sketch becomes *Sunset on the Seine.* Thus Rex swiftly disposes of contemporary French art (facile and meaningless), plunging his viewers instead into his favorite, and menacing, Gothic world.

As Margaret works on her statue, which bears more than a passing resemblance to the Parisian gargoyles, its head slowly begins to shift, cracks appear down its back, and suddenly it collapses, leaving her pinned underneath. Her uncle and guardian, Dr. Porhoët (Firmin Gémier), immediately contacts Dr. Burdon (Iván Petrovich), who operates and performs a miracle in fixing Margaret's spine. The audience behind the glass partition on a balcony overlooking the operating room includes the demented Oliver Haddo. This was Paul Wegener's role; Rex shot him so that his massive body filled the frame, and Wegener responded by holding himself immobile and relying on popping his eyes wide open to indicate rising emotion. Another gesture was to flick his cape over his shoulder dismissively.

He begins to shadow Margaret and Burdon as they romance in the parks of Paris, intercepting them on one occasion to pluck a rose and hand it to Margaret with a bow. Margaret turns to Burdon in confusion; he pats her reassuringly on the arm, remarking of Haddo that "he looks as if he had stepped out of a melodrama." The knowingness of this line suggests that Rex was aware that Wegener could not or would not break with the mode of acting that had made his name as a student of Max Reinhardt and later as the preeminent performer of German expressionist cinema. Now, however, the celebrated German actor lumbers through his role, reliant on his size and his eyes to fill the screen and convey Haddo's threat. Michael Powell's impression of Wegener was that he "was a pompous German whose one idea was to pose like a statue and whose one expression to indicate magical powers was to open his huge eyes even wider, until he looked about as frightening as a bullfrog. . . . He rarely spoke on the set, but every so often his 'Ali, meine Zigarren!' would send his Turkish manservant scurrying to bring a new stogie which he would light with anxious care, while Wegener puffed, his eyes closed to Oriental slits."[14] Alice Terry was, as Rex always ensured, as virginal as ever, so that between her purity and Wegener's immobility, it is hard to credit why her Margaret would run away with the sorcerer. In the original story, she becomes utterly corrupted and wanton; in the film, she remains essentially pure.

Credibility aside, the film is a fascinating tribute to its era. In part, this is due to John Seitz's camera. While critics routinely praised Rex's North African location shooting, the scenes in Paris, Monte Carlo, and the small village of Sospel have an immediacy that is akin to watching old postcards come to life. Another curious consequence of watching this film is how much it both presages and reflects other filmic works. Thus, for instance, the sequence in the casino at Monte Carlo, where the enchanted Margaret gambles at the tables under Haddo's gaze eerily suggests James Bond films. In fact, the authenticity of the casino is an illusion. Rex had wanted to film in the actual casino, but the Monaco authorities refused him access. Instead he had to recreate one in studio and was able to hire the plasterer who had carried out the original work on the casino and use the plaster molds from that job, which he still had. This fascinated Prince Louis of Monaco, who had never been in the actual casino and visited the set to see what it looked like.

In Nice the local inhabitants filled in as extras—for a fairground sequence at the Lion de Belfort, Rex hired four hundred Niçois. Still others crowded into the Old Town to catch a glimpse of Alice and the film's other stars and watch the display of athletes, clowns, dancers, and Russian Cossacks.[15] The same fairground sequence saw Michael Powell make his first appearance on film: "My angelic seriousness must have amused him [Rex], for he suddenly announced on the night of the shooting that I was to be included as comedy relief, Gladys Hamer presumably having been found wanting. I was clapped into a make-up chair, covered in Leichner make-up, had my head shaved, was allotted a battered suit of clothes, a pair of glassless spectacles, a toy balloon, and a bag of bananas—I have said that Rex's comic sense was rudimentary—and was told to be funny. I tried."[16]

Seitz remembered Powell as a little absent-minded. One day on the set, he recalled, Harry Lachman was creating the shot of the carnival: "We used flash powder and cables and so Mickey pulled the switch at the wrong time and one of the Italian electricians was hurt from the blast—lost the hearing in one of his ears." "Anyhow," Seitz added, "we always liked Mickey. He was fine. A very bright guy. He didn't mind mopping the floors or holding the flash."[17]

Other sequences are just as visually rich and filled with horror, with the shadows of German expressionism falling across the film in subtle and less subtle ways. The gift of the flower echoes and reverses a similar gesture in the classic Paul Wegener film *The Golem* (Paul Boese, Wegener, 1920), in which a young woman steps forward and gives him a rose before running away in fear as the creature reaches out to touch her. In this earlier film, which Wegener codirected and scripted, he takes the title role of the Golem, a creature created from a sculpture to act as a servant to the Rabbi Löw (Albert Steinruck), who plans to use him to save the Jewish people. Based on a concept from Jewish scripture, the Golem is obviously similar to Frankenstein's monster, at once terrifying and innocent. Rex had seen and admired *The Golem* and had it in mind when he cast Wegener.

Yet the two productions are quite different. Where the expressionists created a cinematic world of dark shadows, engulfing mists, and off-kilter images as a way of conveying a sense of their characters' inner psychology, Rex had always done the opposite. His films were filled with detail that was intended to make the viewer feel that what they were watching was real, even if the film was set in other times and places, or if it was a fantasy, as *The Magician* was—hence his opening sequences with their documentary-like images of Paris and the later street views from Nice. Shooting with his customary attention to detail, Rex proceeded to deploy miniatures to make his fantasy sequences seem as real as his street scenes. The first full irruption of magic onto the screen is when Haddo hypnotizes Margaret and she falls into a trance. In her dream, as the screen turns red, the faun's head comes alive and metamorphoses into a grotesque Pan with pipes. The next shot takes us into a magical glade, filmed as if it were a voyage into a womb-like orifice, where seminaked and naked dancers caper around a bubbling witches' brew. Now the leering Pan seduces Margaret as she swoons in his arms, before suddenly waking in shock to find Haddo leering at her. Hubert Stowitts, former dance partner of Russian ballerina Anna Pavlova, played Pan with gusto, his body oiled so that he gleams in the light of the fire. Rex brought the wealthy young Fielding brothers, from the neighboring Chateau Fielding in Fabron, on set as fauns. The dance sequence was shot nights on set for nearly a month, using twenty young men and twenty young women, all according to Michael Powell "naked except for a few gauzy rosebuds."[18] The overall effect is an intense and heady sensuality.

The altered ending is another tour de force of horror that anticipates later Universal pictures of the early 1930s—*Dracula* (Tod Browning, 1931), *Frankenstein* (James Whale, 1931), *The Mummy* (Karl Freund, 1932)—whose makers borrowed liberally from Rex's film, particularly for their Gothic castles. Maugham's novel ends with Susie, Burdon, and Dr. Porhoët rushing to England, where Margaret has gone to live with Haddo as his wife. Burdon is convinced that something terrible has occurred and, sure enough, they find that Margaret has unexpectedly died of heart failure. They go to Haddo's strange castle, but he will reveal nothing to them. Recalling the ancient sorcery he has learned, Burdon summons the spirit of Margaret and, knowing now what has befallen her, is filled with the strength to kill Haddo. The threesome enter hidden chambers in the castle to find a room filled with Haddo's horrific experiments with life: glass cases of half-formed, breathing bodies, one of them, the most formed, screaming in eerie, gibberish tones and hurling itself against the walls of the case. They leave, and Burdon burns the castle to the ground.

In Rex's version, the castle is in France, where it is guarded (perhaps inevitably) by a grotesque hunchbacked dwarf. Rex cast the English dwarf Henry Wilson. "In the course of the climax to the film," Michael Powell observed, "he was soaked to the skin, rolled in mud and water, hurled off rocks, hung in chains and was finally blown up in the explosion that demolished the castle—all to his great satisfaction and Rex's sadistic amusement."[19] Now only Arthur Burdon and Dr. Porhoët go to the castle. Arthur runs up the twisted stone stairs to the magician's turret, where he finds Haddo about to slay Margaret so that he can obtain the heart blood of a virgin and thus create life. As a storm sends rain pouring down the window frames and lightning forks across the night sky, the crazed Haddo attacks Burdon and Dr. Porhoët. His chamber of horrors fills with smoke; the screen is momentarily bathed in a red tint. At last Arthur triumphs and rescues Margaret, leaving Dr. Porhoët behind him to burn the magician's recipe. He only leaves when he has set fire to the castle. The final sequence sees the dwarf suspended crazily from the burning remains of his master's home as Burdon walks off to a happy future with Margaret.

The US trade press was scathing: "Rex Ingram has turned out a very slow moving, draggy picture that has but a single thrill and that typical of the old days when the serials were the feature attractions of the average picture bills." The *Variety* critic continued his dismissal of the film by suggesting that Rex's decision to leave Hollywood had been his downfall and that this was a work with "too much of a Continental angle to appeal generally."[20] The French press, for its part, saw nothing Continental about the film, particularly when it came to the casting of France's own highly regarded Firmin Gémier: "As for Gémier, we suffer for him when we see him mixed up in this adventure. We think this great artist is capable of doing better than having wooden chairs thrown at his face, of riding wooden horses in the Fair of Trône or climbing on all fours up the stairs to the villain's lair."[21] Elsewhere the critics were warmer. When *The Magician* opened in Dublin the following year, the *Irish Times* critic found the film to be an "attractive picture," commending the acting of Paul Wegener and Alice Terry.[22]

As we have seen, having a "Continental angle" was a trademark feature of Rex's films right from his first scenarios. Now, living in Europe, he could realize his earliest ambitions and make European films, shot on location and using the great actors and performers of the European tradition. Maybe he was also recalling his childhood fear and pleasure in visiting the Darbys at Leap Castle, with its bloodstained walls and deathly cellars. Either way, the presence on screen and on set of actors such as Wegener and the Serbian Petrovich (who could be made over as a Latin lover type), as well as Stowitts, the theater director Firmin Gémier of the Comédie Française, and sculptor Paul Dardé, lend *The Magician* a real sense of European artistry, with only the rather overwrought plot as a reminder that this was essentially a Hollywood film, made and financed for a Hollywood studio. It is also a reminder of just how, when left on his own to write scenarios, Rex always tended toward melodrama.

Viewed now, *The Magician* is a stronger film than the reviews suggest. Its pacing is swift and its visual construction—the use of light, the tinting of certain sequences, and the Gothic interiors—more than compensate for the less inspiring performances from its leads. It is also a film that reflects its maker's own positioning—halfway between European art and American popular culture.

Endings

Metro had an option to buy the studios in Nice, but before Rex started on *The Magician*, they ceded this option to him on condition that he refund the company two-thirds of the cost of the renovations made by them. In August 1926 Rex returned to America for a visit and to consult with Marcus Loew about the future of the Victorine. Alice accompanied him, as she was to appear in her last film without Rex, John Stahl's *Lovers?* with Ramón Novarro. At this stage Rex was planning to make a start on *The World's Illusion* in September or October of that year.

While they were in America on 23 August, the country was rocked by the announcement of Valentino's death. The national and international outpouring of grief at this unexpected event and the behavior of distraught female fans on hearing of it are now well known. Rex and Alice were as shocked as everyone else. Loew promptly contacted Rex, asking him to be a pallbearer. Loew had heard that a life story was being rushed out, and he wanted in on the publicity. Rex was outraged at the idea of exploiting the event for publicity and assured Loew that he was leaving

America two days before the funeral.[23] Rex also told Alice that he was afraid Rudy would turn over during the procession if he was a pallbearer. "He also said other things but I won't repeat them," Alice told Liam O'Leary.[24] Capitalizing mercilessly on the demise of the world's most famous Latin lover, MGM rushed out a rerelease of *Four Horsemen* and *The Conquering Power*. Once again *Four Horsemen* enjoyed a hugely successful run (and considerable unexpected income for Rex). It also encountered an outraged German response, with the press calling for a boycott of MGM's entire output in Germany.[25]

Alice believed that Rex then paid around five million francs to become the owner of the studio.[26] The history of these transactions (of which more is mentioned below) is somewhat opaque and complicated by what would become a long-standing lawsuit between Rex and his French solicitor, Edouard Corniglion-Molinier. Because of the regulations regarding sales of French property to nonnationals, Corniglion-Molinier bought the Victorine in his name but with Rex's money. At the time, this seemed like a good plan. Later it was to prove otherwise.

Sadly, after *The Magician*, Rex and John Seitz's long working relationship came to an end. Even the dedicated Seitz tired of his director's imperious tendencies, nor did he believe that Rex should be involving himself with matters such as the ownership of the studios. "I do think that the damn studio was the cause of his downfall," Seitz later told author James Ursini. "He used to be very pro-French. He became very anti-French after that."[27] Matters came to a head when Rex changed hotels and Seitz refused to follow him. When the split finally came, Rex was at once furious and dismayed, telling his old friend and collaborator that he, Rex, would never do another good picture.[28]

As it turned out, Rex was not entirely wrong. Although his next picture did have its admirers, his work now began to slide increasingly out of control, with his love of visuals overwhelming often unstructured and dated plots. Seitz, on the other hand, continued successfully in Hollywood, where he lit one masterpiece after another. Howard Strickling left at around the same time, and Frank Scully took his place. "He had integrity and class," Strickling remembered later of Rex. "He wanted everything the best. He was very opinionated and was the producer and director of all his pictures. His word was law. The fact he was not a 'yes man' no doubt caused some people not to admire him as much as they might have. Although all respected him as a man and as a fine artist."[29] Grant and Ota Whytock too went home, and Grant was replaced by another American, Arthur Ellis.

Others added themselves to Rex's entourage, not all equally welcome. The Fieldings were a case in point. Although the brothers acted in *The Magician* and Rex's two next films, Rex confided to Frank that he didn't care for them. He was particularly fed up, he said, when Gerald came to stay in California with them for a long time.[30] Whether this was because Gerald was, according to Anthony Slide, Alice's lover, it is hard to know, particularly when rumors suggested that he was homosexual.[31] Nor, in the home movie footage, do they look anything but amicable. Rex himself was almost certainly having an affair with Rosita Garcia at this time.[32] After her debut in *Where the Pavement Ends,* she rejoined him and Alice in France, taking minor parts in *Mare Nostrum* and *The Magician,* with a more central role in Rex's final film, *Baroud.* Alice meanwhile was sharing an apartment with her sister, Edna. Without anything much in the way of proof, it seems that while Rex allowed himself affairs, however passionate or otherwise they really were, he did not approve of Alice following suit. It was an idiosyncratic moral code, a sort of attenuated liberalism shot through with Victorian prudery. Otherwise, he spent his time on the sculpture that was to become his best-known piece, a pietà of Christ held in the arms of Buddha.

The Garden of Allah (1927)

Rex's next production returned him to the North African locations he so loved and another adaptation. It also brought him back to his childhood, for his new film was based on the book that Sophie Rosa had given him in Kinnitty and that had first ignited his desire to travel to North Africa— Robert Smythe Hichens's *The Garden of Allah.* Colin Campbell had been the first to film Hichens's novel, in 1916 with Helen Ware in the leading role, and it would be filmed again in 1936 by Richard Boleslavsky, with Marlene Dietrich and Charles Boyer. Hichens always maintained that it was Rex's version that he preferred.[33]

The story concerns a young Trappist monk, Father Adrien (Iván Petrovich), who one day, while clearing a tree from his monastery in Algeria, accidentally knocks a young girl unconscious. Tempted by her beauty, he gives in to his desires and embraces her as she returns to consciousness. His actions are reported to the order, and he is forced to do penance. But the call of the world lures him from his monastery. Putting aside his vows of silence, poverty, and celibacy, he reverts to his real name, Androvsky, and sets off into the desert. In Beni-Mora he meets a beautiful English girl, Domini (Alice Terry), a devout Christian, and marries her without telling her about his past. They spend their honeymoon in the desert, but one night a storm brews, and the new wife is lost in the sands. Androvsky turns to God, promising to atone if Domini is found. When this does indeed happen, he returns to the monastery and resumes his vows.

Willis Goldbeck wrote the scenario, and Rex hired Lee Garmes as cinematographer. Garmes had worked in the industry nearly as long as Rex but was still only at the beginning of a long and celebrated career behind the camera. Rex's instructions to him were to light the set like Seitz did, advice that cannot have added to Garmes's confidence. Still, he rose to the challenge of filming in North Africa, rigging up a camera on ropes and pulleys mounted on an old Ford chassis for shots of Arabs praying and introducing Rex to some of the newer innovations from Hollywood.[34] At least when it came to shooting the interiors and the sandstorms, they stayed in France, with the crew churning up sawdust with rows of airplane propellers to create the desired effect. Garmes in turn became a convert to Seitz's "north light" principals: "It was so honest and so real that I decided to follow that for the rest of my career. It's a very simple type of lighting, not difficult to do. You can work fast with it. It's *real*. It's more honest than most of the other lighting is, so I just stuck with it."[35] He also appreciated working with Rex and the sense of family that the unit retained, even after the departure of so many of its members.

In January 1927 the shoot moved to Algiers, to the Trappist monastery of Staoueli, and Hichens, who lived in North Africa during the winter, visited them there. After completing their scenes, the actors returned to Nice, and Alice and her sister went back to New York. The crew continued by bus to Bou Saâda, where Rex had already spent time on the shoot of *The Arab*, to film exteriors. They had to break there, as Rex was ill. While he was recovering, Rex invited Étienne Dinet to eat with them. Dinet was shocked when they told him how films were made, about the money spent, and the fakery behind scene constructions. How could true artists survive, he asked himself, when such practices were commonplace?[36] They also returned to Biskra, another of the locations for *The Arab*. Conditions were trying, the climate was a challenge, and distances long (Biskra was fourteen hours by train from Algiers).

Increasingly the old Ingram collaborators were looking to extricate themselves from a project that had become impossibly personal. As Rex read the Koran and found his ideal world in the sands of North Africa, so his attention to the requirements of Hollywood filmmaking steadily diminished. The creation of plot-driven narratives now finally fell victim to his desire to create vast moving canvases filled with North African life. His films were still going to be works of art, but as entertainment they were falling apart. If he perhaps had chosen to make straightforward documentaries or travelogues, Rex might have found an audience, but he seemed quite indifferent to market requirements, even when it was blatantly obvious that desert pictures were out of fashion.

Harry Lachman was the next to feel the need to move on. Frank Scully had proposed to him that they film a series of two-reel comedies called *Travelaughs.* The idea was, as Michael Powell remembered, "to fill a coach with a bunch of funny-looking tourists, most of them borrowed or stolen from Rex's current productions, and run them around the Riviera (which was always good for quaint hilltowns, the Monte Carlo Casino and bathing girls) and involve them in adventures and escapades."[37] Stills from *The Garden of Allah* show Powell in his role of a comic tourist in this film, and Lachman capitalized on his readiness to try his hand at anything to have him repeat his role, often with hair-raising stunts, in their two first films. Taking advantage of their North African location shooting, the group made a quick two-reeler called *Camels to Cannibals,* featuring the young Englishman: "I now remember that I ended up blacked all over, dressed in a grass skirt, a solar topee and an Eton collar, assisted by Shorty, Rex's jester, as an amiable baby gorilla."[38] Their second production was *Algerian Adventures.* After the *Garden of Allah* shoot was over, Lachman resigned as general manager and headed up a new company that was building studios at Saint-André in Nice. Powell returned to England, where he would eventually become one of the greatest of his country's directors and where he would pursue a commitment to film as art with the same passion, and many of the same consequences, as his gifted, obstinate, visionary mentor.

When the company returned to France, columnist Gladys Hall traveled to Nice to write a feature on Rex and Alice at the Victorine. Bumping into Rex at her hotel, she was shocked at how ill he looked. He'd been "beastly ill" in Africa, he told her, and had lost twenty pounds.[39] As she strolled around the Victorine with Alice and Moreno's wife, Daisy, Hall noticed that it was Alice who was taking care of much of the business, signing checks and dealing with invoices. Next she encountered Rex's father, who was on a visit, and who laughed over his son:

> "I always knew he'd be great at something . . . a genius the boy was . . . I'd quote Shakespeare to him by the hour . . . when he was three . . . brought him up on it . . . and the Bible . . . I'll tell you something, he wasn't much good at mathematics . . . but he was a good boy . . . he always had a great personality."
>
> From Rex, detachedly, "There was never money in the collection box at our house . . . I'd stolen it all . . . "
>
> From his father . . . "Hear him now! That boy's the worst liar in captivity . . . now you can't believe one word he says . . . not one word."[40]

In the villa they come across Rex's sculpture of Christ in the arms of Buddha. His father doesn't like it: "'I hope he never finishes it.'" An argument breaks out about the role of missionaries, with all present siding against the Reverend Hitchcock. He was, Hall observed, "mighty and ecclesiastic and terrifically impressive in his dogmatic faiths, his ironclad, unshakeable beliefs. He shakes his head at his changeling, adorable son. . . . Yet we wonder whether some of Rex's atheism—or is it agnosticism?—may not have come as a reaction, from the very fundamentalism, the very rock-bound rigor of the elder man's beliefs."[41]

When the visitors wonder aloud about Shorty's appearance, the fundamentalism rises to the surface: "'The sins of the fathers . . . '" is the Reverend's reply:

> "But that isn't fair."
>
> "It's God's way . . . "
>
> "Anyway," says Rex, his face buried in Alice's bright hair, "anyway, he's happy . . . he lives for money . . . he's rich and respected among his own people . . . he's happy, that's the main thing."[42]

Not only was Shorty still part of the entourage, but so was an exotic dancer, whose divorce from her Arab husband Rex had just organized on the basis that when she returned home with the money, he would remarry her. Although here she is referred to as "Rabat," the film's credits list her as

"Rehba," and one may guess that this is the same dancer that Rex "acquired" shooting *The Arab*.

Driving away, Gladys Hall mused on her impressions: "Alice, whole-some and sane . . . lovable and loving . . . Rex, indolent and vital and whimsical and perverse . . . and Irish . . . Rex's father, powerful and impressive and reactionary."[43]

According to Liam O'Leary, in March 1927 when Alfred Hitchcock was in Nice, he and Rex met. Rex proffered some advice to the younger man: "You'll never get anywhere with a name like that."[44] Apocryphal or otherwise, it makes for a good story. Another event that might have been equally apocryphal were it not for the material evidence to back it up was the making of Ralph Barton's four-reel home movie version of *Camille*. He shot on 16 mm film, mostly indoors, with scenes taking place in Paris, Salzburg, and New York's Central Park. "We never took it too seriously," he said, "and didn't bother much about costumes and scenery, simply taking a show whenever people were at the house and the mood was on."[45] By now, the caricaturist was famous—not just for his *New Yorker* sketches, but equally for the illustrations he undertook to accompany the publication of his friend Anita Loos's *Gentlemen Prefer Blondes*, which had come out in book form in 1925. Loos returned the favor by writing the screenplay, such as there was, of *Camille*. Barton's famous friends featured prominently, caught on camera as they dropped in to his studios. In the finished version, the Lady of the Camillias has two faces—the good one played by Anita Loos and the bad by Fania Marinoff, Carl von Hechten's wife. Paul Robeson plays the author Alexandre Dumas fils, Charlie Chaplin appears on several occasions, and Somerset Maugham, the Sultan of Morocco (an unwitting participant), George Gershwin, and many other well-known figures feature in an almost plotless rendition of the familiar story. Rex, for no evident reason, makes a quick entry, grimacing horribly to camera, and is credited as "Charles Stewart Parnell" (the nineteenth-century Irish nationalist). He looks like he was having fun. Ralph Barton completed this tour de force in April 1927.

When MGM saw the print of Rex's latest film, they hurriedly reedited it so that it was transformed from a meditative reflection on spiritual values to a kind of exotic suspense melodrama. As Paul Kozak recounts, fortunately Grant Whytock and Willis Goldbeck saw the reedited version at a studio

screening and wired Rex. He in turn invoked the clause in his contract that guaranteed him final cut on his films. Metro backed down.[46]

The Garden of Allah received its New York premiere on 2 September 1927. The *New York Times* was little impressed. By now, the reviewer suggested, audiences were familiar with the romance of the desert and its violent sandstorms: "So many desert stories have been produced in the last few years that this subject has been robbed of much of its original glamour and drama. In the old days of pictures sandstorms were something dramatic, but at present it is just another gust of wind passing over the desert." Even more pertinently, the critic found the acting stiff, bemoaned Alice Terry's inevitable blonde wig, and found Iván Petrovich "frequently guilty of artificial actions and expressions." Nor were Rex's sense of humor and his uncomfortable moments of comedy to their taste. In fact, all that was to the *New York Times*'s taste was the director's pictorial sensibility.[47]

The *Los Angeles Times* was somewhat more favorably disposed to Rex's visual achievement but in full agreement as to the merits, or otherwise, of the screenplay, commenting that "it is a superbly photographed travelogue of the desert, long on beauty but short on drama."[48] Other critics echoed these opinions, agreeing that the film was beautiful to look at but otherwise dull. The *Los Angeles Times* critic did notice that Rex was unusually sympathetic to the Arabs: "The fact alone that the Arabs do not revolt is greatly to the credit of the director who is an idealist always."[49] In New York the Irish societies held a meeting at Carnegie Hall, which they followed with a public denunciation on the grounds that it was "a film in which a Catholic monk is represented as a sensual and sacrilegious weakling, faithless to his vows."[50] In Ireland the censor banned the film for similar reasons, a decision reversed on appeal.[51]

The split with MGM finally came in the summer of 1927 on the completion of *The Garden of Allah*. As long as he had been making films financed by MGM in Nice, Rex had refused to put Louis B. Mayer's name on his credits. The mogul's attempted interference in his latest film now drove him to fury. The ensuing clash of two strong wills saw neither man back down. With the death of Marcus Loew, there was no one to intervene on Rex's behalf. Howard Strickling dearly wished to reunite both men, but neither would make the first move. As Scott Eyman writes, "The fact that Ingram was a prestigious filmmaker whose films didn't really cost the company anything meant little to L.B. Ingram had made it personal."[52]

According to figures supplied by Rex to the *Daily Express, Mare Nostrum* cost £120,000 and had so far realized £400,000, *The Magician* doubled the cost of its production in profit, and *The Garden of Allah* cost just over £80,000 to make.[53] He was still under contract to make *The World's Illusion*, and Mayer was insisting that he return to California, where he could be supervised, to shoot it. Rex refused. Mayer reminded him that under the terms of his contract, if he did not make this film, he could make no other for a year. Rex responded that he would be only too delighted to comply with that stipulation. As he and Alice agreed, he needed a rest. And with that his career at MGM ended.

Travels through North Africa

For the next year, Rex did his best to forget the cinema. At first it was difficult, as his villa in the grounds meant that he kept bumping into the film companies to whom he had rented the studios: "But when I fixed myself up a sculptor's studio where the garage had been, I got down to work. I had never worked harder or with greater satisfaction than I did during the next few months. I kept two or three jobs going at the same time which kept my interest in any one of them from flagging. After that, excepting some stone-cutting jobs, I kept the *fondeurs* in Paris, Rudier and Valsuain, busy for another six months casting my models in bronze."[54]

When the last bronze casting had been shipped to Nice, Rex headed for Marseille and thence by ship to Algiers. After a couple of months in the *bled* (the tribal regions of the Sahara), he went to Morocco, stopping off in Oudja to visit old friends. He met with Gen. Georges Catroux, who was then in command of the Marrakech division of the French army, and reacquainted himself with Gen. Antoine Huré, who was commander in chief of the forces in Morocco. They gave him passes to Cuarzazat and Telouet in the Atlas Mountains. They would permit him to travel no farther, they assured him, because many of the more distant regions were in revolt. But Rex wanted to move on, to the casbahs of Ait-ben-Haddon, Skoura, and Tarudant.

Rex started on his journey with a letter from his friend Marshal Hubert Lyautey, who had served as resident-general of Morocco from 1912 to 1925, in his pocket. When he arrived in Marrakech, another friend, Pasha Si-Thami el Glaoui, gave him a letter of introduction to his son-in-law Si-Hamou, the *caid* of Telouet, instructing him to put his casbah, his mules, and his guides at Rex's disposal. He was also to notify the sheiks at the other towns Rex wished to visit so that he would be guaranteed safe passage. Setting off with his driver, Rex skidded along perilous roads whose dusty surfaces had been turned treacherous with rain. To each side, there were drops of a couple of thousand feet or more. The driver refused to slow down for the bends. Miraculously they reached Telouet unharmed, and there Si-Hamou laid on a display of two hundred dancing girls for Rex's entertainment. They sat down to a feast of baked partridge, smothered in a heavy aromatic sauce, couscous garnished with peppers, raisins, and the yolks of hard-boiled eggs, and in the light of the fire the girls danced for Rex and the *caid*.

The next morning they were up at four o'clock and pressing on for Animeter. Rex spent the day there and in the outlying casbahs of Ounilla, taking photographs. In return for the hospitality he received, he gifted the sheik a thermos flask and demonstrated to him how to use it. He continued on, listening to the Arabs' stories and hearing of their devotion to Marshal Lyautey, one of the few Westerners they genuinely admired. He returned to Nice via Paris and visited Lyautey, who showed him his designs for his tomb, which was to be decorated in Algerian style.

Rex traveled once more to southern Morocco, taking a route through Spain that led him through Murcia, Granada, and Ronda so that he could watch the bullfighting. He was drafting a novel about a bullfighter, with an old minotaur as his central character. Later this would become his second novel, *Mars in the House of Death*, but for now he had to lay it aside. The enforced year's respite from filmmaking had been a delight, filling his imagination with encounters and images that he would spend the rest of his life converting into stories. But, for the moment, Rex was still a filmmaker, with a studio to keep running. He set sail for France and his return to the camera.

10

Final Films

On 13 January 1928, *Tit Bits* carried what was ostensibly a syndicated interview with Rex under the title "Famous Director to Make No More Films." The headline proceeded to quote him as saying "I am sick of Hollywood" before announcing "my reason for turning Mohammedan." On Hollywood, Rex was purported to have said, "Neither God nor Allah is accepted in the homes in Hollywood—they walk there, but are not received; for there the devil reigns paramount." The article also suggested that Rex and Alice's marriage was in trouble, not least because as a "Mohammedan," after he went to Paradise he would be able to enjoy eighty thousand servants and seventy-two wives in addition to those he had before he died.

Rex immediately sued, countering that he was happily married and that far from being sick of Hollywood, it was the place where most of his income was earned, and he confidently hoped to make a great many more films. After a London court hearing on 31 January, *Tit Bits* apologized, and Rex received a settlement that he donated to charity.[1]

How close *Tit Bits* had come to the truth of Rex's inclinations is hard to gauge. Evidently what they published was proven libelous. Yet, as many must have known, Rex was becoming increasingly dogmatic in his beliefs and increasingly convinced that Western culture was being destroyed by capitalism. His refusal to kowtow to Louis B. Mayer or recognize the authority of MGM had made him powerful enemies and placed him outside the most influential filmmaking system in the world. Ironically, he was now quite free to release himself from his Hollywood commitments because of the money Hollywood had enabled him to make and invest, much of it in art and North African artifacts. But he insisted that he was still a filmmaker, and he was certainly planning to remain one. He had not—yet—converted to Islam.

After his enforced idleness, Rex decided to stay on in Nice and run the studio himself. Edouard Corniglion-Molinier became president, with Frank Scully as vice president. Free at last from MGM, what kind of films would Rex now make? The answer was disappointing.

The Three Passions (1928)

One of the reasons for Rex's dismay at the *Tit Bits* article was that in January 1928 he was in the process of signing a contract with Louis Blattner of International Distribution Trust to make a new film, *The Three Passions.* Blattner in turn agreed with United Artists to have the film distributed in the United States. The German-born Blattner was based in England and had already optioned Lion Feuchtwanger's *Jew Süss,* though he would not live to make it. Under the terms of the 1927 Cinematograph Films Act, he was able to claim that *The Three Passions* was a "quota" film. In other words, it was made to satisfy the regulations on the quota of British films that must be released and exhibited in Britain, thus guaranteeing it British and Commonwealth distribution. It was shot as a silent picture but with a synchronized soundtrack that meant that it played, in cinemas equipped with the appropriate equipment, with a score and sound effects. Indeed, it was as a result of his experiments with sound that Blattner was best known, particularly for his "Blattnerphone," designed to reproduce recorded sound to broadcast quality. Synchronized sound was a technological step forward for Rex and the production crew at the Victorine, but by the time *The Three Passions* was in cinemas, in May 1929, American audiences already expected more. The release of *The Jazz Singer* in October 1927 now officially marks the transition to sound filmmaking, and technology had marched swiftly onward from there, with audible dialogue soon becoming the standard. A measure of just how dated Rex's film was on its release is that *The Three Passions* was one of only two silent films to be distributed by United Artists in 1928–1929.

The story was an old-fashioned morality tale of the perils of venality that might not have gone amiss in one of Reverend Hitchcock's sermons. The three passions of the title are wealth, religion, and love. Philip (Iván Petrovich), the son of the shipyard owner Lord Bellamont (Shayle Gardner), grows disgusted with his father's pursuit of money and in an act of revulsion joins an Anglican monastery, where he takes up work in a seaman's mission, putting behind him both his father's wealth and the love of his fiancée, Lady Victoria Burlington (Alice Terry). She determines to lure him back to the world and joins him in his work.

As Rex prepared for his new film, an old friend contacted him. Col. Ben Finney, according to Charles Higham and Roy Moseley, was the heir to a Virginia fortune.[2] In the late 1920s he was killing time in Calcutta waiting to go big-game hunting when he was introduced to a local Anglo-Indian beauty. They saw each other every night for a week and, after one such evening out, as he accompanied her home, he noticed a light on. He took her to her door to be greeted by a very dark-skinned woman whom his companion was anxious to hide from view. Later Merle Oberon would eradicate all traces of her past from her life story and reinvent herself as Tasmanian. But for now, one glimpse of Merle's mother, Charlotte, was enough to send the big-game hunter running scared. He extricated himself promptly from the relationship, throwing a parting promise over his shoulder. If Merle could make her way to the South of France, he would introduce her to his friend, Rex Ingram. He hardly expected to have to honor his promise. Merle did, however, raise the money for her passage, probably from her lover, Victor Sassoon, and arrived with her mother on Finney's doorstep in Antibes. Finney panicked and fled for the second time, only pausing to beg Rex to give his unwanted Anglo-Indian guest an audition. Luckily for Merle, the exotic background that so repelled her lover delighted Rex, and he promptly cast her as an extra in a party scene he was shooting. And so Merle Oberon gained her entree into the pictures as an uncredited extra in *The Three Passions* and remained grateful to Rex to the end of her career.

One of the more intriguing visitors to the set of *The Three Passions* was the venerable Irish playwright George Bernard Shaw, who was staying at the Cap d'Antibes. He and Rex began to toss around the idea of turning Shaw's *Arms and the Man* into a film. According to Harpo Marx, who accompanied Shaw on one of these visits: "We only wanted to watch the shooting for a while, but Ingraham [*sic*] had other ideas. He shanghaied us and put us to work as extras. In our one and only joint appearance before the camera, George Bernard Shaw and I shot pocket billiards in a poolroom scene."[3] It's an attractive image—the stately, bearded Irishman and the small, live-wire American comedian captured shooting billiards in a minor Rex Ingram film—but Alice later told Liam O'Leary that she had no recollection of this ever taking place, nor did her sister, Edna, who was around at the time of the filming.[4] No such scene appears in the completed film.

Also on set for *The Three Passions* were Rex's father and brother, Frank. The latter watched in fascination as his brother meticulously rehearsed each scene. In one, a woman falls to her knees as she sees the body of her husband, who has lost his life in a factory accident, laid out on a stretcher. Rex went down on his knees and showed her how to play the scene, doing it over and over again with her until it was perfect and she was performing it exactly as he told her. Frank was on leave from the army and helped Rex with another scene. In it Leslie Faber portrays Father Aloysius as a man who has forsaken arms for religion. His room is furnished with lances, a shrapnel helmet and military medals. Frank had scoured the secondhand shops of Nice, picking up lances and medals and other appropriate artifacts for the scene. When Rex saw it, he added a crucifix.

Rex's father found some of Rex's new ideas on religion quite unpalatable and did not hesitate to say so. He was constantly outraged at the sight that greeted him every time he walked into the villa at the Victorine of his son's sculpture of Buddha cradling the crucified Christ. Frank, the society columnist Jean Norton, observed, was the opposite of his brother, a fervent "pro-Britisher." To hear the two brothers discussing a subject, she continued, "is to listen to a feast of assorted eloquence."[5]

The Three Passions is, as ever, full of visual treasures. Rex had added the great French cinematographer Léonce Henri (L. H.) Burel to his payroll, sending him to Oxford and London for exterior shooting and around the shipyards of Europe and England so that the factory sets could be constructed with accuracy. The opening sequences, as a result, are striking, with the machinery looming over the workers, at once beautiful and threatening, a look not unlike the new cinema that Sergei Eisenstein and others were creating to celebrate Soviet life. Another delight is the interior of the nightclub where Philip takes Lady Victoria dancing. The walls are covered in vast murals of outsized fruit and exotic motifs, and the ground is patterned in black, painted lines that radiate outward, meeting swirls and semicircles as they run across the floor. No doubt, when played with synchronized sound, these scenes were striking. Burel also helped Rex with Cosmo Hamilton's scenario (which the author subsequently turned into a novel).

Petrovich is handsome, but his part is one-dimensional, and Alice, despite the addition of an elegant cigarette holder, somewhat less than convincing as a femme fatale. In any case their thunder is stolen by the interplay between Shayle Gardner and Clare Eames as his openly and unashamedly adulterous spouse. In one sequence Gardner marches into his wife's bedroom and hurls her lover down the stairs, admonishing her that she is running late for dinner. She responds with the glacial expression of dismissiveness with which she typically treats her arriviste husband. Had the story revolved around them, it might have unfurled with considerably more originality than it does: Lord Bellamont suffers a heart attack as his workers strike, and Philip abandons the mission to take over the factory and settle matters with the strikers. In the scenes in the mission, the relics of the old Ingram world of grotesques and carousers suddenly reappear. The men are misshapen and leering drunks; one threatens Alice in a sequence that seems little interested in arousing pity for society's underdogs and more in demonstrating their instability. In the end the social message counts for little, the love affair is less than convincing, and the photography is forced to carry the film.

The reception was predictable. The *Los Angeles Times* found the film to be a dim shadow of Rex's former glory: "One can scarcely believe in either the reality of what happens, or the delineation of the characters." Only its pictorial qualities were to be recommended as bearing the unmistakable stamp of an Ingram picture.[6] Other papers agreed, with the *Variety* critic advising that "this hokey-pokey wouldn't have meant anything before the talkers and that tells what it's worth now."[7]

The failure of *The Three Passions* was telling. It marked Rex's official break with MGM and his debut as an independent filmmaker. Yet, as so many others were to discover, losing the structure of the studio system, with its regime of control, was not always the catalyst for the future greatness that they had imagined. Even with distribution by United Artists, Rex was fundamentally on his own. He was also out of touch with developments in the art form he had helped to shape, as indeed was Alice, whose performance style—all melodramatic gestures and widened eyes—now looked lamentably old-fashioned. Neither seemed interested in exploring the possibilities of the European art film or developing a new style. The moment had arrived, Alice instead decided, to call an end to her career as a film star. She had never enjoyed it much anyway: "I was always the ingénue, that misunderstood everything, who always had to have an argument, so stupid. . . . With me pictures were just a matter of getting through the day, getting it over with, and I would see a script and look ahead and see that it was going to take a month and I would say 'Oh God,' I would think 'can I stand this' and suddenly the month would be over and the horror was past and I would say 'I hope I don't have to do another one,' but there always seemed to be another until you finally say no."[8]

It seems at this juncture that Rex was facing in two radically different directions. On the one hand, he was increasingly attracted to Islam and the religious beliefs, as well as the way of life, of North Africa. He was studying the Koran and learning Arabic. His villa in Nice was filled with North African hangings and Orientalist art. His sculptures, his conversations, his readings were all leaning toward a quite different view of the world from that of his upbringing. Yet he was committed to a demanding commercial enterprise—running a film studio. To attract visiting productions and to continue to make his own films, he would have to invest seriously in the Victorine, both financially and in terms of personnel. He also urgently needed to make an effort to catch up with new developments in filmmaking.

T. E. Lawrence

Of all the films that Rex might have made at this moment, one was the most obvious. Rex was one of the thirty original subscribers to the early limited edition of T. E. Lawrence's *The Seven Pillars of Wisdom,* but when his copy didn't arrive, he wrote to Lawrence to let him know. Lawrence had no copies of his own left and sent a letter back to Rex: "'I don't think much of it myself as a bit of writing,' he wrote, 'I find writing very uncongenial: and work done so much against the grain doesn't feel happy. So I suggest that you won't miss much.'"[9] Rex was not to be put off and sent another letter to Lawrence, again enclosing a check for thirty guineas but, having read that the explorer and military man was interested in sculpture, accompanied it this time with some photographs of his own sculptures. He labeled each one so that Lawrence would know what they were.

"I like your sculpture," Lawrence wrote back, "and so I must try and get you a copy of my book. Not that it's really a kindness, for the book is no good: but it's the best I can do. My efforts at sculpture, years ago, before the war, were failures also. It's a bore, when you want very much to do something, to find yourself falling down the whole time in the technique of expression. You seem to be fortunate in the direct—sculpture—and in the indirect—the films."[10] In the end Rex accidentally received two copies, returning one to Lawrence's trustee, Professor D. G. Hogarth at Oxford.

He wrote to Lawrence to tell him how much he enjoyed *Seven Pillars*. Lawrence replied, and in a gesture that was well-intended but impractical, Rex dashed off a letter of gratitude to Lawrence suggesting that the military man might like a gift of a bookshelf of books. Lawrence was posted with the RAF in Karachi at the time and politely declined the offer on the grounds that he would have nowhere to put such a bookshelf and wasn't, in any case, much inclined toward possessions. He explained that he was happy not to be writing anymore. He moved camp every two years, and thus possessions were hard to keep, and he had to conceal his few books in his kit box. He was less happy in Karachi than in North Africa: "India makes me homesick for it is a shoddy-feeling place. The people seem ashamed of us, and I feel ashamed of myself before them. The Arabs appealed to me because they had complete self-respect, and no sense of being inferior to the English. That pleases me, for I am Irish too, more or less."[11]

Rex was gripped by Lawrence's story and inquired if Lawrence perhaps had a portrait of Talall (El-Hareidhin of Tafa). He hinted at the question that was closest to his heart: had he ever thought of making a film based on *Seven Pillars*? Referring to the 1927 title of *Seven Pillars*, Lawrence's response was not encouraging: "I do not envy you your film job. It must be a very difficult art, an expression of yourself (and of the author) at two removes. Indeed I wonder if it is even as good as it seems to be. They babble sometimes to me of making a film of 'Revolt in the Desert.' I have no property in it, so I hope they will not. Hollywood offered £6,000 or something, which the trustees turned down. I'd hate to see myself parodied on the basis of my record of what the fellows with me did."[12] Rex concluded that the last sentence was a reply to some army officers he had run across in Suez, who told him that Lawrence was a publicity hound, always being photographed in Arab dress. Rex had defended Lawrence, blaming the journalist Lowell Thomas for the photographs.

Rex now lent his copy of the book to the young British producer/director Victor Saville, who had rented space in the Victorine studios to shoot the war film *Roses of Picardy* (directed by Maurice Elvey). Saville liked to film in the South of France in winter and was delighted to hear that the picturesque village created for *The Magician* had been left intact. Saville relates that he suggested to Rex that *The Seven Pillars of Wisdom* would make a great film, but the latter was convinced that Lawrence would not publish the book commercially, let alone film it.[13] Victor Saville was also friendly with the British producer/director Herbert Wilcox—both men had started in the film business as salesmen—and it may have been through him or just by chance that another version of Lawrence's story nearly came about. Wilcox met with Lawrence, apparently at the behest of the latter's agent. He was unimpressed with the military man, whom he described as "slight and short, about 5 ft. 3 ins. at the most and not very prepossessing."[14] Wilcox's aversion to Lawrence was prompted not least by homophobia; at their meeting, Lawrence outlined his work to the producer, who adjudged it "not good cinema and in spots rather sordid."[15] Of course, time was to prove Wilcox to be very far off the mark in his dismissal of Lawrence's writings. In 1962 David Lean, the British director and lifelong admirer of Rex's cinema, made *Lawrence of Arabia,* a film that is everything and more that Rex would have loved.

In 1928 Rex was prompted to write to *Photoplay* to deny rumors that he and Alice were to separate. "Won't that rumor ever die?" he complained.[16] In that year too he gave an unusually long interview to the *Theatre Review,* looking back on his career and influences. The two most important films of the last two decades, he said, were D. W. Griffith's *Intolerance* (1916) and Charlie Chaplin's *A Woman of Paris* (1923). Other key films from this period were Robert Wiene's *The Cabinet of Dr. Caligari* and Robert Flaherty's *Nanook of the North.* It was the realism of the latter, he said, that inspired his filmmaking, particularly when it came to shooting on location in North Africa: "That is, perhaps, the underlying reason why I am over here, working always in the actual setting of my stories, surrounding principal players with actual characters, rather than made-up supernumeraries. Getting, if necessary, a caravan of Mehris [Meharis], the fleet-footed white camels of the Sahara, when my scene calls for it, instead of renting a dozen lumbering Asiatic two-humped dromedaries from the Selig zoo as a makeshift."[17]

In 1929 it was reported that husband and wife would be commencing work on the first of six "talkies" to be made by Rex Ingram Productions, a film called *Rio Grande,* which Rex would direct with Alice as his star.[18] Nothing came of this, and the only production that Rex did involve himself in that year was to supervise Henri Ménessier's *L'evadée,* an adaption of *The Blue Dahlia,* in which Gerald Fielding acted. Rumors of other productions followed. Publicly Rex embraced the new opportunities of sound technology, though for reasons that were characteristically idiosyncratic:

"I welcome talking films for many reasons," he told a press conference in London. "As a director, it means the happy extinction of beautiful, but dumb stars, whose handling by the director is nerve-racking. Intelligence is going to count at last."[19]

More rumors circulated. Rex was alleged to be working on the sound production of André Berthomieu's film *Broadcasting* (1929).[20] In 1930 Robert Kane was said to have hired Rex to direct for Paramount Pictures at the Joinville Studios. His first film was to be *Le dieu de la mer* (The God of the Sea).[21] Meanwhile, the Victorine was kept ticking over financially through the rental of its space to visiting productions.

In 1931 Rex's old friend Ralph Barton made the headlines for the last time. Around midnight on 19 May, he typed a farewell letter in red ink, which he labeled "OBIT," addressed a short note to his maid (including with it thirty-five dollars), laid a copy of *Grey's Anatomy* on his bed open at the section illustrating the human heart, retired for the night in his silk pajamas, smoked briefly, and then shot himself through the head.

Baroud / Love in Morocco (1933)

Rex had one more film left to make. In 1926 he had invited the French star Pierre Batcheff to Nice.[22] Born Benjamin Batcheff in Harbin, Manchuria, on the border with Russia, the young man came from a privileged Russian-Estonian family that had lost its fortune in the revolution. When he, his mother, sister, and aunt moved without his father to Paris, Batcheff took up acting in an attempt to support them. His debut was on stage, but his real ambition was to appear in cinema. His good looks (startlingly like Novarro's) ensured that he was noticed by a director on the hunt for a young performer.

In 1924 Batcheff appeared in the role of the younger lover in *Claudine et la poussin* (American title *Baby Boy*), directed by Marcel Manchez. The film was a critical success in France and established Batcheff as a star in the making. In 1927 he appeared in Abel Gance's epic, *Napoléon,* playing General Hoche. By this time he had met a formative figure in his private life, Denise Piazza (later Tual). Already married to the antiques dealer Camoin, she became Batcheff's lover and mentor and introduced him to her circle of avant-garde and surrealist friends. Recognizing his beauty and moody talent, she shared his contempt for mainstream filmmaking, which both agreed was filled with vulgar people. When Batcheff received an invitation from Rex to come to Nice in September 1926 to discuss a role in his upcoming film, it might have been expected that the couple would respond well to a director who had made his name as a pictorialist. But Rex's work was too commercial, it seemed, and, besides, he had Batcheff in mind for another of his Latin lover types. Piazza accompanied Batcheff to Nice, a first visit for her, and found a picture-postcard setting: "On sea-front terraces lit up by restaurants, Corsicans with the voice of Tino Rossi sang *Sole mio,* accompanying themselves on guitar. . . . Moonlight and mimosas. A romantic cliché, but one I was living without a concern, at the side of an exceptional individual."[23] Hearing that Rex planned to cast Batcheff as a Berber in an American film that would make him a celebrity across the Atlantic, the exceptional individual and Piazza burst into laughter. The idea of it! Besides, Batcheff intended to quit acting for direction.

Batcheff went on to star with Josephine Baker in *Siren of the Tropics* (Mario Nalpas and Henri Étiévant, 1927), an experience that only underlined his impression of the vulgarity of mainstream filmmaking. By 1928 the young Frenchman had reached the peak of his stardom, but now an opportunity came his way that he relished and that was to make his name in a more enduring manner than in any of his conventional appearances— as the star of Louis Buñuel and Salvador Dali's *Un chien andalou.* The film needs little introduction, having gone on to become a landmark in surrealist cinema. With his reputation in the ascendant and his entrée into surrealist circles guaranteed, Batcheff redoubled his efforts to become a director. At the same time, he threw himself into projects designed to satisfy his social conscience, including organizing film screenings for prisoners and the mentally ill. Time and again, the projects as director fell apart and Batcheff's own health began to suffer. Piazza recommended he change his medicine. He refused and instead, for some reason best known to himself, Batcheff now contacted Rex and asked him if the offer to appear in one of his films was still on the table. Rex, in Piazza's words, "pounced like a tiger on his prey" and cast the young man as Si Hamed in his next project, *Baroud.*[24]

Once again Rex had found a star with Latin lover looks. Once again, he was making a desert film. Ten years previously, this would have guaranteed him funding and accolades. Now it suggested little more than a reluctance to move with the times. Rex found a financier in Mansfield Markham, an aristocratic British producer/director. The screenplay he wrote in conjunction with the Franco-German writer Benno Vigny. The latter had recently published *Amy Jolly, the Woman from Marrakesh* (*Amy Jolly, die Frau aus Marrakesch*), which was the basis for Josef von Sternberg's *Morocco* (1930), starring Marlene Dietrich, and was presumably why Rex hired him. *Baroud* tells of a Frenchman (André Duval) and a Moroccan (Si Hamed) who meet in a French cavalry regiment in North Africa. Their friendship is threatened when André seduces Si Hamed's sister, Zinah (Rosita Garcia). Si Hamed is furious and plans his revenge. Before he can act on his decision, his tribe is attacked, and it is André who comes to their rescue (*baroud* translates as "war"). The film would be shot in sound and, as was common practice in the early years of the talkies, in two versions—one in French, the other in English. For the English-language version, Rex announced he would be playing the lead role of André Duval; in the French version, Roland Caillaux was Duval.

Rex returned to Morocco to film *Baroud,* where, it was reported, the Sultan of Morocco placed some five thousand superb horsemen at his disposal.[25] He spent four weeks in Morocco, moving between Tangier, Rabat, the Atlas Mountains, and Marrakech. To gain a better sense of local life, Rex insisted that the film's crew travel with him in the same carriages that the poor Moroccans used rather than in tourist class. Once in Rabat, he dressed in full Arab costume and prided himself on walking the streets without being recognized as a European. In the Atlas Mountains, he and Burel took to horseback to make the long journey to Thami El Glaoui's casbah at Telouet. El Glaoui is better known to Europeans as the Lord of the Atlas, the fabulously wealthy and powerful Pasha of Marrakech, and Rex was to return there afterward on his own to renew the friendship. Later Rosita Garcia accompanied him, and the twosome dined as the guests of El Glaoui at the palace in Marrakech. Most often Rex traveled alone, immersing himself in the local culture, picking up the stories and meeting the people that would soon fuel his novels and short stories. Voyaging to the Valley of Ounila on one occasion, he heard tell of the medieval fortresses in whose dungeons captives were chained to the wall and never saw the light of day, a legend that gave the name to his collection of stories, *The City without Light.* Yet as much as he identified with North African culture, so too he retained a fascination for the French Foreign Legion and the affairs of the military.

The experience of shooting in sound with such an international cast, many of them nonprofessionals, made life on set frenetic. Alice remembered that "they all had to speak English and you never heard such a racket—the accents made it impossible to understand what was being said and the ones that didn't speak English at all had to learn their lines like a parrot, the sound trucks were not all that they should have been, and Rex was playing *and* directing and it was almost more than he could take. I often wondered how it got finished and released."[26]

One of the reasons *Baroud* did get finished and released, which Alice omits to mention, was that she took over when Rex was unable to direct. But she consistently diminished her own offscreen role in Rex's productions. Even though there is no record of exactly how much of the film's direction one can attribute to her, Alice is credited as codirector, so that if she directed all the sequences in which Rex is on screen, then the major credit ought to go to her. In October of 1931, the *Irish Times* reported that "hitherto it has been his [Rex's] wife who acted, while he directed, but the *rôles* now are reversed, and Miss Alice Terry will direct."[27] Either way, she did not appear before the camera and was around for much of the filming, so she probably ought to receive some considerable credit for *Baroud*'s completion.

The film's editor was Lothar Wolff. Wolff was to become a well-known figure in European and Hollywood cinema after his appointment as chief of the Motion Picture Section of the Marshall Plan Information Service. In the early 1930s he had just completed the switch from publicist—he was responsible for the famous image of Louise Brooks in a bathing suit—to editor and was moving between German and French projects. Nothing had prepared him for the experience, however, of cutting *Baroud*. When Wolff arrived in the Nice studios, he found that Rex had already shot over three hundred thousand feet of film and was still working on the studio sequences. "When Ingram got too frustrated," Wolff recalled, "he found a reason not to shoot that day. I remember once, there were about 500 extras assembled in Arab costumes for a mass scene. He spotted one man, way in back, whose costume wasn't what it was supposed to be (he had a tie on). He cancelled the shooting for the day, stalked back into his villa and had everybody paid off."[28] The production ran out of money, according to Wolff, was refinanced, and lasted for several more months.

Baroud is a film of two parts. One consists of the interior settings and the interaction among the central characters. These sequences suffer terminally from their rudimentary use of dialogue. Lengthy interactions take place without any dialogue, as if Rex had forgotten he was making a "talkie." Conversations, when they do occur, are stilted; gaps spring up between sentences. In order to avail themselves of the concealed microphones, characters deliver their lines in one position, then move to another rather than talking while walking. The French version is little different, with many of the scenes a shot-for-shot match. Although Roland Caillaux is a more accomplished actor than Rex and delivers his lines more convincingly, he adopts many of the same gestures and enjoys the same easy, physical, joshing relationship with Batcheff as Si Hamed. Arabella Fields's Mabrouka, whose role is as Zinah's servant, is the epitome of every stereotype of the devoted, overweight, sharp-tongued "black mammy."

But the other part of *Baroud* is its extraordinary exterior photography, with ranks of Arab horsemen racing across the desert sands, firing their rifles in the air, while in the background musicians play and the crowd dances and sings. As in his previous desert films, Rex revels in local detail. Now, with the addition of sound, he could reproduce the rhythms as well as the visual detail of North African life. One of the most notable differences between this film and its predecessors is the mobile camerawork. Where Rex's trademark had been his use of static setups offset by highly choreographed movement within the frame, now fluid tracking shots follow the horsemen and the dancers, while indoors the camera wanders around exploring the exotic settings and equally exotic inhabitants. Dissolves link sequences, where previously a cut was much more likely. Most uncanny of all is to see Rex appear in his own film. In an early exchange, he stands watching the charging horsemen, then turns to Si Hamed and remarks in self-conscious acknowledgment of his own positioning as actor-director: "They ought to be in the movies!" Soon afterward, in a sequence that must have startled Rex's inner circle, he takes to the floor of the Oasis Bar and dances with the French chanteuse Arlette (Colette Darfeuil), moving with comparative ease for a man who loathed the dance floor. Remarking that she only has eyes for his friend, Rex/André hands Arlette over to Si Hamed: "I adore being in Morocco," she confides. "You are a lot of savages." "Perhaps we are much more civilized than you are," he retorts. "Yet, if you caught a man with your sister, you'd kill him," she replies. "Ah, that's different," he tells her. "There," she concludes. "I knew you were a savage."

Are Rex's Arabs "savages"? From today's perspective, the casting of Western actors in North African roles is offensive, yet the practice still continues and was so commonplace in the early 1930s that it is unfair to critique the film on those grounds. The film's Arab characters are depicted as being masters of a rich culture and one defined by questions of morality and honor, a far cry from Hollywood's regular screen Arabs, then and now. Although they are fierce and warrior-like, they are also rational and humane. Through Batcheff's Si Hamed, Rex provides a most sympathetic portrayal of the young Arab, a man who is torn between his love for his friend André and his duty to punish the infidel for falling in love with his sister. That this is an irreconcilable conflict that can only be concluded by the departure of the European officer, rather than by any symbolic union between colonizer and native, echoes Rex's earlier films of interracial love, *Where the Pavement Ends* and *The Arab*. What is hard to determine is just how much this reflects Rex's own politics. Were these endings motivated as much by his suspicion of convention as by a genuinely liberal set of beliefs?

Certainly for Rex, friendship between European and Arab was both a personal and an ideological imperative. That was why he so admired Marshal Lyautey, captioning a picture of a battalion of Berbers on horseback with the words "Lyautey was the first to realize that with these Moroccan Berbers could he make another France!"[29] Why the Moroccan Berbers should want to make another France does not seem have occurred to him. Lyautey has come to enjoy the reputation of a benevolent colonizer who too held the native peoples of the region in high regard, much prizing their exotic culture. He was not only respectful of their traditions but took an active part in developing the country's infrastructure and modernizing it. Yet he was also a monarchist and a political conservative, much more so than Rex's other hero, Lawrence. Ultimately it seems that Rex, for all his love of North African culture and his admiration for its warrior traditions, struggled to move outside of the imperialist mind-set that defined his generation. *Baroud* hints at a suspicion that there was no place for the European officer in Morocco, yet in truth, for its director, this was not a firmly held conviction.

Rex's last film was also to be Batcheff's. Traveling to visit the set in Nice, Denise Piazza, now his wife, found him in good form, "relaxed and athletic-looking, more handsome than ever."[30] Appearances were deceptive. On his return to Paris, Batcheff once more succumbed to sudden mood swings, and on the evening of 11 April 1932, he confessed to her that he had been taking drugs for years. She hardly had time to recover herself when their friend, the surrealist Jacques Prévert, dropped by, and the threesome went to a nightclub in Montmartre. After a while Batcheff excused himself and returned to the apartment. The following morning, when Prévert dropped off Denise, she found her husband close to death, having left behind a suicide note explaining that he could no longer hurt the people he loved. Prévert called the doctor, but before he could arrive, Batcheff was dead. *Baroud* was released after his death.

Baroud premiered in France in November 1932 at the Gaumont-Palace cinema in Paris to an illustrious audience that included Paul Boncour, the minister for war; Marshal Philippe Pétain; Gen. Henri Gouraud, the military governor of Paris; and a representative of the governor-general of Algeria. It was a grand affair, if perhaps more because of its recognition of Rex's contribution to French cinema than because of the film that was to be released. Once it arrived in the United States, *Baroud* met with an unforgiving reception. With justification the critics picked up where they had left off with *The Garden of Allah*. The *Los Angeles Times* found the new film excessively dated and was equally dismissive of Rex's performance: "To be sure, greater thespians than he reveals himself to be would have gone down to speedy defeat on the face of such dialogue as falls to the lot of all the actors in this little number. Ingram . . . quite evidently faithful to the old silent technique, proceeded on the theory that it scarcely could matter what the characters said, so long as they kept their mouths moving."[31] The *New York Times* was somewhat more positive, its reviewer reveling in Rex's scenery and display of Moroccan characters and concluding of its director's acting that he played "with shy reticence." Rather remarkably, the critic added that "Pierre Batcheff, as Si Hamed, is an inexperienced but seriously effective actor."[32]

The French critics echoed their counterparts in America, their admiration for Rex's filming of North Africa and its peoples only matched by their criticism of the film's narrative construction and use of sound. At least, however, they recognized that Batcheff was far from inexperienced, and the general sentiment was that he carried the film. In Algeria the critic of *Alger-Étudiant* found *Baroud* too restrained, commenting that an African would never have been so easily taken in. Nor did they find it credible that the daughter of a *caid* would have been found wandering through the streets at night, even in the company of her nurse. However, he too praised the exteriors and found the atmosphere of the interiors realistic.[33]

The film was released in the United States under the more alluring title of *Love in Morocco,* perhaps to capitalize on von Sternberg's considerably more successful (and scandalous) *Morocco* or perhaps simply to bring in the old Orientalists. It enjoyed a very limited run before vanishing from the screen. So too did its maker. As a later reviewer wrote, there is a poignancy to the closing moments of the film where Rex as André rides off into the desert toward Marrakech, leaning back from his horse and waving toward the camera, as if bidding farewell to the world of filmmaking.[34]

That turned out to be the truth. Rex's long and extraordinary career as a film director was over.

11

Sculptor, Writer, Artist, Traveler

In 1933 Rex announced in an interview in Paris that he had abandoned cinema and converted to Islam. He told reporters that, since his first visit to Africa eleven years ago, he had been fascinated by the philosophy behind Islam:

> Before the Crash, in America everyone wanted to make a million and to retire, and many managed to do so, even if at the same time they aged prematurely and their final years were unhappy and neurotic. For the 350 million Mohammedans who live by the law of the Prophet, economic problems, as we conceive of them in the West, simply do not exist. There was indeed an economic crisis in Islam that was much worse than the crisis in the world now, and that was 1,311 years ago. At that moment it was decided that people worked too much. Since then, Mohammedans spend much less time working, and spend much more of their day in meditation and contemplation.[1]

He now was taking the Arabic name of Ben Aalem Nacir ed' Deen—Son of a Victorious Savant of Faith. He added that Christians should learn about Islam in order to put into practice the teachings of Jesus.[2]

The satirist Wyndham Lewis had met Rex in the desert when he was shooting *Baroud* and mentions the conversion to Islam, so it seems that Rex took this decision sometime during the making of that film.[3] If the *Tit Bits* article had been libelous in 1928, it was much less so now. French journalists and others who interviewed him were already accustomed to hearing Rex's musings on the spiritual values of the Muslim faith. A few years previously, Maurice Mairgance, later to become a director himself, had been bold enough to counter with a question about Rex's love of collecting ancient weapons. Undaunted by what might have been a somewhat impertinent inquiry, Rex responded happily, "I don't just like oriental weapons. I own several unique items such as the sabre, adorned with precious stones and etched all over, offered to Napoleon by the Mamluks of Egypt." Every morning, he told the reporter, he searched antique shops for items for his collection.[4]

The attraction of Islam for Rex was certainly spiritual, and he was not alone in feeling disenchanted with Western society in the wake of the stock market crash of 1929 and ensuing world economic depression. Nor did he have any difficulty reconciling his love for Eastern spiritualism with his admiration for the warrior spirit of the Berbers and other North African tribes. Still, one can only imagine how shocked he would have been by the vast schism between Islam and the West today. And as he grew older, he became more like his father, even if the outward signs pointed in other directions. In his later films, Rex abandoned racy melodramas for a more elevated moral tone; by *The Three Passions* this fell only a little short of hectoring. The Protestant faith of his upbringing, however, while well equipped to lecture on morality, offered none of the luxurious exoticism of Islam. For Rex conversion was not just a moral choice but an aesthetic one. It was also one his financial independence permitted him to make. Rex himself was not bankrupted by the crash and remained a wealthy man to the end of his life, much of this money derived from the success of *The Four Horsemen of the Apocalypse* and much of it invested in Oriental artifacts.

Before he could abandon himself to his new faith, however, Ben Aalem Nacir ed' Deen had to deal with a significant residue of his old life as the Riviera's most celebrated filmmaker. The Victorine studios were now considered world-class, but Rex's situation there had become a nightmare. Unraveling the legal tangle into which he had been drawn through his ownership of the business is almost impossible. What is certain is that in 1930 he sold the studios in Nice. The sale price was allegedly twelve and a half million francs (approximately $3.125 million). Edouard Corniglion-Molinier drew up the contract for the sale, but Rex apparently only received seven million francs. In 1934 Rex brought Corniglion-Molinier to court, accusing him of embezzling the remainder.[5] The details of the court case are hard to determine. Writing her history of the Victorine, Anne-Elizabeth Dutheil de la Rochère concluded that the case was probably first heard in

Nice in 1930 and finally at a court of appeal in 1936 in Aix-en-Provence. She also believed that a second, parallel case involving Fred Bascot, Corniglion-Molinier's studio manager, accused of falsifying documents for his employer, was heard in Paris in December 1931. In fact, it seems that the case was first heard in Paris in March 1931, when Rex brought a case against Corniglion-Molinier and then again in November 1931, when Corniglion-Molinier countered with an action for slander. What does seem more certain is that no final judgment was reached and that each side sued and countersued over a period of at least six years. In the final case in Aix, where a Monsieur Weill represented him, Rex was ordered to pay costs, but by this stage he was long gone from France, never to return.[6]

Years previously Michael Powell had observed that Rex was outspokenly anti-Semitic.[7] The affair had the additional side effect of increasing this anti-Semitism, as he blamed Jewish factions for cheating him out of his rightful income.[8] Open as he was to friendships across racial and religious divides, he remained obstinately entrenched in this particular mindset. In the same vein, one suspects that his hostility to the Jewish Louis B. Mayer was not informed by professional circumstances alone but equally by personal prejudice.

Freed from filmmaking, Rex began to travel and to write in earnest. Pressing home on one trip through Europe, he found himself within the crowd accompanying the remains of Blasco Ibáñez to his final resting place. The great writer had died in exile on the French Riviera in January 1928 and had stipulated in his will that he not be buried in Spain until it become a republic. Now, five years later, the Spanish government was returning him to his native Valencia. Ibáñez's first wife, Maria, died in January 1925, and he had remarried shortly before his own death. Rex met with his friend's widow, Elena Ortúzar Bulnes, and the two mourners stood side by side on the grandstand, Rex remembering Ibáñez's dream of returning to Spain and starting up a national film company, of his faith in the Mediterranean peoples and their stories, of his love of home: "During the ceremony, the most moving I have ever attended, the Señora held my hand. She wept softly and proudly as the remains were lowered from deck to wharf. Draped over the casket of the returning exile was a banner that bore, in large letters, the title of one of his novels: LOS MUERTOS MAHDAN—THE DEAD COMMAND."[9]

Before finally leaving France, Rex published *The Legion Advances*. The book seems to have received minimal publicity and distribution, and existing copies of it are now few and far between. Nor did it attract attention from any of the critical quarters where one might have expected to find it reviewed. Yet *The Legion Advances,* while far from a classic, is undeserving of such neglect. The writing style suggests that its author was still thinking of Hollywood when he composed it. Chapters fade in and out; locations and characters are introduced with colorful accompanying descriptions. The action is swift, with an ending constructed around the "race against time" formula so beloved of adventure cinema and reminiscent of Rex's earliest scenarios. It is also his most personal work and the only one with an Irish central character—Callaghan, a soldier in the French Foreign Legion. Like so many legionnaires, he is a man who has left behind an unsavory past, in his case in America. He also seems to have left his first name behind him, as all address him simply as "Callaghan." Following a raid on a *caid,* the Arab's daughter Saâdia is orphaned, and Callaghan sets himself up as her avenger and protector. He is, in the words of his superior, like all Celts "a sentimentalist. Discipline irks him; but as a free-lance he has no equal, and he knows how to handle these tribesmen." Expanding further, he remarks that Callaghan has found a new homeland in North Africa."[10] *The Legion Advances* bears a dedication to Marshal Lyautey and an introduction by another friend, Robert Hichens, who lauds the work's authenticity.

A recurrence of native and French phrases was to become customary of Rex's writing and one of its weaknesses: what was authentic in terms of visual construction transferred less comfortably onto the page. Other curious subplots include the appearance of a mysterious Hollywood film star whom nobody recognizes and who disappears from the narrative as unexpectedly as she arrived into it. In Callaghan, a soldier with an intense identification with North Africa, it is easy to see the writer's own alter ego. Here Rex could combine his fascination with the military and his love of the exotic, a love that expresses itself in the book through that most conventional of plot devices, the rescue and seduction of the young native woman. Callaghan's way into native culture is consistently depicted as through its women, whether it be the brothel madam Lalla Fathma, the feisty native Fathmata, or the pliant Saâdia. Callaghan's most loyal companion, otherwise, is his camel, Biedh'a, whom he loves and understands just as Rex and his brother, Frank, loved and understood horses. Horse and woman come together after Callaghan has allowed himself to be seduced by Fathmata;

looking down at her glistening body afterward, "he could not suppress an exclamation of approval—supreme tribute to the beauty of this comely animal."[11]

If these comments make the book sound clichéd—never mind colonialist—it is so in the manner of much filmmaking of the era. It is tempting to see *The Legion Advances* as the film Rex never could make. It is too violent and too sexually explicit ever to have found its way past the growing morality of Hollywood. The Hays Code would never have countenanced Callaghan's attraction to native women, although again the book does make concessions to convention by preventing the ultimate union of Saâdia and the Irishman through a trick of fate. Its colonialist, exoticist imagination is a reminder of Rex's own limitations. Much as he, like Callaghan, might dream of abandoning the spiritual void of the West, he was still steeped in its attitudes and fantasies. Yet despite these considerable weaknesses, and its now anachronistic tone, this is a book that exudes love of place, the adventure of the desert, and the nobility of its people.

In early 1934, Alice and Rex visited Cairo. Both liked it so much that they decided that, as soon as the lawsuit was settled, they would spend six months of each year there. Soon Alice concluded that it was senseless to sit around in Nice and they might as well go immediately. Rex packed up all their possessions, and they set sail in May of that year for Alexandria. The plan was for Rex to return to sculpting, to write, and to collect. By now he held some extraordinary works, including three superb Ottoman sabers, one of which was later acquired by the Metropolitan Museum of Art, and a head of Tuthmosis III from the Court of Suleyman the Magnificent.[12] His collection of the works of the Orientalist painter Théodore Chassériau was also substantial, and he had already loaned his key paintings to the Louvre for their retrospective in May 1933.[13] Before leaving France, he made several bequests to French institutions.

Just what happened to Shorty, Rheba, and the rest of Rex's human "collection" remains undocumented. The one family member who did not make the journey, however, was the adopted son, Kada-Abd-el-Kader. He had long been banished from the golden circle around Rex and Alice. Adoption or not, they seem to have become swiftly disenchanted with the boy, whom they believed had lied to them about his age. Even taking into account changing expectations of social responsibility, the story has a more than unsavory tinge. Although Rex did not immediately act upon his threat of returning him to his native country, the boy was sent back to Tunisia sometime after his appearance in *Mare Nostrum*. Apparently he made his living subsequently as a tourist guide, always introducing himself as the son of Rex Ingram and Alice Terry.[14]

Shortly after their arrival in Cairo, Alice's mother died, and she had to leave immediately for the United States. She found so much to do on her return that she never did go back. Unburdened by material responsibilities and on his own, Rex now was free to lose himself in North Africa. For the next two years, he traveled the length and breadth of the territory. Although he was alone, he was not solitary, meeting with people wherever he went. His memoirs detail his travels, the writing rich with detail and the love of discovery. On one voyage, to the Oasis of Timimoun, deep in the heart of Algeria, he stopped off at the hilltop city of Ghardaïa, in the Sahara. He spent the night with the White Fathers, a French missionary order, whose lives were dedicated to preparing the local population for conversion. Rex admired them, even if he did not believe that they would accomplish their task, and discussed religion with them long into the night as he shared their fine port. This was what he loved—the chance encounters of the road and good conversation, particularly around issues of faith. He accumulated many friends in the French military and stayed in their commands, again traveling hundreds of miles for a visit.

He also journeyed to Syria in an attempt to discover whether there were any likenesses between these descendants of the Phoenicians and his own Galway ancestors who reputedly shared the same heritage: "I was curious to find out which of us had degenerated the more. Heading north from Sûr and Saida—the Biblical Tyre and Sidon, I found grey eyes and long upper lips and a sense of humor that had a Hibernian flavor to it."[15] He followed the routes of the crusaders and in Homs came across slaughtered Russian Cossacks who had fought with the French and whom nobody cared for enough even to bury. Everywhere he moved, Rex witnessed the revolt against French rule, but he was untroubled by any sense of personal danger. He applied the same stubbornness to those who stood in the way of his travels as he had to those who tried to interfere with his filmmaking. Armed with letters of safe passage from his friends in the French military, he simply disregarded all other instructions and, far from the main cities, pressed on into the desert.

In 1935 Rex was finishing the first draft of his memoirs when the Italians invaded Ethiopia, forcing King Haile Selassie into exile. Fantastic stories began to do the rounds of the bars and nightclubs of Alexandria—of mysterious safes found on wrecked aircraft and of plans for a larger Italian invasion of Egypt. The British fleet sailed for Alexandria, and as Rex traveled along the Mediterranean coast, he observed six destroyers at anchor in the bay. He met war correspondents, among them the veteran American journalist Webb Miller and Hubert Renfro Knickerbocker, whose recent book, *Will War Come to Europe?* (1934) had predicted an imminent and vast European war.[16] "Have been working like a dog on a very thick book of memoirs. Over 160,000 words already done," Rex wrote in September of that year to Lee Lawrie, with whom he kept in regular touch. "Maybe I'll get through with it by Xmas. Not sure though. Alice is in California and wants me to pay her a visit there. I might go next year—Jan or Feb. Not sure yet."[17]

He nearly didn't make it home. In Alexandria he went swimming to escape the heat and scraped his shin on a submerged rock. Within a few hours, his leg was swelling and by morning he was unconscious. A doctor was called and gave Rex a series of injections, but the leg kept swelling. He refused to go to the hospital, and the doctor threatened that he would have to amputate. That night, contrary to orders, the Greek nurse who was watching over him lanced his leg and drew enough pus out of it to save him. The ordeal had taken a toll: "From my six weeks bout with Egyptian microbes, on a diet of grapefruit juice, I had acquired an alarmingly ethereal aspect, and the knowledge of how it feels to have a shape like Gandhi."[18] Some time before his illness, Rex had applied for permission from the legation in Cairo to make the pilgrimage to Mecca. Now that permission came through. Rex started to plan his journey, but his doctor urged him that he was in no shape to do so: "Recalling that the hardships of the pilgrimage had been responsible for the death of my friend Étienne Dinet, the orientalist painter, I took his advice."[19] Before he left Egypt, Rex packed up his and Alice's belongings and loaned his precious collection of armor, statues, pictures, and daggers to the Egyptian Museum at Cairo.

Finally he sailed for America, landing in New York on St. Patrick's Day, 17 March 1936, aboard the *Berengaria* from Cherbourg.[20] Alice surprised him by coming to meet him, for the arrangement was that she would wait on his return in Los Angeles. It was Rex's first trip to the United States in ten years, and he arrived with just an old army steamer trunk, two valises, and a sprig of shamrock in his lapel. And it is at this point that he ends his memoirs, as if, at the age of just forty-three, the adventure were over.

Studio City

Rex and Alice moved to 501 North Irving Boulevard but soon afterward bought a house in the Studio City area of the San Fernando Valley, at 11554 Kelsey Street, and built a studio for Rex to work in. Alice's sister, Edna, moved into a bungalow just below theirs on the same lot. It was an unexceptional spot, its major recommendation being a stream that ran through the property, reminding Rex of Ireland. The book of memoirs went for comment to Lee Lawrie and Rex's friend the portraitist Harry Solon.

It was hard to return to America. Much as he loved the sea, Rex found the water off the Los Angeles beaches dirty and oily. The buildings around him were characterless, and in the suburbs the residences looked as flimsy as the sets for motion pictures. "I want to be out of here as soon as I can," he wrote to Lawrie. "Life is too short to be spent in surroundings that are depressing."[21]

Although Rex was largely uninterested in keeping in with the Hollywood set, he and Alice stayed in contact with their oldest friends, of whom Ramón Novarro remained especially close. They went to the movies from time to time and attended the premiere of the new version of *The Garden of Allah* in November 1936. Through the late 1930s and up to 1940, as his passport attests, Rex traveled regularly to Mexico, often staying for several months at a time, often accompanied by Alice. He found himself fascinated by the Mayan and pre-Mayan ruins, admiring the work of these ancient peoples of whom so little was known but whose pyramids resembled those of the Egyptians. Here too he wrote the Mexican sections of his next book, *Mars in the House of Death*.

Mars in the House of Death (1939)

Dedicated to "Alicia," *Mars in the House of Death* opens with an introduction in which the author explains how he watched a man he calls the Minotaur fearlessly unloading bulls at the bullring in Valencia, Spain. Later he joins the Minotaur, a young matador, and the expert on bullfighting, Don Eusebio, at a table for lunch. He listens to the Minotaur tell of how he learned to raise bulls and to fight them. From Don Eusebio he hears the story of the relationship between the Minotaur and the matador, and much later, in Mexico, he finds out what happened there. Since Don Eusebio has no time to set this down on paper, the author has now undertaken to do so. The introduction is written in Guadalajara, Mexico, and dated January 1939.

The story opens in Andalucia in the house of Doña Concepción, a rich widow, whose feckless grandson, Felipe, bears no little resemblance to Julio Desnoyers. A habitué of the brothels of Barcelona, he falls in with Trini, a Gypsy girl, and they have a son, Jesús Enrique, or Chuchito, whose upbringing becomes the responsibility of the Minotaur since Felipe must marry for money. As Chuchito grows up, he shows all the signs of becoming a great matador; meanwhile Felipe has a daughter, Estrella, a frail but beautiful child. In time, he moves with his family to Mexico, where his wife's father made his fortune. There Estrella spends long days with her uncle, the artist Roberto Roqués. Chuchito, now a famous matador, travels to Mexico to fight. In Mexico he begins a lifetime affair with Doña Lisa, a woman somewhat older than him but much younger than her well-connected husband. Back in Spain, Chuchito meets Estrella, and the two commence a strangely inhibited affair, neither realizing that they are half-brother and half-sister. As the book comes to its conclusion, the signs and auguries that had intermittently accompanied the story now return with a vengeance, pointing the reader toward its concluding drama.

Rex's writing is as cluttered as his sets, with detail layered upon detail and with a baroque sense of place and character. Supernatural signs and auguries hang over the central characters. Foreign usages trip up the reader, who is advised to turn to the appendix if they are to understand the many Spanish phrases and bullfighting usages. It is often bawdy—Trini lives above a brothel—and contains vigorous, almost sadomaschistic sex: Lisa passes out as Chuchito claps his hand across her mouth and carries her into the room, only coming to with a rippling ecstasy that makes her realize that she has been ravished. In one scene Rex pays homage to his friend Vicente Blasco Ibáñez by having the Minotaur, Pepe, take Chuchito on a visit to the offices of *El Pueblo,* the republican journal founded by Ibáñez.

Mars in the House of Death is a tale of few surprises, with its central characters seldom departing from type. As in *The Legion Advances,* its author relies on detail rather than delicacy of plot to draw in his reader. As so often in a Rex Ingram film, the background is vivid, with a life of its own, and reading it one feels that he imagined a series of incidents, added color to them in his head, and then linked them together through his characters. Yet there is too much description, too many slightly arch nouns, too much stretching for the obscure word where the everyday would do, for this to flow like the novels of Ibáñez or to match the understated tough-guy prose of that other great writer of bullfighting epics, Rex's Riviera neighbor Ernest Hemingway. Perhaps unexpectedly, Rex decided against illustrating the book himself. Instead he contacted the well-known bull-fighting artist and aficionado of the sport Carlos Ruano Llopis and commissioned a series of illustrations, including one for the front cover.

Time magazine pronounced *Mars* a "colorful, realistic, badly con-structed tale . . . [that] will add more to Ingram's reputation for versatility than to literature."[22] The *New York Times* was kinder, noting how closely the novel resembled a film script but still finding that "the tale though melodramatic is sophisticated, and outside an overburdened plot, inte-grated by a keen intelligence. One or two of these sequences are worthy of any novelist living. They give you to understand why in the history of the moving pictures Rex Ingram belongs with the early immortals."[23] The *Irish Times,* for whom Rex could do no wrong, labeled it a "splendid yarn," advising those who wanted a copy to buy one quickly.[24]

Moving On

In 1938 Rex and Alice sold the house on Kelsey Street and moved to 2041 Pinehurst, but the new purchasers never completed the deal and had to be evicted. While this was happening, Rex and Alice took a trip to Hawaii; he returned shortly afterward, but once more restlessness overwhelmed him, and he went back to Honolulu and then on to Mexico again. On a whim, he wrote to Lee Lawrie with a plan: "I'm going to Egypt next year. If I invite you to come as my guest, will you come? Passage—hotels—everything paid. . . . I would love to see the temples with you, and I've a card from the Egyptian govt to admit me and my party FREE." Elaborating as he writes, he suggests they travel by Hawaii, China, Japan, the Dutch Indies, India, and the Red Sea. The Egyptian Museum at Cairo, he promises, would give Lawrie a new lease on life. And, ominously: "You'll have to take care of Alice if I go wild in any of the ports between San Pedro and Suez."[25]

How wild did he go on these trips? At the end of the day, Rex always answered to Alice. Yet there was an understanding between the now long-married couple that seems to have left each free to conduct their affairs as they chose. With his tireless curiosity and sense of personal invulnerabil-ity, Rex, one senses, found himself in darker places than the memoirs, written for eventual publication as they were, ever described. Lawrie did not take up the offer.

A friendship with the multimillionaire William B. Leeds, who hosted many a celebrity star and writer on his sumptuous yacht *Moana,* saw Rex join the cruiser in summer of 1939. The ship boasted a crew of fifty-nine, a swimming pool, and a reputation for being cursed. He traveled with Leeds from Mexico, through the Panama Canal to Jamestown, Virginia. He seemed unable to stop, now constantly traveling back and forth between Honolulu, Mexico, and Los Angeles. The ship's manifest for one of these journeys—28 June 1940—indicates that Rex had begun listing his occupation as "writer."[26] Finally, at the end of 1941, he moved back to Studio City. Between journeys, in May 1941, the Irishman became a naturalized American citizen.

After one of these trips, Willis Goldbeck bumped into Rex and Alice at Romanoff's Restaurant, a much-loved haunt of the Hollywood set. They had fallen out long before, when Goldbeck was working with David O. Selznick and Rex sent him an actor he wanted him to hire. Goldbeck, who had always felt grateful to Rex for his breakthrough into screenwriting, was unable to persuade Selznick to take the actor on, and Rex had refused to speak to him since. Now Goldbeck went over to Rex and Alice: "And he was pleasant enough but he never forgave me. He was a curious small man in many ways. And yet a generous man, willing to take other people's talent, and give it a chance at least, which very few people will do or would do at that time."[27]

Ill health dogged Rex, and in 1939 he spent a week in the hospital with a recurrence of dysentery originally contracted in Morocco. (By 1943 he was suffering from dangerously high blood pressure and dreading hospitalization: "I am afraid I am a little nervously and restlessly inclined when in bed," he wrote to Lawrie.[28] Only in Cuautla in Mexico had he been able to reduce his blood pressure and this as a result, he believed, of bathing in and drinking its radioactive waters.)[29] Still, he had not quite given up on a return to filmmaking. Certain stories held a particular attraction for him. Guy de Maupassant's "Boule de Suif" (published in 1880) was his favorite, and he managed to interest von Stroheim in taking part. This celebrated short story takes place during the Franco-Prussian War and follows a group of French citizens who are fleeing Rouen in a stagecoach. The passengers comprise a cross section of French society—a prostitute (nicknamed Boule de Suif—Ball of Fat), a petit bourgeois couple who are shop owners, a wealthier couple who own a factory, a count and countess, and two nuns. When they are held up by Prussians, it turns out that they can only proceed if Boule de Suif sleeps with the Prussian officer. Once she has saved them, the other passengers turn their back on the young woman, condemning her "morals."

The plot had everything that appealed to Rex—a wartime background, a virtuous prostitute, and a strong moral message. Regrettably for him, John Ford made his version of the story, *Stagecoach,* in 1939, and even though it was adapted from a different source, the similarities were too strong for him to proceed, had he even been able to. Other projects included adaptations of Victor Hugo's *Toilers of the Sea,* W. B. Trite's *The Gypsy,* and, of course, his own *Mars in the House of Death.* Another long-standing project remained Jakob Wasserman's *The World's Illusion.* None of them came to anything, not least because Rex refused to make a French or Spanish film where the characters spoke in English—he said he couldn't stand a Mexican peon talking Oxford English—and no producer would touch a film where the characters spoke in a foreign language.[30] Only John Huston's *The Treasure of the Sierra Madre,* whose rights Rex had tried to purchase before the war, broke the mold, but then (1948) it was too late. "I would class it as one of the ten great pictures I have seen to date," Rex wrote to Huston:

> There was certainly nothing "españolad" about it. Your father gave a superb performance. I wouldn't have recognized him had his name not been on the screen. The Mexican bandit who objected to being shot without his sombrero, too, was utterly convincing. It was a relief to hear the Mexicans addressing each other in their own language. It gave the picture the factual quality of a newsreel. I'm awaiting your next with impatience. My old cameraman, Johnnie Seitz, comes out once in a while and we talk about your work. He agreed with me after seeing "The Maltese Falcon" that you had more on the ball than any American director since D. W. and Erich von Stroheim.[31]

Rex was also particularly taken by Orson Welles's *Citizen Kane* (1941), which he saw two or three times.[32]

Through following Lee Lawrie's career, Rex retained a strong interest in contemporary sculpture and greatly admired his teacher's *Atlas* at the

Rockefeller Center. On the other hand, "I can't take seriously the crap Picasso turns out for the U.S.," he confided to Lawrie. "When he was young he did some fine things, but I guess he's been kidding the public so long that he's incapable of doing anything that will stand the test of time any more."[33]

Alice meanwhile took up painting. She had started because Edna painted. She found herself enjoying her new pastime, not least because now she had no one she needed to please or answer to. One of her surviving works is a portrait of Rex in middle age. It is a beautiful, wistful painting. In it Rex is tanned, mustached, blue-eyed, with a cravat knotted around his neck. He is gazing beyond the frame with a look that is serious, almost sad, as if something that he had wished for had not come to pass. She also painted a portrait of Rosita Garcia that is quite the opposite, with the starlet looking left out of frame and smiling cheerfully, a little mischievously. Rex reported to his brother that Alice was also teaching three or four hours a night so had her hands full.[34] By February 1941 he had twice rewritten his memoirs, which he now called "A Long Way from Tipperary," and was hoping that he had found a publisher. It was a laborious undertaking. "There were many times I wrote a page over as many as fifty times before I could get it the way I wanted it," he complained afterward.[35] He was never to enjoy the success with his writings that he had as a director, and "A Long Way from Tipperary" failed to see the light of day.

When America entered World War II at the end of 1941, Rex was forty-eight and wanted to enlist again, but his health was now too poor. Instead he went to Washington to advise the government on North Africa, and it seems that he met there with Gen. George C. Marshall.[36] He pressed the authorities to let him play a more active part in the North African campaign, writing to Lawrie, "I'm hoping to get over as I know the ground in Morocco, Algeria and Tunisia so well that I know I could be of use." He was brushing up his languages and translating a novel from Spanish into Arabic for practice.[37] He spent nearly six months in Washington in total and by March 1943 was growing increasingly impatient with the bureaucrats: "They stall and stall and keep you guessing and irritated until you give up, and when you're at the point of relaxing in Mexico or somewhere, they want you at a moment's notice to go to Tombouktou."[38]

By Christmas 1943 he was still hoping to contribute to the war effort, but nothing came of it. He spent the war years collecting, sculpting, and working on a book of short stories. He chafed against being confined to

Studio City, complaining to his father, "I am not happy in this place and it is hard to concentrate and turn out things when there's absolutely nothing that interests you in the life around you. I really got things done in Mexico. Did that bull fight story [*Mars in the House of Death*] in 8 months."[39] He and Alice purchased a ranch beyond Santa Barbara and reared cattle and pigs, or at least Alice did, for Rex soon tired of its management.

During the war his nephew, the little boy who had visited him in Nice, Reginald (Rex) Hitchcock, was fighting in North Africa and contacted his Uncle Reggie to see if he could send him some film for his camera. Rex in turn asked "Patsy," as he always called him, to visit his friend the *caid* of El Hamma, who had lent him horses for *Baroud.* "My regiment had just fought its way through El Hamma and it was not a very opportune moment for social visits!" Major Hitchcock later recalled. Afterward he met friends of his uncle at Bou Saâda, where Rex had shot *The Arab.*[40] Rex had hoped to meet him in Tunis, but the doctors refused to give him the necessary travel inoculations for fear of aggravating his blood pressure, which now registered 215/130.[41] Major Hitchcock sent photos back to his uncle, who, after a few polite words about the forthcoming birth of his nephew's child, whom he hoped would be born on "blessed Irish soil," came to the point. He was concerned about Patsy's technique: "You don't seem to be focussing your pictures very sharply. Perhaps the lens of your camera just needs polishing. It's not a bad idea to have the subjects hold a card with a big black letter on it in front of their faces and focus on that."[42]

Toward the end of the war in Washington, he met Harry S. Truman, and was impressed with the new president, whom he found to be a practical man: "I believe [he] has a very clear sense of his obligation as the first servant of the nation; instead of having a mistaken idea of having the nation's obligations to him, as its lord and master. His determination to govern the country through the elected representatives of the people instead of through a personally selected palace guard is extremely healthy."[43]

Once the war ended, Rex arranged for food parcels from a food store in New York to be sent to his brother Frank and to their father in England. He continued, as he had done for many years, to send the "Old Man," as he and his brother called their father, small amounts of money, though he feared that Reverend Hitchcock was just putting it away for Frank. Rex himself had covered the cost of Frank's care in nursing homes in Davos and Château-d'Oex in Switzerland after he was gassed in the trenches.

Their father's health was poor, but Rex was hoping that it might improve enough for him, Frank, and Reverend Hitchcock to make the long-delayed trip back to Ireland. Perhaps, he suggested, a dose of hormones would do the trick. If so, he would happily airmail a supply of the serum to their father's doctor.[44] He fussed about Lee Lawrie's health as he fussed about his own father's, writing confidentially to the sculptor's second wife, Mildred, that he was worried that Lawrie might contract rheumatism if he continued to work with damp clay in an unheated studio. He would send on some warm clothes, he continued, as well as tobacco and copies of *Life*, *Time*, and the *Reader's Digest*, if Mildred supplied him with Lawrie's measurements.[45] He also regularly sent Lawrie small gifts of money.

In summer 1947 Frank cabled Rex that their father was dying. Rex left immediately, departing New York on 24 July. His ship docked at Liverpool on 5 August; on 6 August Frank met Rex at Euston Station, and they went to London's Dorchester Hotel. From there they traveled to Essex to Reverend Hitchcock's home. "Fortunately," Rex reported to Lawrie, "my visit bucked him up enough to pull him around and he is now well on the way to recovery."[46] It was perfect summer weather, with long warm evenings, and the three men were overjoyed to see each other again. They sat outdoors in the retired rector's garden, laughing and talking together, swapping stories and catching up on the years since the shooting of *The Three Passions* in Nice. On 12 August, Frank reluctantly saw Rex off at Southampton on a troopship, the *Arundel*, to Egypt. En route, off Malta, Rex suffered a heart attack but recovered and continued on. In Egypt he spent a month in the hospital. The Egyptians had previously offered him £50,000 (Egyptian) to hold on to the collection he had loaned them before the war, but Rex was not to be tempted.[47] On arrival, he found that King Farouk had looted the museum and made off with certain of the items. Undeterred, he turned up at the palace and demanded them back. The king's courtiers obliged.

In February 1948 he was in Rabat visiting his old friends Sultan Sidi Mohammed and his grand chamberlain, Si Mameri. From there he went to the El Minzah Hotel in Tangier, where he stayed until 1 March. He traveled on to Spain, with a short stop off in Gibraltar, and always keeping on the move, journeyed from Cordoba to Rhonda, Seville, and Malaga, meeting up with old friends along the way. In Tangier he had another heart attack and another in Seville. The doctor he saw in Seville gave him a new medicine called scillaren, which was less toxic than digitalis but like digitalis acted as a stimulant to the heart. However, it was not, the doctor warned him, a cure.[48] He also warned Rex that he might not survive the trip home to the United States, but Rex was determined to travel so that he might see Alice again and put his affairs in order lest he should die.

On 15 March, Rex sailed on the M/S *Sobieski* from Cadiz for New York. Once back in the United States, he added new rooms to the bungalow to give space to the many books, pictures, furniture, and other artifacts that he had retrieved from the Egyptian Museum. At the east end was the main house, where Alice lived. Rex lived and worked in his studio on the west side. The bungalow gradually began to take on the look of one of Rex's sets, cluttered and rich with detail. Even the walls were precious, set by hand with beautiful fifteenth-century Moorish tiles, while in his study a photograph of his mother, in a frame she had carved herself, stood on an occasional table. Romantic paintings of Arab life by painters such as Dinet and Horace Venet hung where the tiles could not reach. There was one Chasseriau and various of Rex's busts and statues. Among the favorite items in his collection were his swords and other weapons. His sculptures occupied all other available space.

"It's good to have my household gods round me again after their long sojourn in Egypt," he told Lawrie. In the same letter, he responded to his old teacher's critique of his sculpture of his great-great-grandfather, the Chevalier de Johnstone (1719–1805). "I agree with you that the head is a bit timid," Rex wrote, "but that sometimes happens when you think you've a good likeness and are afraid of losing it." The heart attack had left him tired, he complained, and he hadn't been able to summon up enough enthusiasm to do any sculpting for some time.[49]

Around this time, he completed the short stories. The collection was named "The City without Light," after one of its stories, and comprises ten separate narratives. Each one is set in North Africa, and all draw freely on local characters and incidents, usually told from the perspective of a European traveler to the territory. The first of the stories, "Tunisian Interlude," establishes the tone for the remainder. It is set in Sidi Bou Said and tells the story of an American, Bolton, who encounters a young local woman named Yasmina. They make love on their first encounter and then again the next day, but Bolton has to return to New York. Before he leaves, he gives Yasmina a parting gift of a piece of pirate's gold he has worn as an amulet. She in turn gifts him an ornament she has been wearing, and he departs, with the words of an Arab love song she has sung him playing in his head.

With the outbreak of World War II, it is five years before Bolton returns to Africa. When he does, he finds Yasmina's room demolished. He succeeds in running down her former neighbor, Djalloul, who tells Bolton that Yasmina is dead, killed in an attack on an oasis in the south of the country. Bolton and Djalloul stroll together into the Fondouk, a rest house for travelers. There a dervish is performing. Bolton glances around and sees a veiled woman whose eyes look strangely familiar. Intrigued, he requests Djalloul to ask her to speak to him. The dervish continues to perform, crunching scorpions in his mouth; a sheikh then plunges a sword into the man's stomach, and the dervish twists it, displaying his entrails. He leaps into the air and as he falls, he knocks against the woman, whose clothing slips to reveal that she is a leper. Hastily Bolton tells Djalloul that he no longer wishes to meet with Yasmina and presses some money into the Tunisian's hand along with a confused message of sympathy for the leper woman. Djalloul returns to Bolton and passes on her gratitude but fails to mention, perhaps because he did not notice, that she was wearing a pirate's amulet.

Bolton is a successful photographer, painter, and sketch artist, whose activity, photographing locals to illustrate a North African novel, flouts the Prophet's edict against reproducing the human image in any form. As he kicks against his success and the world of capitalism in which he has become trapped, he most resembles Rex, and the story suggests another reason why the latter may have felt he had to cease shooting films, with their "infidel mechanical eye," in North Africa.[50] The love affair with Yasmina is sketchily described, but, Bolton understands, love for the woman is love for the land: "She was a symbol, the symbol of a land, of a race, that had stirred his senses as they had never before been stirred. She was the land, she was the race."[51] In the end he fails to see beyond the surface attractions of the country into the ugliness beneath. This, as ever, was what really fascinated Rex—those twin opposites of beauty and deformity.

Blindness too is the subject of the title story, "The City without Light." Michelle, a young widow, has survived the car crash that killed her wealthy husband. The accident left her blind, but an operation by a French eye surgeon, Max, has restored her sight, and she has come to Morocco to visit her late husband's properties. There she becomes drawn to a sanctuary for the blind and meets a mysterious, unseeing dervish, Aziz, who later appears to her in an erotic dream. She persuades Max to operate on the dervish. After one of the company's properties is blown up, Michelle demands a meeting with the *caid* of Es-Siba, who is behind the anticolonialist campaign. He turns out to be no else but Aziz, the dervish. They begin to meet clandestinely, and from Aziz she learns of her late husband's exploitation of the local people. She in turn determines to build a hospital for the blind. The story ends without resolving whether this felicitous union between the charismatic native lord and the sympathetic Frenchwoman will bring new understanding to both races.

It is the gap between the Western eye and the frenetic, often cruel pulse of North Africa that the stories return to over and again. In another, "Double Spread," an antiques seller capitalizes on the West's love of stories of primitive Africans to promote his new collection. In some, the Western travelers achieve an insight into the shortcomings of their concept of civilization. In others they remain unaware of the wealth of the local culture.

Stylistically the writing is uneven, again overloaded with description and often awkward and slightly stilted, as if Rex could never quite lose himself in this art, just as he could never abandon self-consciousness enough to be a good actor. His female characters are one-dimensional, sexually giving but never afforded the luxury of a personality. His men are decent if somewhat lost Westerners, at sea in a foreign land. By contrast, the native men are assured, dominant, at home.

It is not surprising that Frank, who was working informally as Rex's agent, could not find a publisher for his brother's stories. One can read much like another, and the writing style is not accomplished enough for a market of readers who grew up with T. E. Lawrence and now were discovering Paul Bowles. Yet that stilted prose, with its hesitancies and its sudden appropriations of Arabic words in the midst of English sentences, leaves one with a strong reminder of its author's presence. In particular, those alternations between enthusiasm and inhibition are resonant with how Rex had lived his life, that sense of a man who would plunge into adventure only to recognize that the dream of fully losing himself in another place or time could never be realized.

Tempting as it is, it would be misleading to think of these as wasted years. Undated home movie footage from around this time shows quite another side of Rex's life with Alice at the bungalow. Relaxed and cheerful, he dives into their pool and plays games with their Pomeranians, taunting one mercilessly with a rubber duck. Guests, including his lover Rosita Garcia and Alice's lover Gerald Fielding, stroll in and out of the frame. Von Stroheim mugs to the camera. They dress up in costumes—Rosita Garcia in traditional peasant garb, Fielding in Rex's Canadian air force uniform, and Rex as a cowboy. Two men, who appear to be a gay couple, pose. Alice for the most part is out of sight, presumably operating the camera, although in one sequence she appears, just as relaxed as her spouse, laughing and smoking a cigarette. Watching Rex in this easy-come, easy-go atmosphere, one understands just something of his and Alice's disregard for the conventions of married life. One also understands how a return to Ireland, with its strict Catholic moral outlook, was quite out of the question.

In June 1949, after a disastrous screening of his *The Elusive Pimpernel* (1950) for Samuel Goldwyn, Michael Powell was, as he writes, reminded once more "about Hollywood and its treatment of its children."[52] Hearing that his erstwhile protégé was in town, Rex invited Powell over for a visit. The two men hadn't seen each other since Powell had left the Victorine studios in 1928, and the younger man wondered about visiting Rex and Alice after their fortunes and his had now so radically reversed. Nor had they parted on the best of terms, with Rex out of sorts over Powell's departure to work with Harry Lachman. Howard Strickling insisted, however, and so Powell and his wife, Frankie, made their way to Rex and Alice's home. As soon as they arrived, Powell's reservations vanished; Rex was as good looking as ever, the gold bracelet still on his wrist, the gold necklace around his neck, Alice on his arm. Rex in his turn was warm in his praise for Powell and his manifest achievements, inscribing for him a copy of *Mars in the House of Death* with the words "Am very proud of you, Micky— more power to you. Keep on showing them!"

Rex continued to suffer from fatigue, and in the spring of 1950 he took a trip to Haiti to relax. There he met up with his old friend from Nice, Max de Vaucorbeil. They were together every day, swimming in the pool, eating together at restaurants, taking trips to the country, meeting people. Max thought Rex well, even though he had to rest for a couple of hours each afternoon. Rex flew home from Port-au-Prince.

From there he traveled to Cuba and Vera Cruz. In Vera Cruz he contracted malaria and was forced to lie up for several weeks. By the time he returned to Alice, Rex was gaunt and ill-looking. With some treatment and rest, he began to return to health; still his blood pressure remained obstinately high. He settled back to life at 11554 Kelsey Street, exploring his family connections, reading, and always extending his collection of memorabilia.

As he appeared to recover, Rex began to feel like working again. He had become interested in Haitian writer Ralph Korngold's popular account of the Haitian revolution of 1791–1804, *Citizen Toussaint,* which was published in 1944. He thought it would make an exciting film and wanted to start on a script. He returned to his bust of the Chevalier de Johnstone, whose life he had been researching and who, he was delighted to discover, had been a lothario as well as a distinguished military man. Back in December 1949 he had sent a picture of his work so far to his father, for whom he intended the sculpture as a gift. Rex's doctor was strongly opposed to this rush of activity and in July 1950 insisted that his patient have a series of X-rays. It would be easier, the doctor and Alice agreed, for Rex to stay in Park View Hospital while the X-rays were being taken, as the procedure always made him nervous and this would cut down on travel between home and hospital.

Alice went to see him in the hospital twice a day, and on 21 July she sat with him for an hour or two. He was due to travel to a clinic in the Valley the following day for blood tests, so Alice arranged to come to the hospital at nine the next morning to collect him. Her birthday was on 24 July, and Rex told her to pick out something nice for herself from him, adding, "I will see you in the morning. Be sure to get something pretty."[53]

Alice left and shopped for an hour. When she arrived home, the telephone was ringing. It was the hospital, asking her to come immediately, as Rex was unconscious. When she got back to the hospital, he was in a coma and passed away a short time afterward. He had suffered a cerebral hemorrhage, and his heart was too weak to take the shock.

12

The Life, the Legacy

Rex Ingram was fifty-seven years old when he died. Working on his new film in Nice, Max de Vaucorbeil could not get over the news. He went up to their old studios and found it hard to look at them and to see the villa where they had been so happy for so many years. Men who had worked with Rex soon came over to him to share their grief at his passing. For them, Max wrote in a sympathy letter to Frank, Rex would "always remain like a god."[1]

Lee Lawrie too was heartbroken to hear of his student's premature death, writing to Reverend Hitchcock: "Sometimes we hear someone spoken of as a 'shining light.' Reginald, wherever he happened to be, whether in the class-room, in a gathering of people, or at work, radiated the fine elements of his personality. I believe he had more abilities and a finer grace in exercising those abilities than I have seen in anyone else I have ever known."[2] One can only imagine the retired clergyman's feeling of loss and Frank's. The latter's lingering sense of bereavement permeates the letters he wrote to Liam O'Leary when O'Leary was researching his book on Rex. They are memorials, meticulously recalled, to an older brother.

On 26 July 1950 Rex's funeral service was held at Forest Lawn Cemetery in Glendale, California. Ramón Novarro accompanied Alice. Those of the old crowd who could make it were there: Constance Talmadge, Claire du Brey, Antonio Moreno, and Gilbert Roland attended, as did John Seitz and Grant Whytock. According to Anthony Slide, the group also numbered four of Rex's mistresses, all of whom Alice invited to the postfuneral party on the grounds that she was the only one who could call herself Mrs. Rex Ingram.[3]

The passing of Rex Ingram caused barely a ripple in the news columns. He was by now a forgotten name, a relic of an era of filmmaking that had long been supplanted—by talking pictures, Technicolor, television. Indeed, several of the obituary writers confused him with his namesake the actor

Rex Ingram, who was, disconcertingly for him one imagines, still alive. Many of the people who had worked with Rex were also gone: Valentino spectacularly; June Mathis the year after Valentino; Barbara La Marr outrageously; Edward Connelly quietly. Lewis Stone died the following year, in 1953. Some lived on to long and acclaimed careers, notably John Seitz and Willis Goldbeck, although Harry Lachman had directed his final film in 1942. Ramón Novarro was now enjoying something of a revival. Irving Thalberg had died of pneumonia in 1936; the year before Rex's death, Dore Schary fired Louis B. Mayer from MGM.

Rex's protégé Michael Powell, in partnership with Emeric Pressburger, went on to direct a series of brilliant visual fantasies that transformed the image of British cinema. In 1960 he staged a comeback with *Peeping Tom* that so shocked the critics that it took decades, and a new generation of cinefiles, to retrieve his reputation. He is now celebrated as one of the greatest British filmmakers of all time.

Rex left behind an estate valued at over $200,000. All his personal effects were left to Alice Terry along with one-half of the estate. He had also set up a trust fund that was to provide her with an annual income of $500 for the rest of her life. Upon her death, the trust was to be divided equally between his father and his brother.[4] Edna took over the management of the estate (she also seems to have had a hand in managing Alice, refusing to allow Gerald Fielding to move in). The balance was set aside to care for Rex's father and brother. Frank by then had gained a reputation as an unerring chronicler of life in the trenches with the publication of his military diary, *Stand To*, in 1937; he also wrote and illustrated a series of books on horsemanship: *Rudiments of Riding* (1930), *Saddle Up!* (1933), and *To Horse!* (1938). After he was invalided from the British army, he was appointed to the position of Military Knight of Windsor. He died in Beaconsfield, England, in 1972. Reverend Hitchcock had remarried, to Annie Traill, daughter of the former provost of Trinity College, Anthony Traill, but she died in 1943. He died shortly after his older son, in 1951. When Frank was going through his possessions after his death, he found in his wallet the photograph of the bust of the Chevalier de Johnstone that Rex had sent him.

Although the name Rex Ingram has nearly vanished from film history, remakes of his films started during his lifetime and continued after his death. Richard Boleslawsky remade *Garden of Allah* in 1936, John Cromwell remade *Prisoner of Zenda* in 1937, George Sidney remade

Scaramouche in 1952, and Vincente Minnelli remade *The Four Horsemen of the Apocalypse* in 1962. In 1948 Spanish director Rafael Gil remade *Mare Nostrum,* tweaking the plot to suggest that the Allies had been victorious over Nazi Germany thanks to Franco.

Of course, it was Rex's first great star who would remain most famous of all. In 1951 Lewis Allen directed *Valentino,* with Anthony Dexter taking the title role. In an effort to make the Italian's life story more concise and more glamorous, Allen elided June Mathis's part in favor of a plotline that had Valentino discovered by Joan Carlisle (Eleanor Parker), soon to be wife of William King (Richard Carlson), a big-name Hollywood director, though not of *The Four Horsemen of the Apocalypse.* Instead he directs Carlisle and Valentino in *The Sheik.* Carlson's "King" is a bland, pipe-smoking all-American who defends his wife's honor even when he knows she has been trysting with Valentino. Alice was not amused by the film's suggestion that she had an affair with Valentino and in 1953 successfully sued Columbia, the film's distributor. The case was settled out of court for a sum rumored to be in the region of $750,000.[5] Valentino's sister and brother also sued on the grounds that the film defamed him. This did not prevent more versions of the Valentino story appearing, notably the television film *The Legend of Valentino* (1975), with Franco Nero in the lead, and Ken Russell's deliriously outré *Valentino* (1977), starring the ballet dancer Rudolf Nureyev. The latter is notoriously inaccurate, cost a fortune to make, and nearly ended Russell's career. Russell himself later disowned it but not before he cast himself as Rex in a re-creation of the familiar shot of the director on a platform behind a megaphone on the set of *Four Horsemen.* In the shot Russell/Rex has one arm casually draped around his (male) assistant's shoulder.

It's a Shame That It Couldn't Have Gone On and On

Alice survived her husband long enough to see a new generation of historians and scholars rediscover their films. Liam O'Leary began his research on Rex Ingram in the 1950s and contacted Alice then. They kept in touch by correspondence for many years, up until the publication of *Rex Ingram: Master of the Silent Cinema* in 1980 and afterward. Film historian Anthony Slide became a regular guest at her house. On 10 January 1970, Kevin Brownlow arranged for the Academy of Motion Picture Arts and Sciences to screen *The Conquering Power.* He contacted Alice and, knowing how she guarded her privacy, invited her to a private screening of Rex's film: "I thought she'd refuse and she said: 'Could I bring my sister?' So they turned up, Alice Terry, her sister, the cameraman Seitz, the editor Grant Whytock, and several other people from the Ingram crowd. They all gathered and saw this fascinating film."[6]

"I was a little afraid it would fall apart at the seams, pop and crackle, after all it was made 50 years ago," Alice wrote O'Leary. But she was thrilled when the titles came on the screen, and apart from a few scratches the print was perfect. Suddenly she found herself face to face with her younger self: "I was quite pleased with the girl who played 'Eugénie Grandet,' but outside of being a bit coy—she wasn't as bad as I had imagined for 50 years the photography was excellent and the direction perfect—no laughs in the wrong place—all in all it was a very enjoyable morning. Johnny Seitz was there too. The public screening that night was packed."[7]

Other film historians made the pilgrimage to meet Alice. In April 1958 John Seitz accompanied the writer and film curator George Pratt to Alice's home so that he could interview her. Pratt, a lifelong fan of Alice, noticed that "immediately apparent was a sturdy sense of humor—quite unexpected from the calmly radiant image on the screen. She now laughed at herself, I surmised, over situations in the past which at the time probably weren't funny to her at all. But perhaps she had always done that, always recovered herself quickly."[8] She often thought of her life with Rex and of the extraordinary man she had married: "I never quite understood Rex," she told Liam O'Leary, "but I think that was why I was in love with him. I think the minute you understand somebody you have had it."[9]

Alice continued too to mull over their legacy: "Saw *Garden of Allah* yesterday. I must say that Iván [Petrovich] seemed less of an actor than I remembered—but I liked it better than I thought I would."[10] Sometimes she thought of the ending of Rex's career with regret: "Whenever I think of the studio in Nice—*The Three Passions* and *Baroud*—I always feel a bit sad for they were the last pictures Rex made—it's a shame that it couldn't have gone on and on."[11] Alice Terry succumbed to Alzheimer's disease in a Burbank hospital on 22 December 1987.

By then, in 1979, a substantial portion of Rex's highly valued collection of art and artifacts had been anonymously put up for auction in Los Angeles. Many of the pieces are now in private collections, but one, Chasseriau's *Scene in the Jewish Quarter of Constantine* (also known as *Two Jewish*

Women of Constantine, 1851), is held at the Metropolitan Museum of Art in New York. In 1988 further items were auctioned in Los Angeles, this time including his collection of ancient weapons.

In 1980 the Cork Film Festival honored Rex and another forgotten Irish director, Herbert Brenon. Liam O'Leary organized a retrospective and exhibition at the Galway Film Fleadh (Festival) of 1990. The Pordenone Silent Film Festival held a major centenary retrospective in 1993 with Kevin Brownlow and David Gill's restored print of *Four Horsemen* as its centerpiece, and this was mirrored by a retrospective and exhibition at the Irish Film Centre in Dublin. This was followed in 1994 by the inclusion of all of Rex's extant MGM and Metro-Goldwyn films as part of the *MGM 70 Years: Rediscoveries and Classics* season at the Museum of Modern Art in New York. Since then the restored *Four Horsemen* has continued to astonish generations of filmgoers with its extraordinary virtuosity.

It is that virtuosity that makes the films of Rex Ingram so distinctive. In those few short years of early cinema, when everything seemed possible, he believed that he could create true artworks that anyone, from any walk of life, could enjoy. This spirit of optimism prompted him to declare in 1922:

> Slowly but surely, the cinema is coming into its own, taking its place, if not beside sculpture and painting as an art, most certainly ahead of the spoken drama. The motion picture's unlimited possibilities where sweeping, smashing dramatic effects are desired; the many opportunities it affords to accomplish results not to be dreamt of behind the footlights; the intimacy that can be made to exist between the audience and the characters in the film play—all go to prove that this great new art—until recently termed "industry"—potentially combines that which fine sculpture, fine painting, and the best the theatre has to offer can give us.[12]

Cinema, he believed, was the foundation for civilization.

In his own practice, Rex gradually came to realize how valuable his training as a sculptor was. As the sculptor organizes his work to fit a certain space, so the director must place people within given lines and deploy light and shade to lend the film its pictorial quality. Most of all, this training influenced his close-ups, for with light a director could model a head as a sculptor would, "to give something of a stereoscopic quality to the soft, mellow-toned close-up, which takes the place of the human voice on the screen and helps to make the audience as intimate with the characters as if they had known and seen them constantly in everyday life."[13] If sculpting with light and shadow brought characters to life and, literally, filled in their backgrounds, so the successful director, Rex believed, must mix with people from all walks of life, be familiar with the cultures of the world, be an avid reader of books, and have the power to visualize the written word. He remained fascinated with beauty and its underside, the grotesque, combining both in his films and then later in his writings. In the heyday of his Hollywood career, as he made one hit after another, his aspirations for the motion picture chimed with an influential school of thought within Hollywood itself. Critics, writers on film, and certain sectors of the public welcomed the new medium— and Rex's pictures in particular—for their refusal to distinguish between art and commerce.[14] As the industry developed, however, and took on the form that is now more familiar to worldwide audiences, Rex's artist-centered filmmaking became less and less relevant. His final North African films were a testament to his love for the people and places with which he was now so preoccupied, and as travelogues they were works of extraordinary beauty, but as stories they fell far short. And so his movies fell from favor and his work slipped out of fashion.

After completing *Mars in the House of Death,* Rex wrote to Lee Lawrie: "I have so much work to do simplifying what I write. If I keep at it long enough I think I will turn out something worth while [*sic*]—that is to say from a creative point of view, making no concessions to box office—which I seldom did anyway, and when I did I messed things up."[15] In a way, he was right: his films seldom were made with the box office in mind, if for a while the box office loved them. Yet, behind these words, there is a yearning for success, for artistic reward, that perversely he found in no other career, neither writing nor sculpture.

The success of two homages to the silent era of film production, Martin Scorsese's *Hugo* and Michel Hazanavicius's *The Artist,* both released in 2011, introduced a new generation of filmgoers to the romance of those early days of filmmaking. In 2012, Pablo Berger followed these with the Spanish silent film version of the Snow White story, *Blancanieves.* As we revisit the history of those incredible film pioneers, their daring, and their sense of the possibilities of filmmaking, challenge us to keep that tradition alive. If writing this book can contribute in any small way to that, it can only do so because its subject was a man of such brilliance.

Acknowledgments

This is not the first book about Rex Ingram. In 1980 Liam O'Leary published *Rex Ingram: Master of the Silent Cinema;* this book is indebted to O'Leary's scholarship and I have drawn liberally on his research. Since its publication, many of the films that had been believed lost have been rediscovered and made available for viewing. New sources of information have emerged, and I am grateful to Maj. R. K. B. Hitchcock for permission to view and quote from the unpublished short stories and family papers and for the support and enthusiasm of the Hitchcock family for this project.

I am hugely indebted to Geoff Balkan for his safekeeping of Rex Ingram's memoirs, "A Long Way from Tipperary," as well as the other items, including the home movie footage, now held in the archives of Trinity College Dublin. I would also like to thank Paul Kozak for allowing me to read his unpublished master's dissertation on Rex Ingram and for donating it to the Trinity College Dublin archives. I have benefited enormously from the advice of Kevin Brownlow and Anthony Slide, whose extensive knowledge of Rex Ingram and the silent era they have so kindly shared with me. Quotations from Brownlow's privately held interviews with Willis Goldbeck and Grant Whytock are reproduced with kind permission. I welcome Thelma Schoonmaker's enthusiasm and support, both on her behalf and on Martin Scorsese's, for the wider project of reviving Rex Ingram's reputation.

At Trinity College Dublin, I would particularly like to thank Simon Williams for his support of this project over the last several years; Aidan Delaney for work on the Rex Ingram website (https://www.tcd.ie/film/rexingram/); Catherine Morris for suggestions and advice; Robin Adams, Jane Maxwell, Bernard Meehan, and the staff of the library and archives; and my colleagues and students in the School of Drama, Film and Music. I would like to acknowledge the financial assistance of the Arts and Social Sciences Benefaction Fund in providing extra funding for the website, research, and travel.

Without the generous invitation from Michael Kenneally to take up a position as the Peter O'Brien Visiting Scholar in Canadian Irish Studies at Concordia University in the fall of 2012, I would not have been able to complete this book on schedule, and I am enormously grateful to all of those responsible for that invitation, including the O'Brien family.

I have benefited in so many ways from collaborating with Bill Grantham and Rachel Lysaght on the wider Rex Ingram project, now including their forthcoming documentary on Ingram, and this would be a lesser book without their collegiality. I would also like to thank Judith Gantley at the Princess Grace Irish Library, Kevin McGee at the Nenagh Silent Film Festival, and Barry Monahan at University College Cork for invitations to speak on this research and for the feedback I received on those occasions. I have met so many people through the writing of this book that I cannot begin to acknowledge them all, but I would like to mention two longtime Ingram enthusiasts, Inez Nordell and Michael Ford, who were in on this project from the start. At a very late stage in writing this, I met Leonhard Gmuer and am full of admiration for his knowledge about Ingram and the Ingram circle, now published as *Rex Ingram: Hollywood's Rebel of the Silver Screen* (epubli GmbH, 2013).

I would like to thank all those who assisted me at the Margaret Herrick Library, Ned Comstock at the University of Southern California library, Jared Case at George Eastman House, staff at the MoMA Film Study Center, the French National Library, and the British Film Institute. I am especially indebted to Fiona Ross, former director of the National Library of Ireland, and Honora Faul, Sandra McDermott, and Colette O'Flaherty at the NLI for access to the Liam O'Leary archives, an ongoing project, I hope.

I would like to thank Tom Slater for sharing his knowledge of June Mathis with me and many others who responded to my queries and offered help, including Charles Barr, Elaine Burrows, Josef Gugler, Greg Harm, Richard Koszarski, Nils Liljeberg, Lobster Films, Joseph McBride, Neil McGlone, Nathalie Morris, Thaddeus O'Sullivan, Rick Spector, Amanda Vaill, Jake M. Wien, and Abdenour Zahzah. At the very last moment, Kaveh Askari and Douglass Daniel rescued me from what would have been a major omission (the Ingram correspondence at Library of Congress), and I cannot thank them enough.

Pat McGilligan has been, once again, the most generous mentor any biography writer could hope for, and I have turned to him over and again for help with this book. It has been a pleasure working with the University

Press of Kentucky, especially Anne Dean Dotson, Mack McCormick, Bailey Johnson, Don McKeon, and the anonymous readers of this book.

As ever, it is my long-suffering family who deserve most of my thanks for living with the current obsession, especially Willie, Conal, Eoin, and Paddy, but also Clare, my mother-in-law, and my own mother, Anne Barton.

Notes

Abbreviations

AMPAS   Academy of Motion Pictures Arts and Sciences (Margaret Herrick Library)

LOC   Library of Congress

LOLA   Liam O'Leary Archive, National Library of Ireland (uncataloged)

TCD MS 11448   Rex Ingram collection at Trinity College Dublin archives

Introduction

1. Ricciotto Canudo, "Reflections on the Seventh Art," in *French Film Theory and Criticism*, ed. Richard Abel (Princeton, NJ: Princeton University Press, 1988). Although Canudo's essay was originally published in 1923, he had been refining this notion over the course of several articles and years.

2. Sewell Stokes, *Pilloried!* (Edinburgh: Riverside, 1928), 62.

3. Michael Powell, *A Life in Movies: An Autobiography* (London: Faber, 2000), 164.

4. "Knowledge of Film Tricks Fatal to Fun," *Los Angeles Times*, 17 September 1922, III-32.

5. James Joyce, *Finnegans Wake* (London: Penguin Books, 1992), 568.

6. E-mail correspondence with Thaddeus O'Sullivan, 16 April 2013.

I. Childhood in Ireland

1. *Thom's Official Directory 1891*, 1632.

2. William Butler Yeats, "The Man and the Echo," in *The Collected Poems of W. B. Yeats* (London: Wordsworth Poetry Library, 1994), 298–99.

3. Liam O'Leary, questions to Maj. Francis Clere Hitchcock, undated manuscript, LOLA. Hitchcock responded that his brother read Yeats but did not name specific works.

4. Rex Ingram, "A Long Way from Tipperary," unpublished memoirs, TCD MS 11448, 1.

5. Ingram, "A Long Way," 10.

6. Information taken from the census of 1901, http://www.census.nationalarchives.ie (accessed 11 November 2012).

7. Ingram, "A Long Way," 15–16.

8. Ibid., 31.

9. Ibid., 45.

10. The term "big house" is loosely used to describe the houses of the Irish landed gentry. See Terence A. M. Dooley, *The Decline of the "Big House" in Ireland: A Study of Irish Landed Families* (Dublin: Wolfhound, 2001).

11. Letter from W. J. Kinsella to Liam O'Leary, 20 May 1980, LOLA.

12. Ingram, "A Long Way," 53.

13. See Noel Guerin, "Darbys of Leap," *Irish Midlands Ancestry* (1999), http://www.irishmidlandsancestry.com/content/family_history/families/darbys.htm (accessed 7 September 2012).

14. F. R. Montgomery Hitchcock, *Types of Celtic Life and Art* (Dublin: Sealy, 1906), 123.

15. Ibid., 23.

16. Ibid., 52.

17. R. D. Greer, "Letters to the Editor," *Irish Times*, 25 November 1972, 13.

18. Letter from Rex Ingram to Kathleen Hitchcock, "Sunday 18" (no further information supplied), LOLA. Hastings Killingley died in World War I, aged 21.

19. St. Columba's College Records (copy), 4 July 1950, LOLA.

20. Letter from Blacker Bridge to Liam O'Leary, 23 September 1959, LOLA.

21. Letter from Colonel Bridge to Liam O'Leary, 31 July 1959, LOLA.

22. Transcript of card, 30 May 1910, LOLA.

23. Transcript of card, dated only October, LOLA.

24. Ingram, "A Long Way," 85–86.

25. Ibid., 103.

26. Ibid., 110–11.

27. Ibid., 114.

28. Liam O'Leary, *Rex Ingram: Master of the Silent Cinema* (Pordenone, Italy: Le Giornate del Cinema Muto; London: British Film Institute, 1993, 1980), 21–22.

29. Ingram, "A Long Way," 130.

2. New York Bohemia and the Lure of the Movies

1. Ingram, "A Long Way," 135.

2. Quoted in ibid., 170.

3. O'Leary, *Rex Ingram*, 25.

4. *Yale Record*, 18 June 1912, 898.

5. Page torn from the *Yale Record* and sent to Liam O'Leary by Francis Clere Hitchcock. Sketch is dated 1914. LOLA.

6. *Directory of the Living Non-Graduates of Yale University, Issue of 1914*, unpublished document, http://www.google.ie/url?sa=t&rct=j&q=&esrc=s&source=web&cd=6&ved=0CFkQFjAF&url=http%3A%2F%2Fwww.library

.yale.edu%2Fmssa%2FYHO%2FDirectory_of_the_Living_non-graduates
.pdf&ei=d3HYT_H8M4SXhQfdwqWvDw&usg=AFQjCNGYFnhza2QQH7dV5
7jsW8kMbDkGyQ&sig2=LMPd302-MvirfT0H2wLiJA (accessed 13 June 2012).

7. Ingram, "A Long Way," 186.

8. Ibid., 188. In other accounts, Rex says that he first saw *A Tale of Two Cities* when staying on Long Island with Horace Newsome. In these versions, this reads like the moment of revelation when he discovers cinema, but it is very unlikely that he would not have seen films when at Yale.

9. Bruce Kellner, *The Last Dandy, Ralph Barton* (Columbia and London: University of Missouri Press, 1991), 32.

10. Ingram, "A Long Way," 198.

11. Erika Doss, *Benton, Pollock, and the Politics of Modernism: From Regionalism to Abstract Expressionism* (Chicago and London: University of Chicago Press, 1991), 15.

12. Ibid., 15.

13. Ibid., 37.

14. Kellner, *Last Dandy,* 12. I am indebted to Kellner's biography for background on Barton.

15. Ibid., 34.

16. Ibid., 35.

17. Ingram, "A Long Way," 214.

18. Ibid., 217.

19. Rex Ingram, "Letter to Aunt Lizzie," 15 September 1913, TCD MS 11448. Aunt Lizzie was probably his great-aunt, Elizabeth Jane Lambert, sister to his paternal grandmother, Frances. My thanks to Bill Grantham for this information.

20. The transitional period is usually considered to have lasted from around 1907 to around 1917.

21. Ingram, "A Long Way," 219.

22. Ibid., 223.

23. Rex Ingram, "Letter to Aunt Lizzie," 25 December 1913, TCD MS 11448.

24. Ingram, "A Long Way," 241.

25. Letter from Seymour Stern to Liam O'Leary, 2 May 1966, LOLA.

26. Albert E. Smith and Phil A. Koury, *Two Reels and a Crank* (Garden City, NY: Garland, 1985), 193.

27. Kristin Thompson, "Narration Early in the Transition to Classical Filmmaking: Three Vitagraph Shorts," *Film History* 9, no. 4 (1997): 410–34, 411, and Barry Salt, "Vitagraph Films: A Touch of Real Class," in *Screen Culture: History and Textuality,* ed. John Fullerton, 55–72 (Eastleigh: John Libbey Publishing, 2004), 56.

28. Ingram, "A Long Way," 258.

29. "The Moonshine Maid and the Man," *Moving Picture World,* 19 December 1914, 1680.

30. Letter from Rex Hitchcock (Ingram) to Cissie, 17 March 1915, LOLA.

31. Thomas Hart Benton, *An Artist in America* (New York: University of Kansas City Press, 1951), 38.

32. Henry Adams, *Tom and Jack: The Intertwined Lives of Thomas Hart Benton and Jackson Pollock* (New York: Bloomsbury, 2009), 153.

33. Benton, *An Artist*, 38. Ingram's later film *Broken Fetters* (1917) had a Paddy Sullivan in the cast, so this might be the film.

34. Ingram, "A Long Way," 260–61.

35. Ibid., 267.

36. Edward Montagne, "Then and Now," *Film Daily*, 7 June 1925, 23.

37. Edward Weitzel, "Should a Mother Tell?," *Moving Picture World*, 17 July 1915, 506–7.

38. "The Song of Hate," *Variety*, 17 September 1915, 25.

39. "Triangle Here at Auditorium," *Los Angeles Times*, 7 November 1915, III-3.

40. "The Blindness of Devotion," *Variety*, 12 November 1915, 22.

41. An article in *Variety* suggested that Rex was also using the pseudonyms "Captain Wilbur Lawton" and "Captain John King," both of which appear in the credits of *The Wonderful Adventure* and *A Woman's Past*, respectively, and on no other films, so this could be true. See "Film Flashes." *Variety*, 10 December 1915, 20. The scenario of *A Woman's Past*, held at 20th Century-Fox Collection, USC Cinematic Arts Library, is credited to Rex Ingram. Quotation from page 31.

42. Rex Ingram, "The Criminal," *New York Call*, 9 May 1915, Rex Ingram Scrapbook, AMPAS. My thanks to Leonhard Gmuer for advising me on the correct date of publication.

43. Ingram, "A Long Way," 290–91.

3. Rex Ingram, Director

1. Ingram, "A Long Way," 304.

2. For an analysis of the structures at Universal, see Mark Garrett Cooper, *Universal Women* (Urbana, Chicago, and Springfield: University of Illinois Press, 2010).

3. Ingram, "A Long Way," 314–15.

4. "The Great Problem," *Variety*, 7 April 1916, 22.

5. "Broken Fetters," *Variety*, 23 June 1916, 20.

6. Ingram, "A Long Way," 332–33.

7. Margaret I. MacDonald, "Broken Fetters," *Moving Picture World*, 1 July 1916, 103.

8. Ingram, "A Long Way," 345.

9. Cleo Madison, undated letter to Liam O'Leary, LOLA.

10. "The Dual Personality of an Actress," *Moving Picture Stories* 8, no. 187 (1916): 28–29. Available on http://www.silentera.com/articles/movPicStories/1916/

v018n0187/pp28–29.html (accessed 3 June 2012). On Cleo Madison's marriage, see Cooper, *Universal Women*, 182.

11. Ingram, "A Long Way," 347.

12. Kaveh Askari, "Art School Cinema: Rex Ingram and the Lessons of the Studio," in *Film History* (forthcoming).

13. "The Chalice of Sorrow," *Variety*, 29 September 1916, 26.

14. "Black Orchids," *Variety*, 29 December 1916, 22.

15. Ingram, "A Long Way," 347.

16. Ibid., 348.

17. Myrtle Gebhart, "An Easy-Chair Career," *Picture-Play Magazine*, February 1923, 84.

18. Madison, undated letter.

19. Ingram, "A Long Way," 348.

20. Ibid., 349.

21. Ibid., 351–52.

22. Quoted in Ingram, "A Long Way," 353.

23. Ibid., 356.

24. Ingram, "A Long Way," 357.

25. In Peter Bogdanovich, *John Ford* (London: Studio Vista, 1967), 47.

26. Ingram, "A Long Way," 359.

27. Ibid., 361.

28. Liam O'Leary, "An Interview with Alice Terry," undated, transcribed, LOLA.

29. Letter from Maj. Francis Clere Hitchcock to Liam O'Leary, 20 August 1960, LOLA.

30. Note on back of photograph from Maj. Francis Clere Hitchcock to Liam O'Leary, undated, LOLA.

31. Letter from Ministry of Defence to Liam O'Leary, 2 May 1966, LOLA.

32. Gordon Sparling, "J. Booth Scott, November 1966," *Canadian Journal of Film Studies* 5, no. 2 (Fall 1996): 124–34, 126.

33. Ingram, "A Long Way," 373.

34. Ibid., 375–79.

35. Ibid., 380.

36. Ibid., 400.

37. Ibid., 404.

38. Ibid., 410.

39. Ibid., 416–17. I can find no record of a Swigstrom at Universal.

40. In O'Leary, *Rex Ingram*, 57. The original interview with Erich von Stroheim took place in London in 1954. Recording held at LOLA.

41. Letter from Alice Terry to Liam O'Leary, 14 April 1971, LOLA.

42. Letter from Alice Terry to Liam O'Leary, 6 October 1970, LOLA. Confusingly, there was another silent-era film actor called Alice Terry. To distinguish

between the two, one needs to remember that Alice Terry was always credited as "Alice Taafe [sic]" in her films of the teens.

43. O'Leary, "Interview with Alice Terry."

44. Ingram, "A Long Way," 442–43.

45. Ibid., 443.

46. Letter from Alice Terry to Liam O'Leary, 4 April 1960, LOLA.

47. Letter from Alice Terry to Liam O'Leary, undated, LOLA.

48. Ingram, "A Long Way," 450–51.

49. Ibid., 452.

50. In Paul Enright Kozak, "Rex Ingram: The Films of a Forgotten Master of Silent Screen Arts as Recalled by Friends and Contemporaries, and a Modern Viewpoint" (MA thesis, University of Southern California, 1978), 85. In fact the Moviola came into general usage in 1924.

51. Kevin Brownlow, "Interview with Grant Whytock," California, 1970, private collection. Reproduced with kind permission of Kevin Brownlow.

52. Ingram, "A Long Way," 454.

53. George C. Pratt, "'If You Beat Me, I Wept': Alice Terry Reminisces about Silent Films," *Image* 16, no. 1 (1973): 17–22, 20.

54. "Little to Recommend This in Either Story or Production," *Film Daily,* 6 June 1920, 13.

55. Jesse L. Lasky with Don Weldon, *I Blow My Own Horn* (New York: Doubleday, 1957), 147.

56. Ingram, "A Long Way," 459.

57. "Oral History with John F. Seitz," conducted by James Ursini, May 1971 to May 1972, Louis B. Mayer Oral History Collection, American Film Institute.

58. Ibid.

59. O'Leary, "Interview with Alice Terry."

60. Letter from Lee Lawrie to Rex Ingram, 19 May 1920, Rex Ingram Scrapbook, AMPAS.

61. Ingram, "A Long Way," 463.

62. O'Leary, "Interview with Alice Terry."

63. Letter from Alice Terry to Liam O'Leary, 4 April 1960, LOLA.

64. Letter from Alice Terry to Liam O'Leary, undated, LOLA.

65. Selma Robinson, "A Rex-Ray View of Alice Terry," *Motion Picture Magazine* 28, no. 10 (1924): 24–25, 106–7.

4. Apocalypse at Metro

1. Metro Pictures Corporation Weekly Pay Roll, 2 July 1921, sheet number 6, Special Collections, AMPAS.

2. Terry Ramsaye, *A Million and One Nights: A History of the Motion Picture through 1925* (New York: Simon & Schuster, 1986), 797.

3. Vicente Blasco Ibáñez, *The Four Horsemen of the Apocalypse,* translated by Charlotte Brewster Jordan (New York: E. P. Dutton, 1918), 178.

4. I am indebted to A. Grove Day and Edgar C. Knowlton Jr.'s *V. Blasco Ibáñez* (New York: Twayne, 1972) for much of the following background information.

5. Ramsaye, *A Million and One Nights,* 799.

6. Ibid.

7. Thomas J. Slater, "June Mathis: A Woman Who Spoke through Silents," in *American Silent Film: Discovering Marginalized Voices*, ed. Gregg Bachman and Thomas. J. Slater (Carbondale: Southern Illinois University Press, 2002), 202.

8. Natacha Rambova, *Rudolph Valentino: A Wife's Memories of an Icon,* ed. Hala Pickford (Hollywood, CA: 1921 PVG Publishing, 2009), 150.

9. Gladys Hall, "A Maker of Young Men," *Motion Picture Classic* 19, no. 1 (1924): 22.

10. Ibid. Emphasis in the original.

11. Of the many biographical accounts of his life, see in particular Emily Wortis Leider, *Dark Lover: The Life and Death of Rudolph Valentino* (London: Faber, 2003). The classic academic analysis of Valentino's fandom is chapter 3 of Gaylyn Studlar's *This Mad Masquerade: Stardom and Masculinity in the Jazz Age* (New York: Columbia University Press, 1996). See also chapter 11 of Miriam Hansen's *Babel and Babylon: Spectatorship in American Silent Film* (Cambridge, MA, and London: Harvard University Press, 1991).

12. Rudolph Valentino, "Rudolph: My Life Story," *Photoplay,* April 1923, 53, 96, 97.

13. In Samuel Goldwyn, *Behind the Screen* (London: Grant Richards, 1925), 188.

14. Metro Pictures Corporation Weekly Pay Roll, 2 July 1921, sheet number 12, Special Collections, AMPAS.

15. In Robert Florey, *La lanterne magique* (Lausanne: Cinémathèque suisse, 1966), 162 (author's translation).

16. Metro Pictures Corporation Weekly Pay Roll, 13 August 1921, sheet number 12, Special Collections, AMPAS.

17. Ingram, "A Long Way," 477.

18. Katherine Lipke, "Most Responsible Job Ever Held by a Woman," *Los Angeles Times,* 3 June 1923, 13, 16.

19. In William Butler Yeats, *Michael Robartes and the Dancer* (London: Kessinger, 2003), 9.

20. Ibid., 19

21. Lipke, "Most Responsible Job," 16. Surely the drag sequence in Jean Renoir's *La Grande Illusion* of 1937, also featuring Erich von Stroheim, is an homage to this.

22. Ingram, "A Long Way," 472.

23. Ramsaye, *A Million and One Nights,* 800.

24. Richard Koszarski, *Hollywood on the Hudson: Film and Television in New York from Griffith to Sarnoff* (New Brunswick, NJ: Rutgers University Press, 2008) 18.

25. In Richard Koszarski, *An Evening's Entertainment: The Age of the Silent Feature Picture, 1915–1928* (Berkeley, Los Angeles, London: University of California Press, 1994), 134.

26. Grace Kingsley, "Picture Taxes Art Resources," *Los Angeles Times,* 29 August 1920, III-1.

27. Rehfeld stayed on as Rex's assistant but later lost a leg in a streetcar accident. June Mathis stayed faithful to him, selecting him as director for *The Greater Glory* in 1926.

28. Pratt, "'If You Beat Me, I Wept,'" 20.

29. Leider, *Dark Lover,* 114.

30. O'Leary, *Rex Ingram,* 94.

31. Rambova, *Rudolph Valentino,* 37n.

32. Ibid., 290.

33. Ibid.

34. In Goldwyn, *Behind the Screen,* 189–90.

35. In "Ideaed Directors," *New York Times,* 13 February 1921, V1-2.

36. In Goldwyn, *Behind the Screen,* 189. Elsewhere Rex attributed this decision to Alice. See Robinson, "A Rex-Ray View of Alice Terry," 24.

37. Rumors have long circulated that Rex Ingram in fact directed that particular sequence in *Regeneration,* so alike are they, but there is no evidence to support this.

38. The version I am referring to is Kevin Brownlow's restoration.

39. Alexander Walker, *Stardom: The Hollywood Phenomenon* (London: Joseph, 1970), 154.

40. A widely discussed newspaper editorial fulminated on the degeneration into effeminacy by the American male, who now was reputed to make up his face in public washrooms and of whom the epitome was Valentino. "Editorial," *Chicago Tribune,* 6 July 1926.

41. Andrei Tarkovsky's antiwar film *Ivan's Childhood* (1962) also references Dürer, and it would not be surprising if the great Russian artist/director were paying homage to Rex Ingram's film.

42. Ingram, "A Long Way," 480.

43. "A £500,000 Film with 12,000 Performers: 'The Four Horsemen of the Apocalypse,'" *Illustrated London News,* 12 February 1921, 209.

44. Kingsley, "Picture Taxes."

45. "The Four Horsemen," *Film Daily,* 14 February 1921, 4.

46. *Variety,* 8 April 1921, 1.

47. "The Screen," *New York Times,* 7 March 1921, 16.

48. Edwin Schallert, "Reviews," *Los Angeles Times*, 10 March 1921, III-4.

49. "Four Horsemen of the Apocalypse," *Variety*, 18 February 1921, 40.

50. Ingram, "A Long Way," 482.

51. Schallert, "Reviews," III-4.

52. Ramsaye, *A Million and One Nights*, 801, and *Variety*, 18 March 1925, 27.

53. John Bull, *Film Daily*, 30 December 1922, 4.

5. Conquering Metro

1. In Florey, *La lanterne magique*, 162 (author's translation).

2. Ingram, "A Long Way," 484.

3. Rambova, *Rudolph Valentino*, 37–39, and "Oral History with John F. Seitz."

4. Kellner, *Last Dandy*, 70–71.

5. Valentino, "My Life Story," 97, 98.

6. "Oral History with John F. Seitz."

7. Ibid.

8. Ingram, "A Long Way," 485.

9. Ibid., 483.

10. DeWitt Bodeen, "Rex Ingram and Alice Terry, Part One," *Films in Review* 16, no. 2 (1975): 73–89.

11. Lasky, *I Blow My Own Horn*, 146–47.

12. Telegram from Jesse Lasky to Adolph Zukor, 25 June 1921, Adolph Zukor Correspondence, AMPAS, http://digitalcollections.oscars.org/cdm/singleitem/collection/p15759c0113/id/185/rec/1 (accessed 14 May 2013).

13. Lasky, *I Blow My Own Horn*, 147.

14. "In 'Conquering Power' Ingram Outdoes 'Four Horsemen' Says the National Board of Review," *Moving Picture World*, 19 November 1921, 412.

15. Edwin Schallert, "The Conquering Power," *Los Angeles Times*, 11 August 1921, III-4.

16. "Screen: A Maker of Pictures," *New York Times*, 10 July 1921.

17. Schallert, "Conquering Power," and Jolo, "Conquering Power," *Variety*, 8 July 1921, 27.

18. "Rex Ingram Story Ran High on Cost," *Los Angeles Times*, 27 March 1922, III-3.

19. Mary O'Hara, *Flicka's Friend* (New York: G. P. Putnam's Sons, 1982), 157.

20. "Turn to the Right," *New York Times*, 6 February 1922, 11.

21. Leed, "Turn to the Right," *Variety*, 27 January 1922, 34.

22. Letter from Howard Strickling to Liam O'Leary, 12 August 1971, LOLA.

23. In Kozak, "Rex Ingram," 149n.

24. Letter from Alice Terry to Liam O'Leary, 4 April 1960, LOLA.

25. Rudolph Valentino, "What's the Matter with the Movies?," *Illustrated World*, May 1923, 342, 44, 422, 26.

26. Leed, "Turn to the Right," 39.

27. "Turn to the Right (Review)," *Picture-Play Magazine,* April 1922, 62.

6. Swashbucklers and Other Romances

1. "Oral History with John F. Seitz."

2. Elizabeth Lonergan, "Directors I Have Met," *Pictures and Picturegoer,* April 1923, 34.

3. Anthony Hope, *The Prisoner of Zenda* (London and New York): J. M. Dent and Sons and E. P. Dutton, 1894), 164.

4. Ingram, "A Long Way," 484–85.

5. A Special Correspondent, "A Famous Film Star: Ramón Novarro in Dublin; How He Reached Hollywood," *Irish Times,* 20 April 1936, 8.

6. "'It's Just Wonderful How Fate Works!' Ramón Novarro on His Film Career," *Image* 16, no. 4 (1973): 16–26, 19.

7. In DeWitt Bodeen, *More from Hollywood: The Careers of 15 Great American Stars* (South Brunswick, NJ, and New York: A. S. Barnes, 1977; London: Tantivy, 1977), 196.

8. Quoted in Frank Javier Garcia Berumen, *Ramón Novarro: The Life and Films of the First Latino Hollywood Superstar* (New York: Vantage, 2001), 13.

9. O'Leary, "Interview with Alice Terry."

10. "'It's Just Wonderful,'" 196.

11. Ann Joyce, "Countess Helga, of Hollywood," *Pantomime,* 18 February 1922, 11.

12. Adela Rogers St. Johns, *The Honeycomb* (Garden City, NY: Doubleday, 1969), 171.

13. Brownlow, "Interview with Grant Whytock."

14. In Koszarski, *An Evening's Entertainment,* 130.

15. According to DeWitt Bodeen, Metro forced Rex to film an alternative happy ending, but this was not used. Bodeen, "Rex Ingram and Alice Terry, Part One," 87.

16. Kevin Brownlow, "Interview with Willis Goldbeck," 4 March 1970. I am grateful to Kevin Brownlow for allowing me to consult this item from his private collection.

17. O'Leary, "Interview with Alice Terry."

18. Ingram, "A Long Way," 487.

19. Ibid.

20. O'Leary, "Interview with Alice Terry."

21. Anthony Slide considers the possibility that Rex Ingram was a gay man without finding any convincing grounds that he was, in "The Silent Closet," *Film Quarterly* 52, no. 4 (1999): 24–32. While researching his book, Liam O'Leary asked Jean de Limur if he thought Ingram was homosexual. De Limur replied that he thought Ingram was asexual, though this also seems unlikely. That undated audio recording is held at LOLA.

22. Inez McCleary, "Rex Ingram—Idol Smasher," *Picture-Play Magazine*, February 1923, 83, 99.

23. Grace Kingsley, "Flashes, Postpone Wedding," *Los Angeles Times*, 14 October 1921, III-4.

24. Kozak, "Rex Ingram," 238.

25. "Alice Terry Married to Rex Ingram," *Los Angeles Times*, 6 November 1921, II-5.

26. Herbert Howe, "When Alice Played a German Soldier with a Beard," *Photoplay*, February 1925, 98.

27. Lorna Moon gave birth to three children out of wedlock, one of whom, Richard de Mille, was adopted by Cecil B. DeMille but was in reality the child of his brother, William. The other two children were another son and a daughter. Moon's novel *Dark Star*, set in her home town of Strichen in Scotland, was banned by the Strichen library for too closely resembling some of the community's members.

28. Edwin Schallert, "Reviews: Myths and Fancies," *Los Angeles Times*, 18 September 1922, II-9.

29. "The Prisoner of Zenda," *New York Times*, 1 August 1922, 14.

30. Rush, "Prisoner of Zenda," *Variety*, 4 August 1922, 34–35.

31. "'The Prisoner of Zenda' (Review)," *Picture-Play Magazine*, July 1922, 69.

32. Grace Kingsley, "Rex Ingram to Join Exodus to Europe," *Los Angeles Times*, 13 June 1921, II-7.

33. Edwin Schallert, "Westward Is Loew's Course," *Los Angeles Times*, 30 October 1921, III-33.

34. Grace Kingsley, "Flashes: Rex Ingram's Plans," *Los Angeles Times*, 5 January 1922, III-4.

35. Edwin Schallert, "Playdom: Ingram Going East," *Los Angeles Times*, 19 April 1922, II-9.

36. "Making Your Own Movies," *Screenland*, April 1922, 35.

37. "New Faces," *Film Daily*, 4 October 1922, 1.

38. "Newspaper Opinions," *Film Daily*, 6 October 1922, 4.

39. "Oral History with John F. Seitz."

40. "Trifling Women," *New York Times*, 4 October 1922, 23.

41. "Newspaper Opinions," 4.

42. Helene G. Bellis, "Vive Le Rex!," *Photoplay*, July 1923, 8.

43. Herbert Howe, "Close-Ups and Long Shots," *Photoplay*, November 1923, 55.

44. Herbert Howe, "How He Makes Them Act," *Photoplay*, December 1923, 53, 106–7.

45. John Russell, *Where the Pavement Ends* (London: Thornton Butterworth, 1919), 65.

46. This is a lost film. Quotations taken from "Where the Pavement Ends Intertitles" (transcript), LOLA. Suspension points in original.

47. Kozak, "Rex Ingram," 27.

48. Ibid., 368n.

49. Ingram, "A Long Way," 501. For the crew's recollections of the shoot, see Kozak, "Rex Ingram," 267–78.

50. St. Johns, *The Honeycomb,* 171.

51. See Thomas J. Slater, "The Vision and the Struggle: June Mathis's Work on *Ben-Hur* (1922–24)," *Post Script* 28, no. 1 (2008): 63–78, and Kevin Brownlow, *The Parade's Gone By* (London: Secker & Warburg, 1968), 366–414.

52. "Oral History with John F. Seitz."

53. Novarro quoted in Brownlow, *The Parade's Gone By,* 391.

54. Edwin Schallert, "Playdom: South Sea Romance; Rare Impression by Latest Ingram Picture," *Los Angeles Times,* 2 April 1923, II 7.

55. "'Where the Pavement Ends' (Round up of Reviews)," *Film Daily,* 4 April 1923, 4.

56. Fred, "Where the Pavement Ends," *Variety,* 5 April 1923, 36.

57. Bodeen, "Rex Ingram and Alice Terry, Part One," 86.

58. Brownlow, "Interview with Willis Goldbeck." The "assistant" was probably Curt Rehfeld.

59. Ingram, "A Long Way," 503. Jean-Antoine Houdon was a famed French sculptor of the nineteenth century.

60. Various figures from $800,000 to more than $1 million have been attached to the budget.

61. Peter White, "What Every Woman Wants," *Picture-Play Magazine,* June 1922, 24.

62. Herbert Howe, "Finds Kings and Jokers," *Los Angeles Times,* 19 August 1923, III-33, III-39.

63. Lasky, *I Blow My Own Horn,* 110–11.

64. Cecil B. DeMille, "Picture Secondary in Cinema Success," *Los Angeles Times,* 18 July 1923, WF5.

65. "23 Roadshows," *Film Daily,* 6 August 1923, 1.

66. Edwin Schallert, "Playdom: 'Scaramouche,'" *Los Angeles Times,* 18 January 1924, A11.

67. "'Scaramouche': Metro (Round up of Reviews)," *Film Daily,* 5 October 1923, 2.

68. Fred, "Scaramouche," *Variety,* 4 October 1923, 22.

69. "'Scaramouche': Metro (Round up of Reviews)."

70. Bodeen, "Rex Ingram and Alice Terry, Part One," 88–89.

7. Escape to the Desert

1. Flyer for *The Arab,* TCD MS 11448.

2. "Film Folk Embark to Old World," *Los Angeles Times,* 1 October 1923, I-3.

3. "Mr Rex Ingram to Visit Dublin," *Irish Times,* 10 October 1923, 3.

4. Grace Kingsley, "Flashes: Ingram to Sahara," *Los Angeles Times,* 3 October 1923, III-1.

5. Letter from Alice Terry to Liam O'Leary, undated, LOLA.

6. Dooley, *Decline of the Big House*, 286.

7. F. R. Montgomery Hitchcock, "Letters to the Editor," *Irish Times*, 19 April 1922, 6. His was one of a sequence of letters to the *Irish Times* on this theme; see also John N. Fryday, "Letters to the Editor," *Irish Times*, 15 April 1922, 8.

8. Quoted in Dooley, *Decline of the Big House*, 269.

9. "Ingram Takes up Life Abroad as Expatriate," *Los Angeles Times*, 15 October 1923, I-7.

10. "This Industry of Ours," *Film Daily*, 12 November 1923, 2.

11. Anthony Slide, *Inside the Hollywood Fan Magazine: A History of Star Makers, Fabricators, and Gossip Mongers* (Jackson: University Press of Mississippi, 2010), and André Soares, *Beyond Paradise: The Life of Ramon Novarro* (Jackson: University Press of Mississippi, 2010).

12. Ingram, "A Long Way," 512, 511.

13. François Pouillon, *Les deux vies d'Étienne Dinet* (Paris: Éditions Balland, 1997), 84.

14. Ibid., 90.

15. Abdenour Zahzah, "Parcours. Acteur, scénariste, réalisateur, producteur . . . ," *El Watan*, 7 February 2008, http://www.elwatan.com/archives/article .php?id=86604 (accessed 7 November 2012).

16. Roy Armes, "Women Pioneers of Arab Cinema," *Screen* 48, no. 4 (2007): 517–20.

17. Herbert Howe, "On the Road with Ramon," *Motion Picture Magazine* 33, no. 2 (1927): 26–28, 108–116.

18. Pratt, "'If You Beat Me, I Wept,'" 21.

19. Howe, "Oracle Speaks," 27.

20. Ibid.

21. Howe, "On the Road," 115.

22. Herbert Howe, "Sheikhs Have Inhibitions," *Los Angeles Times*, 17 February 1924, B11, 13.

23. "Oral History with John F. Seitz."

24. Ingram, "A Long Way," 517.

25. Howe, "Sheikhs Have Inhibitions," B13.

26. Ingram, "A Long Way," 525.

27. "Ingram Decides to Quit Screen for Art Career," *Los Angeles Times*, 4 March 1924, A13.

28. Grace Kingsley, "Flashes: Home from Africa," *Los Angeles Times*, 22 March 1924, A7.

29. Herbert Howe, "Rex Ingram Buys Moorish House and Plans to Take Up Residence There Soon," *Los Angeles Times*, 16 March 1924, B11.

30. "A Tragic Decision," *Picture Show*, 14 June 1924, n.p.

31. Howe, "Rex Ingram Buys Moorish House."

32. Rex Ingram, "What Is a Director?," *Photoplay,* August 1921, 109.

33. Richard Koszarski, *Von: The Life and Films of Erich von Stroheim* (New York: Limelight Editions, 2001), 164–65, and Peter Noble, *Hollywood Scapegoat: The Biography of Erich von Stroheim* (New York: Arno, 1972), 52.

34. Edwin Schallert, "Playdom: The Real Desert," *Los Angeles Times,* 28 July 1924, A7.

35. "The Arab (Review)," *Film Daily,* 6 July 1924, 8.

36. "Newspaper Opinions New York," *Film Daily,* 17 July 1924, 4.

37. Lait, "The Arab," *Variety,* 16 July 1924, 22.

38. I have only been able to view a poor-quality print of this film with Russian-language intertitles. The beginning and the ending are missing.

39. Grace Kingsley, "Flashes: To Join Mate," *Los Angeles Times,* 10 September 1924, A11, and Grace Kingsley, "Flashes: Ingram to Work," *Los Angeles Times,* 20 September 1924, A7.

40. Howe, "Rex Ingram Buys Moorish House," B11.

41. Pratt, "'If You Beat Me, I Wept,'" 21–22.

42. Harry Carr, "Harry Carr's Page," *Los Angeles Times,* 6 August 1924, C2.

43. Susan Delson, *Dudley Murphy, Hollywood Wild Card* (Minneapolis: University of Minnesota Press, 2006), 70.

8. Escape to Nice

1. Letter from Harry Lachman to Liam O'Leary, 29 August 1960, LOLA.

2. For a detailed examination of the financial affairs and the development of the Victorine studios in this period, see Anne-Elizabeth Dutheil de la Rochère, *Les studios de la Victorine, 1919–1929* (Paris and Nice: Association française de recherche sur l'histoire du cinéma, Cinémathèque de Nice, 1998).

3. Fonds Serge Sandberg, French National Library, 4-COL-59/506.

4. Ibid., 4-COL-59/508.

5. Anthony Slide, *Silent Players* (Lexington: University Press of Kentucky, 2002), 378.

6. De la Rochère, *Les studios de la Victorine,* 202.

7. Letter from Rex Ingram to F. Scott Fitzgerald, 27 October 1926, in Matthew J. Bruccoli and George Parker Anderson, *F. Scott Fitzgerald's* Tender Is the Night: *A Documentary Volume* (Detroit: Gale, 2003), 58.

8. Author's interview with Maj. R. K. B. Hitchcock, Devon, 8 July 2001.

9. Powell, *A Life in Movies,* 97.

10. See Calvin Tomkins, *Living Well Is the Best Revenge: Two Americans in Paris, 1921–1933* (London: Deutsch, 1972), and Amanda Vaill, *Everybody Was So Young: Gerald and Sara Murphy; A Lost Generation Love Story* (London: Little, Brown, 1998).

11. "Americans in France," *Continental Life,* 24 January 1925, 7.

12. F. Scott Fitzgerald, letter to John Peale Bishop, September 1925, in F. Scott Fitzgerald, *The Crack-up, with Other Pieces and Stories* (Harmondsworth: Penguin, 1974), 272.

13. F. Scott Fitzgerald, *Tender Is the Night* (London: Penguin, 1999), 197.

14. Powell, *A Life in Movies,* 124.

15. Ibid., 135.

16. Letter from Waldo Peirce to Harry Salpeter, 2 May 1936, box Barrett-Peirce, accession number 8402, Clifton Waller Barrett Library of American Literature, University of Virginia Library. Some punctuation has been altered for the sake of readability.

17. "Oral History with John F. Seitz."

18. O'Leary, "Interview with Alice Terry."

19. Jacques Faure, "Les Américains chez nous: Rex Ingram," *Mon Ciné,* 30 December 1926, 6, 7, 8.

20. Powell, *A Life in Movies,* 150.

21. Brownlow, "Interview with Grant Whytock."

22. The version screened on TCM (on 5 December 2010) runs just over 101 minutes. According to Paul Kozak, one rumor had it that "when the picture was refilmed in Mexico in 1948 with Maria Felix and Fernando Rey, the producing company bought the original material for use in their version as stock footage." Kozak, "Rex Ingram," 347n.

23. In Delson, *Dudley Murphy,* 72.

24. Ingram, "A Long Way," 530.

25. Helen Klumph, "Mare Nostrum Is Artistic Hit," *Los Angeles Times,* 21 February 1926, 23, 25.

26. Mordaunt Hall, "Mare Nostrum (1926) Spurlos Versenkt!," *New York Times,* 16 February 1926, 22.

27. "De Mare Nostrum à la veuve joyeuse," *Cinéa,* 15 May 1926, 13.

28. Michel Lefevre, "Mare Nostrum," *Les Spectacles,* 18 March 1927, n.p.

29. "A Film of the Week: 'Mare Nostrum' at the Metropole Cinema," *Irish Times,* 6 September 1927, 8.

30. Laurent Véray, "1927: The Apotheosis of the French Historical Film?," trans. Bill Krohn, *Film History* 17, nos. 2–3 (2005): 334–51, 342–43.

31. For more on Frank Harris, see Philippa Pullar, *Frank Harris,* Penguin Classic Biography (London: Penguin, 2001).

32. Ingram, letter to F. Scott Fitzgerald, in Bruccoli and Anderson, *F. Scott Fitzgerald's* Tender Is the Night, 58.

33. Alice Terry, letter to Liam O'Leary, 14 April 1971, LOLA.

34. F. Scott Fitzgerald, *Tender Is the Night: The Melarkey and Kelly Versions,* introduced and arranged by Matthew J. Bruccoli (New York and London: Garland, 1990), 295.

35. Ibid., 301–2.

36. Ibid., 303.

37. Ibid., 309.

38. Ibid.

39. Ibid., 329.

40. Ibid., 331.

41. F. Scott Fitzgerald, "Jacob's Ladder," *Saturday Evening Post,* 20 August 1927, http://ebooks.adelaide.edu.au/f/fitzgerald/f_scott/short/chapter10.html (accessed 28 July 2011).

42. Fitzgerald, *The Crack-Up,* 49.

43. Fitzgerald, *Tender Is the Night,* 32.

44. Malcolm Lowry, Miguel Mota, Paul Tiessen, and F. Scott Fitzgerald, *The Cinema of Malcolm Lowry: A Scholarly Edition of Lowry's "Tender Is the Night"* (Vancouver: University of British Columbia Press, 1990), 165–66.

45. Powell, *A Life in Movies,* 141.

46. Ibid., 142.

47. Ibid.

48. "Oral History with John F. Seitz."

49. Brownlow, "Interview with Willis Goldbeck."

50. "Oral History with John F. Seitz."

51. Sewell Stokes, *Isadora: An Intimate Portrait* (London: Panther, 1968 [first published 1928]), 38, and Jean Negulesco, *Things I Did . . . and Things I Think I Did* (New York: Linden / Simon & Schuster, 1984), 75–77.

52. Victor Seroff, *The Real Isadora* (New York: Avon, 1972), 438.

53. Isadora Duncan, "A Philosophy of Life," *Riviera Season,* 17 February 1926, 18–19.

9. The Magician of the Riviera

1. "Bathing Adventure at Nice," *Manchester Guardian,* 20 June 1927, 9.

2. Claude McKay, *A Long Way from Home* (New York: L. Furman, 1937), 272.

3. Ibid., 274.

4. Ibid., 276.

5. Letter from Harry Lachman to Liam O'Leary, 29 August 1960, LOLA.

6. Letter from Maj. Francis Clere Hitchcock to Liam O'Leary, 27 October 1959, LOLA.

7. Ingram, "A Long Way," 536.

8. Leider, *Dark Lover,* 365.

9. Letter from Alice Terry to Liam O'Leary, 4 April 1960, LOLA.

10. Stokes, *Pilloried!,* 63.

11. W. Somerset Maugham, *The Magician: A Novel, Together with a Fragment of Autobiography* (Harmondsworth: Penguin, 1978), 8.

12. Oliver Haddo [Aleister Crowley], "How to Write a Novel! After W. S. Maugham," in *W. Somerset Maugham: The Critical Heritage*, ed. Anthony Curtis and John Whitehead (London: Routledge, 1997), 56.

13. Maugham, *The Magician*, 33.

14. Powell, *A Life in Movies*, 154–55.

15. Uncredited author, *Continental Life* 6, no. 93 (1926): 7.

16. Powell, *A Life in Movies*, 155.

17. "Oral History with John F. Seitz."

18. Powell, *A Life in Movies*, 156.

19. Ibid., 157.

20. Fred, "The Magician," *Variety*, 27 October 1926, 64.

21. "Le Magicien," *Cinéa*, 1 May 1927, 31.

22. "A Film of the Week, 'The Magician' at the Grafton Cinema," *Irish Times*, 11 October 1927, 6.

23. Ingram, "A Long Way," 553.

24. Letter from Alice Terry to Liam O'Leary, 14 April 1971, LOLA.

25. For an extended account of the German boycott, see the typescript by Reinold E. Thiel titled "The Four Horsemen of the Apocalypse, Mare Nostrum, Contemporary German reactions," LOLA.

26. Letter from Alice Terry to Liam O'Leary, undated, LOLA.

27. "Oral History with John F. Seitz."

28. Ibid.

29. Letter from Howard Strickling to Liam O'Leary, 12 August 1971, LOLA.

30. Letter from Maj. Francis Clere Hitchcock to Liam O'Leary, 28 August 1960, LOLA.

31. Slide, *Silent Players*, 379.

32. This has been confirmed by her nephew, Professor Larry Daley, from papers he holds. E-mail to the author, 22 August 2011.

33. Robert Smythe Hichens, *Yesterday: The Autobiography of Robert Hichens* (London: Cassell, 1947), 245.

34. Kozak, "Rex Ingram," 380.

35. Ibid., 140.

36. Jeanne Dinet-Rollince, *La vie de E. Dinet* (Paris: G. P. Maisonneuve, 1938), 192.

37. Powell, *A Life in Movies*, 164.

38. Ibid., 170.

39. Gladys Hall, "At Home with the Ingrams," *Motion Picture Magazine* 33, no. 6 (1927): 52, 53, 80, 82, 83, 87.

40. Hall, "At Home," 83 (punctuation and capitalization in original).

41. Ibid., 87.

42. Ibid.

43. Ibid.

44. O'Leary, *Rex Ingram,* 183.

45. Quoted in Kellner, *The Last Dandy,* 152.

46. Kozak, "Rex Ingram," 386.

47. Mordaunt Hall, "A Delight to the Eye: 'Garden of Allah' Is Rich in Beauty but Poor in Drama, " *New York Times,* 11 September 1927, X-5.

48. Norbert Lusk, "City Mourns Marcus Loew," *Los Angeles Times,* 11 September 1927, C13.

49. Ibid.

50. Cited in a letter from Mrs. Thomas McGoldrick to Gov. Carl E. Milliken, Motion Picture Producers and Distributors of America, 2 October 1927, *The Garden of Allah* Production Code Administration file, AMPAS.

51. Kevin Rockett, *Irish Film Censorship: A Cultural Journey from Silent Cinema to Internet Pornography* (Dublin: Four Courts, 2004), 82. Rockett also notes (p. 333) that the censor recommended the banning of *Mare Nostrum* because of its anti-German message, but the film certainly played in Ireland, possibly in a different version.

52. Scott Eyman, *Lion of Hollywood: The Life and Legend of Louis B. Mayer* (London: Robson, 2005), 132.

53. G. A. Atkinson, "Rex Ingram Makes a Full Confession," *Daily Express,* 19 December 1927, 3. Paul Kozak, however, states that *Mare Nostrum* has stood for years on Metro's books as being $260,000 short of recouping its loss (as the costs of refurbishing the Victorine were written off against it). Kozak, "Rex Ingram," 345n.

54. Ingram, "A Long Way," 556. Just what happened to these sculptures is a mystery. Apparently Rex did not sell any, and it is unclear whether he attempted to and failed, or decided not to. Other than three listed by the Smithsonian Institution as held privately, no others seem to have survived.

10. Final Films

1. "Film Producer's Libel Action: Sequel to Fictitious Interview," *Irish Times,* 1 February 1928, 6.

2. Charles Higham and Roy Moseley, *Princess Merle* (New York: Simon & Schuster, 1983), 28–33. The following account is taken from Higham and Moseley's biography, and much of their information came from Merle Oberon's nephew, Capt. Harry Selby. What Selby did not tell them was that he had discovered that he was in fact Merle Oberon's half-brother. The dates in *Princess Merle* are incorrect.

3. Harpo Marx and Rowland Barber, *Harpo Speaks!,* The Lively Arts (London: Virgin, 1989), 255.

4. Letter from Alice Terry to Liam O'Leary, undated, LOLA.

5. Jean Norton, "Rex Ingram," *Daily Express,* 26 January 1926, 8.

6. Edwin Schallert, "Rex Ingram Production Is Typical," *Los Angeles Times,* 8 February 1929, A11.

7. Sime, "Three Passions," *Variety*, 8 May 1929, 20.

8. O'Leary, "Interview with Alice Terry."

9. Ingram, "A Long Way," 548.

10. Quoted in ibid., 549. Kevin Brownlow dates this letter to 5 October 1926 in *David Lean: A Biography* (London: Richard Cohen, 1996), 405n9.

11. Quoted in Ingram, "A Long Way," 550. Kevin Brownlow dates this letter to 21 July 1927 in *David Lean*, 405n10.

12. Ibid.

13. Victor Saville and Roy Moseley, *Evergreen: Victor Saville in His Own Words* (Carbondale: Southern Illinois University Press, 2000), 32.

14. Herbert Sydney Wilcox, *Twenty-Five Thousand Sunsets: The Autobiography of Herbert Wilcox* (Oxford: Bodley Head, 1967), 204.

15. Ibid.

16. *Photoplay*, March 1928, 2.

17. Rex Ingram, "Art Advantages of the European Scene," *Theatre Magazine*, January 1928, 24, 64, 66.

18. "Alice Terry Preparing for Talkers in France," *Film Daily*, 12 November 1929, 2.

19. "Rex Ingram to Direct Two British Talkie Productions: Views on Industry's Future," *Kinematograph Weekly*, 25 April 1929, 27.

20. "L'activité cinégraphique," *Cinéa*, 15 July 1929, 23.

21. "Kane Signs Rex Ingram," *Film Daily*, 25 November 1930, 2, and "Rex Ingram's First," *Film Daily*, 21 December 1930, 8.

22. Biographical information on Batcheff taken from Phil Powrie and Éric Rebillard, *Pierre Batcheff and Stardom in 1920s French Cinema* (Edinburgh: Edinburgh University Press, 2009).

23. Denise Tual, *Au coeur du temps* (Paris: Carrère, 1987), 95 (author's translation).

24. Ibid., 132.

25. Our Cinema Correspondent, "The Screen: A Colossal Business; 'Alice in Wonderland' to Be Filmed," *Irish Times*, 6 July 1931, 4.

26. Letter from Alice Terry to Liam O'Leary, 4 April 1960, LOLA.

27. Our Cinema Correspondent, "The Screen: Hollywood Loses Millions; Rex Ingram as Actor," *Irish Times*, 5 October 1931, 4.

28. Lothar Wolff, "Reminiscences of an Itinerant Filmmaker," *Journal of the University Film Association* 24, no. 4 (1972): 83–91.

29. Rex Ingram collection, TCD MS 11448. It looks as if he intended placing this as a news item in the press.

30. Tual, *Au coeur du temps*, 132.

31. Philip K. Scheuer, "Melodrama of Algiers Opens," *Los Angeles Times*, 5 March 1934, 6.

32. "On the Sands of Morocco," *New York Times,* 20 March 1933, 3.

33. Raymond Bacri, "Baroud," *Alger-Étudiant,* 18 March 1933, 7.

34. David Atfield, "Fascinating Farewell to Film by the Great Rex Ingram," Internet Movie Database, http://www.imdb.com/title/tt0022655/reviews (accessed 27 October 2012).

11. Sculptor, Writer, Artist, Traveler

1. "Rex Ingram abandonne le cinéma et se fait mahométan," 2 July 1933, otherwise uncredited clipping, Rex Ingram clippings file, French National Library. Translation by the author.

2. Ibid.

3. Wyndham Lewis, *Journey into Barbary,* ed. C. J. Fox (Harmondsworth: Penguin, 1987), 94–96.

4. Maurice Mairgance, "Rex Ingram a quitté la France pour le Maroc," *Ami du Peuple,* 22 June 1929 (author's translation).

5. "Irishman's Action at Nice: Alleged Embezzlement of £66,000," *Irish Times,* 28 November 1934, 7.

6. De la Rochère, *Les studios de la Victorine,* 197–99. Multiple reports on this case appeared in the press, both in France and in the United States. See, for instance, "Rex Ingram poursuit en justice un français connu pour abus ce confiance," *Paris Midi,* 15 March 1931, and "Rex Ingram on Slander Charges," *Film Daily,* 8 November 1931, 8.

7. Powell, *A Life in Movies,* 148.

8. Letter from Maj. Francis Clere Hitchcock to Liam O'Leary, 15 November 1960, LOLA.

9. Ingram, "A Long Way," 574.

10. Rex Ingram, *The Legion Advances* (London: Ivor Nicholson & Watson, 1934), 83.

11. Ibid., 177.

12. For a picture of his "Yataghan from the Court of Suleyman the Magnificent," see Metropolitan Museum of Art, http://www.metmuseum.org/Collections/search-the-collections/40003187 (accessed 11 March 2013).

13. The Metropolitan Museum of Art now holds Rex's copy of Chassériau's *Scene in the Jewish Quarter of Constantine.* See Metropolitan Museum of Art, http://www.metmuseum.org/Collections/search-the-collections/110002428 (accessed 11 March 2013).

14. See entry on Kada-Abd-el-Kader on the Internet Movie Database by Steve Crook: http://www.imdb.com/name/nm0434255/bio (accessed 7 November 2012), and Soares, *Beyond Paradise,* 231n.

15. Ingram, "A Long Way," 579.

16. Ingram, "A Long Way," 579–84.

17. Letter from Rex Ingram to Lee Lawrie, 28 September 1935, box 9, Lee Lawrie papers, LOC.

18. Ibid., 584.

19. Ibid., 585.

20. Ancestry.com, New York Passenger Lists, 1820–1957, online database (accessed 6 April 2012).

21. Letter from Rex Ingram to Lee Lawrie, 12 August 1936, box 9, Lee Lawrie papers, LOC.

22. "Romantic's Return," *Time,* 2 October 1939.

23. Fred T. Marsh, "Mars in the House of Death," *New York Times,* 1 October 1939, 102.

24. "Novels," *Irish Times,* 30 November 1940, 5.

25. Letter from Rex Ingram to Lee Lawrie, 29 November 1938, box 9, Lee Lawrie papers, LOC.

26. Ancestry.com, Honolulu, Hawaii, Passenger and Crew Lists, 1900–1959, online database (accessed 6 April 2012).

27. Brownlow, "Interview with Willis Goldbeck."

28. Letter from Rex Ingram to Lee Lawrie, 20 April 1943, box 9, Lee Lawrie papers, LOC.

29. Letter from Rex Ingram to Maj. Francis Clere Hitchcock, 28 May 1943, private collection.

30. "Oral History with John F. Seitz."

31. Letter from Rex Ingram to John Huston, 17 September 1948, John Huston Papers, AMPAS.

32. Letter from Alice Terry to Liam O'Leary, 14 April 1971, LOLA.

33. Letter from Rex Ingram to Lee Lawrie, 5 March 1947, box 9, Lee Lawrie papers, LOC.

34. Letter from Rex Ingram to Maj. Francis Clere Hitchcock, 28 May 1943.

35. Letter from Rex Ingram to Lee Lawrie, undated, box 9, Lee Lawrie papers, LOC.

36. Letter from Alice Terry to Liam O'Leary, undated, LOLA, and author's interview with Major Hitchcock, Devon, 8 July 2001.

37. Letter from Rex Ingram to Lee Lawrie, 14 December 1942, box 9, Lee Lawrie papers, LOC.

38. Letter from Rex Ingram to Lee Lawrie, 7 March 1943, box 9, Lee Lawrie papers, LOC.

39. Letter from Rex Ingram to Reverend Hitchcock, 25 October 1945, private collection.

40. Letter from Maj. R. K. B. Hitchcock to Liam O'Leary, 18 October 1959, LOLA, and author's interview with Maj. R. K. B. Hitchcock, Devon, 8 July 2001.

41. Letter from Rex Ingram to Maj. Francis Clere Hitchcock, 28 May 1943.

42. Letter from Rex Ingram to "Patsy" (Maj. R. K. B. Hitchcock), 6 December 1946, private collection.

43. Letter from Rex Ingram to Lee Lawrie, undated, box 9, Lee Lawrie papers, LOC.

44. Letter from Rex Ingram to Maj. Francis Clere Hitchcock, 24 July 1947, LOLA.

45. Letter from Rex Ingram to Mildred Lawrie, undated but presumably Christmas 1945, box 9, Lee Lawrie papers, LOC.

46. Letter from Rex Ingram to Lee Lawrie, 1 December 1947, box 9, Lee Lawrie papers, LOC.

47. The sum is mentioned in a letter from Rex Ingram to Lee Lawrie, 29 November 1938, box 9, Lee Lawrie papers, LOC. At that time, the Egyptian pound was stronger than the British pound, so this was a significant offer.

48. Letter from Rex Ingram to Maj. Francis Clere Hitchcock, 28 March 1948, LOLA.

49. Letter from Rex Ingram to Lee Lawrie, 7 December 1949, box 9, Lee Lawrie papers, LOC. It is possible that this is meant to be "household goods," not "gods."

50. Rex Ingram, "Tunisian Interlude," in "The City without Light" (unpublished short stories), private collection, 1.

51. Ingram. "Tunisian Interlude," 10.

52. Michael Powell, *Million-Dollar Movie: The Second Volume of His Life in Movies* (London: Heinemann, 1992), 58.

53. Letter from Alice Terry to Liam O'Leary, undated, LOLA.

12. The Life, the Legacy

1. Letter from Max de Vaucorbeil to Maj. Francis Clere Hitchock, 7 September 1950, LOLA.

2. Letter from Lee Lawrie to Reverend Hitchcock, 11 August 1950, LOLA.

3. Slide, *Silent Players*, 380.

4. "Rex Ingram Widow Bequeathed Estate," *Los Angeles Times*, 29 July 1950, A1.

5. "Alice Terry Suit over Valentino Film Settled," *Los Angeles Times*, 6 January 1953, A1.

6. "Kevin Brownlow Interview (Part IV)," Ann Harding's Treasures, http://annhardingstreasures.blogspot.ca/2010/11/kevin-brownlow-interview-part-iv.html (accessed 13 November 2012).

7. Letter from Alice Terry to Liam O'Leary, undated, LOLA.

8. Pratt, "'If You Beat Me, I Wept,'" 18.

9. O'Leary, "Interview with Alice Terry."

10. Letter from Alice Terry to Liam O'Leary, 14 April 1971, LOLA.

11. Letter from Alice Terry to Liam O'Leary, undated, LOLA.

12. Rex Ingram, "Directing the Picture," in *Hollywood Directors 1914–1940,* ed. Richard Koszarski, 84–91 (New York: Oxford University Press, 1976 [first published 1922]), 85.

13. Ibid., 89.

14. For a detailed discussion of the interplay between art and film in this era, see Askari, "Art School Cinema."

15. Letter from Rex Ingram to Lee Lawrie, 29 May 1939, box 9, Lee Lawrie papers, LOC.

Selected Bibliography

Abel, Richard, ed. *French Film Theory and Criticism*. Princeton, NJ: Princeton University Press, 1988.

Adams, Henry. *Tom and Jack: The Intertwined Lives of Thomas Hart Benton and Jackson Pollock*. New York: Bloomsbury, 2009.

Bachman, Greg, and Thomas J. Slater, eds. *American Silent Film: Discovering Marginalized Voices*. Carbondale: Southern Illinois University Press, 2002.

Benton, Thomas Hart. *An Artist in America*. New York: University of Kansas City Press, 1951.

Berumen, Frank Javier Garcia. *Ramon Novarro: The Life and Films of the First Latino Hollywood Superstar*. New York: Vantage, 2001.

Blasco Ibáñez, Vicente. *The Four Horsemen of the Apocalypse*. Translated by Charlotte Brewster Jordan. New York: E. P. Dutton, 1918.

Bodeen, DeWitt. *More from Hollywood: The Careers of 15 Great American Stars*. South Brunswick, NJ, and New York: A. S. Barnes, 1977; London: Tantivy, 1977.

Bogdanovich, Peter. *John Ford*. London: Studio Vista, 1967.

Brownlow, Kevin. *David Lean: A Biography*. London: Richard Cohen, 1996.

———. *The Parade's Gone By*. London: Secker & Warburg, 1968.

Bruccoli, Matthew J., and George Parker Anderson. *F. Scott Fitzgerald's* Tender Is the Night: *A Documentary Volume*. Detroit: Gale, 2003.

Cooper, Mark Garrett. *Universal Women*. Urbana, Chicago, and Springfield: University of Illinois Press, 2010.

Curtis, Anthony, and John Whitehead. *W. Somerset Maugham: The Critical Heritage*. Critical Heritage Series. London: Routledge, 1997.

Delson, Susan. *Dudley Murphy, Hollywood Wild Card*. Minneapolis and London: University of Minnesota Press, 2006.

Dinet-Rollince, Jeanne. *La vie de E. Dinet*. Paris: G. P. Maisonneuve, 1938.

Dooley, Terence A. M. *The Decline of the "Big House" in Ireland: A Study of Irish Landed Families*. Dublin: Wolfhound, 2001.

Doss, Erika. *Benton, Pollock, and the Politics of Modernism: From Regionalism to Abstract Expressionism*. Chicago and London: University of Chicago Press, 1991.

Dutheil de la Rochère, Anne-Elizabeth. *Les studios de la Victorine, 1919–1929.* Paris and Nice: Association française de recherche sur l'histoire du cinéma, Cinémathèque de Nice, 1998.

Eyman, Scott. *Lion of Hollywood: The Life and Legend of Louis B. Mayer.* London: Robson, 2005.

Fitzgerald, F. Scott. *The Crack-up, with Other Pieces and Stories.* Harmondsworth: Penguin, 1974.

———. *Tender Is the Night.* London: Penguin, 1999.

———. *Tender Is the Night: The Melarky and Kelly Versions.* Introduced and arranged by Matthew J. Bruccoli. New York: Garland, 1990.

Florey, Robert. *Deux ans dans les studios américains.* Plan-de-la-Tour: Éditions d'aujourd'hui, 1984. Paris: Jean-Pascal, 1926.

———. *La lanterne magique.* Lausanne: Cinémathèque suisse, 1966.

Fullerton, John, ed. *Screen Culture: History and Textuality.* Stockholm Studies in Cinema. Eastleigh: John Libbey Publishing, 2004.

Goldwyn, Samuel. *Behind the Screen.* London: Grant Richards, 1924.

Grove Day, A., and Edgar C. Knowlton Jr. *V. Blasco Ibáñez.* New York: Twayne, 1972.

Hansen, Miriam. *Babel and Babylon: Spectatorship in American Silent Film.* Cambridge, MA, and London: Harvard University Press, 1991.

Hichens, Robert Smythe. *Yesterday, the Autobiography of Robert Hichens.* London: Cassell, 1947.

Higham, Charles, and Roy Moseley. *Princess Merle.* New York: Simon & Schuster, 1983.

Hitchcock, F. R. Montgomery. *Types of Celtic Life and Art.* Dublin: Sealy, 1906.

Hope, Anthony. *The Prisoner of Zenda.* London and New York: J. M. Dent and Sons and E. P. Dutton, 1894.

Ingram, Rex. "The City without Light." Unpublished MS.

———. *The Legion Advances.* London: Ivor Nicholson & Watson, 1934.

———. "A Long Way from Tipperary." Unpublished MS.

———. *Mars in the House of Death.* New York: Knopf, 1939.

Joyce, James. *Finnegans Wake.* London: Penguin, 1992.

Kellner, Bruce. *The Last Dandy, Ralph Barton: American Artist, 1891–1931.* Columbia and London: University of Missouri Press, 1991.

Koszarski, Richard. *An Evening's Entertainment: The Age of the Silent Feature Picture, 1915–1928.* Los Angeles: University of California Press, 1994.

———. *Hollywood Directors 1914–1940.* New York: Oxford University Press, 1976.

———. *Hollywood on the Hudson: Film and Television in New York from*

Griffith to Sarnoff. New Brunswick, NJ: Rutgers University Press, 2008.

Koszarski, Richard. *Von: The Life and Films of Erich Von Stroheim.* New York: Limelight Editions, 2001.

Kozak, Paul Enright. "Rex Ingram: The Films of a Forgotten Master of Silent Screen Arts as Recalled by Friends and Contemporaries, and a Modern Viewpoint." MA thesis, University of Southern California, 1978.

Lasky, Jesse L., with Don Weldon. *I Blow My Own Horn.* New York: Doubleday, 1957.

Leider, Emily Wortis. *Dark Lover: The Life and Death of Rudolph Valentino.* London: Faber, 2003.

Lewis, Wyndham. *Journey into Barbary: Travels across Morocco.* Edited by C. J. Fox. Harmondsworth, Middlesex: Penguin, 1987.

Lowry, Malcolm, Miguel Mota, Paul Tiessen, and F. Scott Fitzgerald. *The Cinema of Malcolm Lowry: A Scholarly Edition of Lowry's "Tender Is the Night."* Vancouver: University of British Columbia Press, 1990.

Marx, Harpo, and Rowland Barber. *Harpo Speaks!* The Lively Arts. London: Virgin, 1989.

Maugham, W. Somerset. *The Magician: A Novel, Together with a Fragment of Autobiography.* Harmondsworth: Penguin, 1978.

McKay, Claude. *A Long Way from Home.* New York: L. Furman, 1937.

Negulesco, Jean. *Things I Did . . . and Things I Think I Did.* New York: Linden / Simon & Schuster, 1984.

Noble, Peter. *Hollywood Scapegoat: The Biography of Erich von Stroheim.* New York: Arno, 1972.

O'Hara, Mary. *Flicka's Friend.* New York: G. P. Putnam's Sons, 1982.

O'Leary, Liam. *Rex Ingram: Master of the Silent Cinema.* Pordenone, Italy: Le Giornate del Cinema Muto; London: British Film Institute, 1993, 1980.

Pouillon, François. *Les deux vies d'Étienne Dinet.* Paris: Éditions Balland, 1997.

Powell, Michael. *A Life in Movies: An Autobiography.* London: Faber, 2000.

———. *Million-Dollar Movie: The Second Volume of His Life in Movies.* London: Heinemann, 1992.

Powrie, Phil, and Éric Rebillard. *Pierre Batcheff and Stardom in 1920s French Cinema.* Edinburgh: Edinburgh University Press, 2009.

Predal, René. *Rex Ingram, 1893–1950.* Paris: Anthologie du cinéma, 1970.

Pullar, Philippa. *Frank Harris.* Penguin Classic Biography. London: Penguin, 2001.

Rambova, Natacha. *Rudolph Valentino: A Wife's Memories of an Icon.* Edited by Hala Pickford. Hollywood, CA: 1921 PVG Publishing, 2009.

Ramsaye, Terry. *A Million and One Nights: A History of the Motion Picture through 1925*. New York: Simon & Schuster, 1986.

Rockett, Kevin. *Irish Film Censorship: A Cultural Journey from Silent Cinema to Internet Pornography*. Dublin: Four Courts, 2004.

Russell, John. *Where the Pavement Ends*. London: Thornton Butterworth, 1919.

Saville, Victor, and Roy Moseley. *Evergreen: Victor Saville in His Own Words*. Carbondale: Southern Illinois University Press, 2000.

Seroff, Victor. *The Real Isadora*. New York: Avon, 1972.

Slide, Anthony. *Inside the Hollywood Fan Magazine: A History of Star Makers, Fabricators, and Gossip Mongers*. Jackson: University Press of Mississippi, 2010.

———. *Silent Players: A Biographical and Autobiographical Study of 100 Silent Film Actors and Actresses*. Lexington: University Press of Kentucky, 2002.

Smith, Albert E., and Phil A. Koury. *Two Reels and a Crank*. Garden City, NY: Garland, 1985.

Soares, André. *Beyond Paradise: The Life of Ramon Novarro*. Jackson: University Press of Mississippi, 2010.

St. Johns, Adela Rogers. *The Honeycomb*. Garden City, NY: Doubleday, 1969.

Stokes, Sewell. *Isadora: An Intimate Portrait*. London: Panther, 1968.

———. *Pilloried!* Edinburgh: Riverside, 1928.

Studlar, Gaylyn. *This Mad Masquerade: Stardom and Masculinity in the Jazz Age*. New York: Columbia University Press, 1996.

Tomkins, Calvin. *Living Well Is the Best Revenge: Two Americans in Paris, 1921–1933*. London: Deutsch, 1972.

Tual, Denise. *Au coeur du temps*. Paris: Carrère, 1987.

Vaill, Amanda. *Everybody Was So Young: Gerald and Sara Murphy; A Lost Generation Love Story*. London: Little, Brown, 1998.

Walker, Alexander. *Stardom: The Hollywood Phenomenon*. London: Joseph, 1970.

Wilcox, Herbert Sydney. *Twenty-Five Thousand Sunsets: The Autobiography of Herbert Wilcox*. Oxford: Bodley Head, 1967.

Yeats, William Butler. *The Collected Poems of W. B. Yeats*. London: Wordsworth Poetry Library, 1994.

———. *Michael Robartes and the Dancer*. London: Kessinger, 2003.

Index

Index

Index